Created and Directed by Hans Höfer

INSIGHT GUIDES
CReTe

Original edition by Gerhard Sasse
Translated by Marianne Rankin

HOUGHTON MIFFLIN COMPANY

APA PUBLICATIONS

CRETE

Third Edition
© **1995 APA PUBLICATIONS (HK) LTD**
All Rights Reserved
Printed in Singapore by Höfer Press Pte Ltd

Distributed in the United States by:
Houghton Mifflin Company
222 Berkeley Street
Boston, Massachusetts 02116-3764
ISBN: 0-395-73858-X

Distributed in Canada by:
Thomas Allen & Son
390 Steelcase Road East
Markham, Ontario L3R 1G2
ISBN: 0-395-73858-X

Distributed in the UK & Ireland by:
GeoCenter International UK Ltd
The Viables Center, Harrow Way
Basingstoke, Hampshire RG22 4BJ
ISBN: 9-62421-076-4

Worldwide distribution enquiries:
Höfer Communications Pte Ltd
38 Joo Koon Road
Singapore 2262
ISBN: 9-62421-076-4

ABOUT THIS BOOK

Crete, the cradle of European civilisation, an island of myths and legends where Asia and Africa meet, is the subject of one of four *Insight Guides* to the country. It joins *Insight Guide: Greece*, *The Greek Islands* and *Athens* in the award winning series which has more than 180 titles covering the world. Produced by Apa Publications, the series has editorial offices in London and Munich, and Apa has its own printing plant in Singapore.

Using Apa Publications' well tested formula of quality journlism and fine pictures, the writers and photographers of *Insight Guide: Crete* were recruited by the Munich editorial office. The contributors set out to capture the island's many different aspects in a fresh and original way, drawing on their specialised knowledge of the place. Above all, their aim is to convey their own affection for Crete and its people.

The Authors

The project editor of *Insight Guide: Crete* and author of most of the chapters in the book is **Gerhard Sasse**, who while travelling in Africa and North and Central America, learned about very different and exotic cultures. "Fascinating though these cultures are," he says, "they are normally viewed from a distance. Crete, however, is different; you find yourself becoming more and more involved in the classical Minoan civilisation the more you learn about it."

Gerhard Sasse's love affair with Crete has endured since his first visit to the island in 1969. He knows the islanders and has many friends among them, but he has no illusions about them either, and he appreciates their individualism and strength of character.

Gerhard Sasse's enthusiasm for Crete is equally shared by his wife, **Nadja Sasse**. A Bulgarian born in Sofia, she is a painter as well as a writer. She has lived in Germany since the mid-1970s and has visited Crete for a long stay nearly every year since, taking her sketch pads and notebooks with her. Because she speaks Greek like a native, she is able to explore aspects of life in Crete which remain hidden from the ordinary tourist, whether it is to gather information from an association of hothouse plant growers or to talk with a scholar out in a remote part of the island digging for remains of an ancient culture.

The author of the historical section, **Hans-Gerd Schulte**, has written essays on pre- and early history. He has also worked on several contemporary historical radio plays. A lawyer by profession, he has a wide range of talents, which was exactly what was required for probing an elusive subject such as early Cretan history. Faced with a lamentable lack of facts, the historian turns detective, searching for clues and details.

Author and sociologist **Gerhard Wilhelm** combines a keen interest in great explorers (Evans and Schliemann, as well as Freud and Jung) with studies of matriarchal societies. This combination of factors in the Minoan civilisation has always fascinated him. His work on Arthur Evans on the one hand, and the social system of the Minoans on the other,

Gerhard Sasse

Nadja Sasse

Hans-Gerd Schulte

enabled him to bring these threads together for *Insight Guide: Crete* in a coherent, descriptive manner.

Takis Touglitos comes from Athens and is now a Berlin-based film-maker and script-writer. He has some pertinent comments to make on the subject of superstition which he has included in his lucid picture of everyday life on the island. He has elaborated on his thoughts and ideas about the mysticism of the Cretans and other Greeks in his own book on the subject.

The youngest contributor, **Stella Stephaniki**, was born on Crete. She lives on Haniá and works as a travel agent in Paleóhora. As a courier, she was able to furnish details which were extremely useful in the compilation of this *Insight Guide*. Stella Stephanaki also advised on the sections about Haniá, Réthimnon and West Crete.

The Photographers

The popularity of *Insight Guides* with travellers is not only due to the interesting and well-researched text. A great part of the appeal of these travel guidebooks is the wonderful photography. Apa Publications aim to give the photographs a role far beyond one that is merely illustrative: the pictures blend with the text, and give a picute of the place by themselves.

The team working on this book was a combination of seasoned Apa photographers and enthusiastic newcomers. Together they have succeeded in capturing the varied and elusive, even illusive atmosphere of the is-

land: the true character of the island without the usual clichés.

Marcus Brooke had already shown his talent in *Insight Guide: Greek Islands*, as had **Michele Macrakis**, who comes from Athens. It is the first time, however, that the sensitive photographs taken by **Regina Hagen**, who comes from Munich, have been included in an *Insight Guide*. She also had the difficult task of compiling the photographic material for the final choice to be made by the publisher in Singapore.

The photographer and artist **Udo Gerner**, who has known Crete for many years, was able to bring his own eye and understanding to the places he shot. He is capable of giving well-worn scenes and themes a completely new perspective.

Nomi Baumgartl is another contributor who has had her photographs published regularly in leading international magazines.

Once again **Gerd Pfeiffer** proved himself a friend in need and contributed photographs in areas where certain subjects were found lacking.

Other valuable photographic contributions came from **Jens Schumann**, **Stefan Seidel** and **Hans Wiesenhofer**.

Under the patient guidance of **Dr. Dieter Vogel**, manuscripts and photographs found their way, often by circuitous routes, to Munich, and into the final volume. The maps were drawn by **Berndtson & Berndtson** in Germany and the English translation was **Marianne Rankin**.

Travel Tips for this edition have been entirely revised by **Tanya Colbourne**, a Canadian writer who lives on the island.

Gerhard Wilhelm

Stella Stephaniki

Udo Gerner

CONTENTS

History

Places

Features

Maps

TRAVEL TIPS

Compiled by Tanya Colbourne

For detailed information
see page 241

CRADLE OF EUROPE

The shape of Crete is reminiscent of a gnarled branch, or perhaps a snail. A wise old Cretan likened the island to the crown of King Minos – tempered and battered by numerous battles and wars but, above all, ravaged by time.

With an area of about 8,350 sq. km, it is the largest of the Greek Islands and, after Sicily, Sardinia, Cyprus and Corsica, the fifth largest island in the Mediterranean Sea. From west to east, the island is over 256 km long, and between 15 and 60 km wide.

Crete lies between the 34th and 35th degrees of latitude, on a plane with Tunisia and Syria and, with more than 300 days of sunshine a year, it's the most pleasant of all the Mediterranean islands. It is, without doubt, also the most significant of the islands; for here, more than 4,000 years ago, European culture first blossomed with the "Minoan" civilisation.

There are so many different sides to Crete that there is certainly something here for everyone. The northern coast is the tourist area, with wonderful beaches, while the southern coast is still relatively deserted and undeveloped. Those looking for solitude can take refuge in the peninsulas of Gramvoússa, Rodopoú and Akrotíri, or just go up into the mountains.

There's beautiful scenery wherever you look, but it's not of the soft and gentle kind. It is quite a rugged place, in stark contrast to the friendly openness of the inhabitants.

Plant lovers can find many different species unique to the island. If you are interested in caves, there's no lack of choice: there are more than 3,000 of them, all different. Then there's the Samaria Gorge, 18 km long, which makes it the longest in Europe, and several shorter gorges, no less spectacular.

Crete is exceptionally rich in places to see. Most of these can be easily reached on the 2,000 km of asphalt road. Apart from excavation sites of the Minoan period – especially Knossós, Festós, Agía Triáda, Mália and Káto Zákros – there are many interesting Greek-Dorian and Roman sites; then a wealth of Byzantine cultural monuments – over 1,000 churches, chapels and paintings; in the towns there are old buildings from the time of the Venetian and Turkish occupations. Between Hrissoskalítissa in the far west and Toploú in the east, there are more than 30 impressive monasteries strung out across the island.

Preceding pages: Wood carving of Venizelos, Anoyia; octopus hung out to dry; goatherd near Frangokastello; small fishing catch; traditional Cretans; Greek coffee. **Left**, the legendary bull carrying Europa.

Up until the second half of the 19th century the early history of Crete lay buried in the myths of late Greek civilisation. It was hidden for over 4,000 years since the first of the splendid palaces were built. But even the earliest legends attest to the high level of cultural development. We hear of the god-like Minoan dynasty and its great sense of justice and beauty. The Minoans loved dancing and sport and their settlements reflect their ability to combine the practical and the

well as numerous other finds and continuing excavations, while not providing evidence of the godliness of the Cretan kings, certainly point to the existence of an independent culture far in advance of the later Mycenaean civilisation.

Today the evidence revealed by excavation and research completes a picture of the art, architecture, religion and everyday life of Europe's first very advanced civilisation. Revelations about the Cretan-Minoan epoch

aesthetic. It was this social complexity which made Crete the first great historical centre in Europe, now so richly documented in Crete's museums and excavated sites.

Homer, Herodotus, Horace and Ovid all tell of Zeus, who took on the form of a bull and won the daughter of the Phoenician king. He carried her on his back over the sea to Górtin. Under the evergreen plane tree they created Minos, Sarpedon and Radamanthys. Minos, the wise yet powerful and severe demigod/king was the first of their offspring.

The sensational discoveries made by the archaeologist Arthur Evans after 1900, as

have led to a revision of theories on early Greek history. But despite this, articles still abound in which European history merely has its prelude in Crete. In some, Cretan culture loses its unique attributes and is just seen as part of a "Minoan-Mycenaean" culture.

Neolithic Period (up to 3000 BC): Up to now there has been no evidence of Palaeolithic or Mesolithic habitation on Crete. It is assumed that in Neolithic times a hunting and gathering culture immigrated to the island, perhaps

Preceding pages: fresco from Knossós. Above, courageous Europa takes the bull by the horn.

as early as the 7th millennium. At first these early islanders lived in caves, such as the Eileíthya Cave near Amnissós or the Geráni Cave near Réthimnon. Later they built primitive dwellings of stones and bricks. This development took place before the "Neolithic Revolution" – the advent of cultivation of the ground.

With the introduction of agriculture, the use of fire for the production of pottery and the taming of wild animals and the breeding of cows, sheep and goats, a unique island civilisation developed. Through fishing and sea voyages, contact was made with the neighbouring islands of Gávdos, Día and the Cyclades. Tools such as hammers, cudgels and axes were made from stone, occasionally from bone. Pottery vessels were made without the aid of a wheel. The pots had a rustic appearance with a simple shape, and were decorated with polished patterns and slits. Some discoveries of marble and baked idols (Neolithic pieces in the Archaeological Museum in Iráklion – abbreviated as "AMI" in cabinets 1 and 2) point to the worship of the Mediterranean Goddess of Fertility, the Great Mother, Mother Earth. But there was still very little indication of the unique way in which early civilisation on Crete was to develop in the future.

Prepalatial Period (3000–2000 BC): At the beginning of the Cretan Bronze Age, in the early 3rd millennium BC there was a further wave of immigration to the island from the Aegean and Asia Minor. These newcomers were relatively more advanced. They had the potter's wheel and also had experience in obtaining and working copper, which soon became a valued commodity for the far-reaching sea trade. Furthermore, glassy, volcanic obsidian was imported from the islands of Mélos and Yiáli. New trading routes and cultural links were established with Anatolia and Syria, Cyprus, the Cyclades, Libya and Egypt.

These contacts with neighbouring civilisations – some of which were highly developed – combined with Cretan receptivity and inventiveness, led to the rapid evolution of the original and unique Mediterranean culture of the Minoan palatial civilisation.

It was probably during this period, referred to as Prepalatial, that Knossós and Festós got their names, both of which reflect the influence of Asia Minor. The first mansions such as Mírtos and Vassilikí were occupied and larger buildings were erected, some with a second storey. The practice of burying the dead in beehive tombs began, as demonstrated by finds in Lébena and Krási and in Fourní near Arhánes. These innovations show the process of change during the early years of Minoan culture. The architectural high point of this burial culture will be seen later in Pylos and Mycenae.

The ceramics of the Prepalatial period still show signs of the New Stone Age as the wheel was seldom used and the pieces were not baked in an oven but over an open fire. The Pírgos style, which was influenced by the rich Cycladic culture (AMI, cabinet 3), demonstrates the distinct further development of late Neolithic ceramics. A vivid example of the polished lattice pattern is the often reproduced dark chalice-like cup (AMI, No. 74855).

Dating from the same period too, is an example (AMI, No. 2719) of a pyx, a shallow, round steatite box with a lid, decorated with slit patterns and with a handle in the shape of a dog lying down. Other variations in the style of creative works in clay are the Agios Onoúfrios style with its profusion of line decorations; the early Vassilikí style characterised by uneven baking; and the Barbotine style with three-dimensional decoration (examples in AMI, Room 1, cabinets 3, 4, 6, 9, 12).

Just as remarkable as the ceramic art was the technique of stoneworking which developed. The stone pitchers found on the island of Mólchos in Mirabello Bay (AMI, cabinet 7) are notable for their attractive shape and the natural texture of the material. The harmony of shape and decoration of the vessels is particularly impressive.

There were also innovations in the art of seal moulding. Small *objets d'art* used for decoration or protection were made in a variety of designs. Precious stones, rock crystal and ivory were used, and shaped into geometrical and figurative forms, pyramids or cylinders. The rich variety of ideas is astonishing. The seal-makers produced graceful animal representations and even, more rarely, depictions of human figures.

In metallurgy too, there were new trends being developed. Goldsmiths had reached a high level of skill as early as the Prepalatial era (AMI I, cabinets 5, 14, 16, 17, 18a). The Cyclades were still the leaders in the artistic field (compare AMI I, cabinet 18a, found on Crete) but by the end of the Prepalatial

erected, making excavations under the foundations difficult. However, parts of the courtyard were sometimes accessible as in the old palace theatre arrangement in the West Courtyard at Festós and at the Louloures in Knossós, where round, well-like sacrificial shafts were built on Prepalatial foundations. In general, the new palaces differed little from the old, except in one major respect: the new palaces were far larger, and eventually almost took on the dimensions of small towns.

Archaeological finds seem to indicate that

period they had been superceded by Crete.

Early Palatial Period (2000-1700 BC): At the beginning of the 2nd millennium, there was more successful development in Cretan life. As the population increased, the first palaces were built and set in prominent positions, such as on the heights of Knossós and Festós. The palace of Mália was built on somewhat more modest lines. In order to prepare the ground for building, the hilltops were flattened. Then the unique and unprecedented residences were built with hundreds of rooms adjoining in labyrinthine form.

Later, on the same sites, new palaces were

there was a monarchical central power in Knossós. The growing influence of the Cretan rulers paved the way for the development of an island kingdom, giving Crete economic and political pre-eminence in the whole of the Aegean. This in turn led to the "Pax Minoica", an extended period of peace, during which extensive fortifications were unnecessary and all the arts reflected the people's peaceful way of life.

Due to its favourable situation at the intersection of east Mediterranean trade, Crete's fleet was able to make wide-ranging contacts. Cretan ships sailed as far as Italy and

Ugarit, Troy, Melos and to Lerna in Argolis.

At these Mediterranean trading posts, many Kamáres style pots have been found. The name was derived from the site of origin on Crete, a grotto in the Ida Mountains below the snowcapped peak of Psíloritis, where the infant Zeus is said to have grown up. In ceramic terms, the Kamáres style denotes the Late Palatial period, but it still holds decorative elements from an earlier period. Its main features are its wide variety, range of colours and, above all, its beauty.

Grottos such as the Kamáres Cave and

the body, hands or chest – indicate the extent of the power ascribed to the goddess of nature. This tradition of votive offerings to the deity has continued unbroken on Crete since Minoan times.

The palaces were not merely the dwelling places of the rulers, but were also centres of production and administration. It has been discovered that even at the beginning of the Early Palatial period, a script composed of hieroglyphics was in use. This was only preserved on a few objects and tablets (AMI II, cabinet 25), all documents in ink having

other mountain shrines were the destinations of pilgrims. People laid down offerings to placate the goddesses of fertility and maturity, and those of birth and death. Finds from this period also reveal the way the pilgrims were dressed. The women had wide skirts and elaborately coiled hair. The men wore loincloths and carried daggers in their belts. Some offerings – depictions of sick parts of

Left, partridge fresco from a caravanserai; the colourful "eggs" are symbols of fertility. **Above**, griffin fresco from the small throne room in Knossós.

been lost. This still undeciphered first European picture writing possibly had its origins in Egyptian hieroglyphics. In this script each word had a sign, whereas in the Linear-A script which developed from it, from about 1700 BC onwards, each syllable had a sign. Despite many years of study, this script has still not been deciphered either. It most probably corresponded with the far-reaching bureaucratic necessities of the palatial trade organisation. It is assumed that the few clay tablets which have been preserved contain references to stocks and trade. However, it is the invaluable and singular Festós Disc which documents the transition to the Late Palatial Minoan period. This is a clay disc embossed on both sides with hieroglyphics, the text of which, reading from the outside to the centre in spirals, would perhaps give more cultural information. The text is composed from 45 syllables but, unfortunately, it has never been deciphered. It has been dated at about 1600 BC.

The end of the early palaces came suddenly. In fact, in about 1700 BC they were all destroyed almost simultaneously. Their destruction is generally attributed to a massive

earthquake, although it has been put forward that a warring invasion from North Africa could have been responsible. But the rapid rebuilding of the palaces and the continued development of Minoan civilisation contradict this theory.

Late Palatial Period (1700–1375 BC): The extensive sea trade which provided the basis for the flowering of Minoan culture also served to supply the island with any materials it lacked. Lead, silver, copper, steatite, jasper, rock crystal, manganese and ochre, all essential for the paintings, were extracted from the island itself. There was local timber

too; cypress trees abounded. But copper was imported from Cyprus, gold from Nubia, ivory from Syria, obsidian from the island of Melos and papyrus from Egypt. Tin was of great importance as it was increasingly used in bronze alloys, and it was imported from Asia Minor.

In fact, the whole development of Minoan civilisation can only be understood against the background of this economic exchange. In the civilised lands of the Near East, particularly in Egypt, Cretan products were greatly sought after. Not only was wine in high demand, but also olive oil, timber, ceramic pots, bronze weapons and many other products. Foreign trade from Crete was extensive, reaching as far as Ugarit and Phoenicia, and is attested to by finds of Cretan wares in Syria and Yugoslavia as well as in inscriptions found in Egypt.

After the destruction of the old palaces, new ones were built, including Knossós, Festós and Mália – which have been the destination of numerous visitors for years. In 1900, the English archaeologist Arthur Evans and his team, led to the site by Greeks, caused a sensation by unearthing the palace of Knossós. At almost the same time, Federico Halbherr and Luigi Pernier were at work in Festós. These excavations were continued after 1950 by Doro Levi.

Mália was revealed by the Cretan archaeologist Joseph Hatzidákis from 1915 until 1920 when French teams took over. A fourth palace was discovered in 1960–61 in Zákros in eastern Crete, although its existence had been suspected for some time, and since 1962, it has been researched by Nikolas Pláton. These excavations are of particular interest as large parts, some preserved beneath the sea, have been found untouched.

One can safely assume that Crete will come up with further archaeological finds in the future. The number of excavation sites is considerable and in some recently revealed building complexes, researchers believe they have found more Minoan palaces: Tourkoginotiá/Arhánes, Prophítis Iliás, Monastiráki, Hamálevri and Haniá.

The four palaces already excavated are

similar in some respects, but they are not imitations of the residences of Mari or Ugarit nor are they comparable to the palaces of Anatolia, Egypt or Mesopotamia. Most notable are the north/northeast facing quadrangles and the asymmetrical layout of the buildings and the irregular shape of the outer walls. There are no facades to provide outside shelter while extending the living space. This gives a clear indication of how the Minoans lived.

Other unique features are the palace halls, open at the sides, and the enormous staircases, the "bathrooms" too, lying lower than the adjoining rooms, the light shafts and gardens in terrace form with porticos. The upper rooms were used for offices, sanctuaries and staterooms.

The whole ensemble is quite spectacular. The labyrinthine arrangement of the building is evident from its ground-plan. Huge *pithoi* fill the storerooms, there are cult rooms, workshops of various kinds within the palace complex, administrative offices and, finally, the royal staterooms. The whole ensemble gives a unique indication of a palace life which endured for more than half a millennium.

Outside the palace buildings, both at Festós and Knossós, there were theatre-like courtyards and stairways, with "processional paths" leading at an angle (Festós) or at right angles (Knossós) linking the steps to the "small" palace, which at Knossós was at a distance from the main building.

Around the palaces and also in other parts of the island, townships with several thousand inhabitants grew up becoming regional centres and marketplaces. The freedom loving nature of the Cretans was reflected in the towns. Of course, the architecture of a town was greatly influenced by its location; for example whether it was built on a slope (Festós, Psíra, Arkolohorí) or on a level plain (Mália). The geographical position of Zákros, Gourniá and Palékastro called for

narrow streets, while at Mália and Knossós there were blocks of houses divided by courtyards and gardens.

In this completely original and varied style of building even the mostly flat-roofed stone town houses showed a highly developed sense of creativity. Excavations have revealed more details, as in the simple two-storey brick house in Gourniá with a storeroom on the ground floor, and living rooms above. Its counterpart is House E at Mália. This "villa" has about 50 rooms on the ground floor, with bathrooms and a room decorated with murals.

It is respectfully, if inaccurately, called the "Small Palace".

The variety of housing at Knossós can be seen from about 50 faïence plaques, part of a complete picture, giving an indication of the facades of the houses at the beginning of the Late Palatial period (AMI II, cabinet 25). The two- and three-storey houses are of varied design; the ochre-coloured windows indicate that there was a covering of transparent material. A clay model of a typical, fairly large house complete with light shaft and balcony was found in 1970 at Arhánes. Even more attractive are the houses of

Left, a nice find from Soúnia – an octopus decorates the drinking vessel. **Right**, richly ornamental cup in Kamáres style.

31

Akrotíri on the island of Santorini (Thira), which were preserved in the volcanic matter, and which reflect the building designs on Crete (Late Palatial period, phase II, late Minoan Oia).

In the countryside, life was less varied and free. Although on the length and breadth of the island there was no one olive tree exactly like another, the eternally repeating demands of the viticulture and olive harvest, and the uniformity of agriculture and cattle raising left little scope for the development of the individual. Various forms of collective

many apartments with a two-roomed porter's lodge (Villa B); they also had running water. It was noticeable, however, that country life gradually became more refined and civilisation developed as a consequence of the cultivation of nature.

Life in the new Palatial society unfolded in many directions. There were bullfights and processions, dances and plays, which can clearly be seen as early forms of the different categories of sport, religion and theatre. Religious life was primarily influenced by the cycles of nature and the seasons of the year

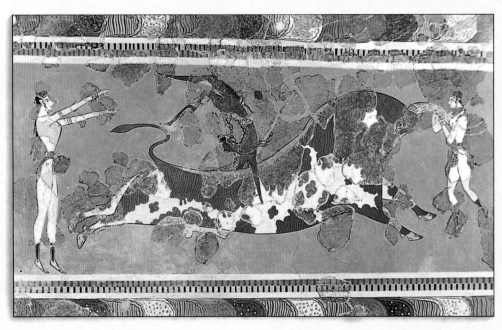

ownership, as well as clan associations, had been a feature of Cretan life for centuries. But now clear social divisions became evident and the old order was broken up. This is shown in various excavated country houses, which clearly reflect the difference between rich and poor. Houses from the area between Kouse and Siva were poor, without kitchen, lavatory or even a stable. Then there was the typical country house in Achládia, with servants' rooms and a reception room next to the entrance and, at the top of the spectrum, the splendid and plush Minoan villas. Each of the "manor houses" of Tílissos comprised

which determined growth. Despite the fact that Crete was an important trading and sea power, the fundamental growth of plants and ripening of crops was still a mystery. The autumnal withering and dying was observed with awe and hope was always renewed with the advent of rebirth in spring. The wonder at nature's regeneration had found expression in the concept of a great Mother Nature. She was the mother, and also the wife of the younger, lesser god who died each year, yet always came back to life. As Díktynna, Briómartis or Eileithyía, with regional variations, this goddess was also recognised in neighbouring regions and she appeared impressed on seals and golden rings, which are among some of the most valuable finds of the Late Palatial period.

Some of the scenes captured on such rings – and again the difference between country and Palatial life is evident – indicate that many events took place out of doors, as shown on the golden ring of Isópata (AMI VI, cabinet 87, No. 424). Other cult events, however, are depicted as taking place in stone areas (golden ring from Mycenae, National Museum Athens No. 3179), or

began to diminish. Some were still revered, but new centres of worship had sprung up as well. In the caves, for example, the power of the great goddess was manifest. The goddess of women in labour, the birth helper, was sought in the Grotto of Eileithyía, even the poet Homer has recounted this. The Cave of Psichró was thought to have been the birthplace of the young god who later became known to the Greeks as Zeus.

Numerous votive objects, sacrifice tables, small statues, tools and double axes give an insight into this religion of nature, which

staircases, which lead one to visualise a theatre-like central courtyard (ring from Arhánes, AMI VI, cabinet 88, No. 989). There is still much to learn about the origins and early history of European theatre.

Ceremonies and processions featured in the religious sphere. With the development and transformation of new Palatial customs, the significance of the holy caves, the importance of which dated back hundreds of years,

Famous exhibits from the Museum of Iráklion: left, the bullfight fresco of Knossós; above, the Festós Disc.

endured for a considerable period of time.

The bull games, where the worldly and religious ceremonials were inextricably bound, were held in the theatre area. The bull was worshipped in Eastern cultures as a godlike creature. Stylised bull horns were found dating from the 6th millennium BC in Catal Hüyük in southern Anatolia. On Crete the bull was probably the embodiment of virility. The mythological union of the beautiful bull and Pasiphae, wife of Minos, may have its origins in Minoan theories about fertility. Minoans believed that the holy marriage between the god of heaven and the Great

33

Mother resulted in the fertility of the earth and its flowers, plants and trees. The ubiquity of bull worship is indicated by sculptures and horns and their proximity to the double axes. This cult aspect must not be overlooked when one admires the agile athletes and incredible acrobats.

The bull games certainly caused the deaths of athletes from time to time. Occasionally, there may have been a sacrificial offering of one of the bulls, but on the whole the games were nowhere near as gory as bullfights are now. The venue for these tests of courage

seems to have been the so-called "royal road", a narrow street leading to the wider theatre area, which in itself was probably less suitable. The discovery of a long stone foundation edging the street, which could well have offered seating for spectators along the way, would certainly seem to indicate this arrangement.

Details of the games are shown in various representations: one of Crete's most beautiful murals has the games as its subject (AMI XIV). The unique representation of movement, one of the most important characteristics of Minoan art, is nowhere more evident

than in the ivory sculpture of the suspended somersaulting bull leaper (AMI IV, cabinet 56) which is prized as one of the first examples of such movement in art. In addition, the cult container from the Small Palace in Knossós, the stone bull's head with lifelike rock crystal eyes, the golden horns and the wonderful slit and relief decoration covering the head, demonstrate the special place held by this revered animal (AMI IV, cabinet 51, No. 1368).

A totally different aspect of Minoan art is seen in a ceramic model, dating from a somewhat later period, from Palékastro (AMI X, cabinet 132, No. 3903). Three women are dancing a round, with a lyre player in the centre. They are holding hands, and make a circle around the musician. Their long, bell-like robes accentuate their light swaying movements. This alluring scene is described by Homer with the words: "…circling round, just like the rounded wheel the seated potter wields…"

In the ancient world, Crete was the cradle of dance, and several signet rings show ecstatic dancers. Some dances have even been handed down to the present day. Scenes of dancing are documented in the miniature frescoes at Knossós. Almost a thousand years later, the Greek poetess Sappho wrote in verse:

The Greek women,
Harmony in their light feet,
Danced around the altar of Eros,
Stepping on softly swelling flowers.

The dance for the protection of the newborn offspring of Zeus has its origin on the island of Crete. So do the choral songs in praise of Dionysos from which Attic drama was later to develop.

Special mention must be made of some treasures of the purely Minoan Late Palatial works of art. In ceramics, where the forms become more slender, two new styles emerged with the building of new palaces. The flora style came a little earlier with its dark colours on a light background. Very naturalistic, particularly in the depiction of grasses (AMI IV, VIII), this was used to portray the world of plants. The marine style eloquently expressed the other dominant side of island life: octopuses, corals, shells and starfish. Here, particular attention should be paid to the works from eastern Crete (AMI IX, cabinets 120, 125; AM Agios Nikólaos, room 3).

However, some of the most remarkable pieces of art in the world must be the famous snake goddesses from the central sanctuary of Knossós (AMI IV, cabinet 50) whose interpretation as depicting mother and daughter is still controversial. Even though the third figure, like some of the others, is not complete, the clothing of these sacred figures clearly indicates the various fashions of the Late Palatial era. The arms and upper parts of the older goddess are covered with snakes, cult-like attributes of the female godheads. They may be seen as chthonian animal companions of the Earth Goddess, although in Minoan times they were looked upon as protective house demons.

Some of the most glorious works of Minoan art are to be found in the unique murals. It is here, above all, that the whole depth of the love of life and the glorious creativity of Cretan artists is expressed. Here the combination of the grace and originality in the depiction of the themes and the rich colour composition are shown at their height.

Alfresco, but also applied dry, the paintings adorned the walls and filled the surfaces of the rooms. Simple but durable mineral and metallic oxide colours glowed red, blue and green. They conjured up ornamental spirals and lines, painted over stucco relief work with bull scenes and pictures of cult festivals in the miniature frescoes. Here in the Mycenaean versions as well, and particularly in the Minoan paintings which were uncovered on Santorini, the attractive youthfulness of this art has been well preserved and can still be appreciated today.

Even Níkos Kazantzákis was spellbound

Left, large portrait of a beauty of Knossós in blue.
Above, Earth Mother with snakes from the Palace of Knossós.

by the murals: "…large almond shaped eyes, black swaying braids, noble, dignified women with bare breasts, with lush, sensual lips, and birds, pheasants, partridges, blue apes, kings' sons with peacock feathers on their heads, wild holy bulls, maiden-like priestesses with snakes winding around their arms, blue boys in wonderful gardens: joy, strength, wealth, a secret world, Atlantis arisen from the depths of Cretan soil looked at us with huge black eyes, but with sealed lips. What world is this, I wondered, when will she open her mouth and speak? What

great deeds had been performed by these ancestors from the soil of Crete upon which we stand?"

In about 1450 BC, this colourful splendour came to a sudden end. The cities and palaces of the Minoan civilisation collapsed in ruins. What actually happened? Was it the eruption of the volcano of Santorini – which was more devastating than the eruption of Krakatóa in 1883 (36,000 were left dead) – and the ensuing earthquake and tidal wave which caused the destruction of Minoan culture?

Today, the catastrophe of Santorini is dated at about 1500 BC, 30 or 50 years before the destruction on Crete. However, it is, still possible that there were many indirect repercussions, as the Cretan trading fleet must have suffered great losses.

But the complete destruction of all the palaces – apart from Knossós – and the cities? The theory of an islandwide fire following the eruption of the volcano can no longer be upheld today. The facts do not support any other thesis, so all we are left with is hypothesis.

Nevertheless, what is certain is that after this setback, or perhaps even much earlier

structive battle. So it is possible that Crete came under the influence of the Mycenaeans in two stages.

First – we assume – Knossós and other places were conquered, much of them destroyed or possession taken of them. The influence of political seizure of power, with all the accompanying adaptations and influences, may have taken place as described by Horace. Writing centuries later, Horace refers to the replacement of Greek domination by the Romans: "The Greek land was conquered, elevating the rough possessor."

than this, Mycenaean regents ruled in the palace of Knossós, which they altered and subsequently developed in a completely different way.

At Haniá too, the Linear-B clay tablets were found (up to then only secured in Knossós). The discoveries in Tourkogitonía/ Arhánes and Agiá Triáda from this period (1600–1450 BC) point to a Mycenaean presence in numerous other places in Crete – perhaps even earlier, as is now argued.

Great social inequality may have led to disputes bordering on civil war, but there is no evidence to suggest an islandwide de-

It is at Knossós in particular that the slow process of change can be seen. The previously unknown and all-conquering Mycenaean war chariot was in use – although the Cretans used it mainly for outings. The throne room in the palace of Knossós was erected during this period.

The royal grave of Isópata, to the north of Knossós, is definitely Mycenaean, as can be seen from its unfamiliar construction and arrangement of rooms. The warlike, masculine character of the new rulers is also evident in the knights' graves near Festós, which contained swords, daggers and spears

– extremely unusual grave furnishings on peaceful Crete.

Also attributable to this warring spirit are the mercenary figures in the fresco scene *Leader of the Blackamoors* from Knossós (AMI XIV, No. 3); and in general the subjects of the murals became harsher during that time (for example the *Procession* fresco, AMI XIV, No. 21).

Even in Egypt, which continued to be a trading partner of the island, the change in Cretan clothing to a loincloth tapered at the front was observed. Another change was that valuable script documents were mainly the book-keeping lists, although mention was made of some of the Greek gods. On the Knossós tablet V-52, four godheads are referred to, among whom was almost certainly the goddess Athena.

There is a dispute over the exact dating of the Knossós tablets, and also there are discussions over the date of the change from Linear-A to Linear-B, as well as over the deciphering itself.

In areas under foreign domination, ceramics too evolved a new style known as the

Linear-A, the script used for the palace book-keeping, was replaced by the more fitting Linear-B. This script, which was preserved on baked clay tablets, records an early form of the Greek language.

The Mycenaean Greek script was discovered in a sensational effort of deciphering by Michael Ventris in 1952. The same language was also spoken in Pylos in the Peloponnese where similar tablets were found. These

Left, a sarcophagus found in the Palace of Agía Triáda. **Above**, a golden ring from a chamber tomb in Mycenae.

"Palace Style". Although the Minoan creative skill is still in evidence, for example in stoneworking, there are signs of decay. Now, instead of the octopus motif, reflecting the graceful Minoan style of movement, on a palace style amphora we see a swarm of battle helmets.

Around the year 1375 BC, the Palace of Knossós was destroyed – this time completely – and with it disappeared several other Minoan settlements and Mycenaean centres on the island, all of which served as invaluable testimony to the first great European civilisation.

The cause of the destruction of the Palace of Knossós and disappearance of several Minoan settlements and some Mycenaean centres is obscure. It is possible that there was an unsuccessful uprising on the island against the foreign overlords. Perhaps the governor was evicted by Mycenaean mainland forces. However, from around the start of the Post Palatial Period (1375–1000 BC), the Mycenaeans held parts of central Crete

While Crete was in decline, politically, culturally and artistically, Cretan artefacts were used and further developed in the new centres of power. Cretan artists who had emigrated contributed to this development, so the dramatic depiction of the conquest of a walled city on a silver rhyton from Mycenae (National Museum of Athens, Mycenaean Room, cabinet 27, No. 481) is probably an example of Cretan metalworking. This is

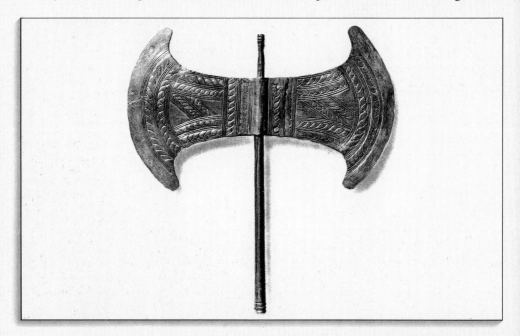

and were already extending their influence.

Other Greek tribes forced their way onto the island and Crete's influence abroad began to decline. The significance of what was now essentially a Mycenaean province of the Greek "community" (*koiné*), which included other islands such as Sámos, Rhodes and Chíos as well as parts of Thessaly and Asia Minor (e.g. Milet), was no longer what it had been. Mycenae and Tyrins, Thebes and Pylos, Sparta and Athens were now far more important as fortified centres of Mediterranean power which continued to suffer from internal disputes.

in fact the oldest example of historical representation in the Occident.

The lesser importance of Crete does not exclude the presence of a Mycenaean king on the island. Cretan participation in the Trojan War with a fleet only just smaller than that of Agamemnon is considered most likely since the discovery of graves in Besik Bay near Troy and Homer relates in *Iliad*:

But the renowned spear thrower Idomemeus led the Cretans,
Who came from Knossós and the fortress of Gortyn,

Lyktos, Milet and Lycastos on chalk shimmering cliffs,
Phaestos, Rhytion too, those populous towns
Others too, from Crete of a hundred cities,
These Idomeneus led, he of the skill with the lance,
And Meriones, like the murderous Ares,
They were followed by a squadron of eighty dark ships.

This time of decline, which may be referred to as the "Cretan-Mycenaean Civilisation", is also known as the time of "Reoccupation" when the palaces and buildings which had been destroyed were resettled. Unfortunately, there is very little documentation of this period. The construction of a new palace cannot be proved, although it is assumed, but the small shrine of the double axes does date from this time. Life went on as usual in the cities of Festós, Knossós, Górtis and Agía Triáda, and life began in a new way in what were, according to tradition, cities founded by the new rulers, such as Tegea, Pergamos and Lappa.

The sudden turning point is clearly evident in the far-reaching changes in artistic expression. The typical Mycenaean stylisation in ceramic decoration and the degeneration in thematic representation is proof of artistic decline, particularly in stonework. A typical example of Mycenaean art is the "Goddess with uplifted hands".

The decline of Minoan culture, which had so long stimulated and enriched that of the Mycenaeans, caused a paralysis in Mycenaean artistic development, which was apparent further afield than Crete. Art cannot be taken captive; culture cannot be conquered. The destruction of the artistic prerequisites led to the destruction of the Minoan culture itself. Crete shared with other places the history of Mycenae, which was not to last much longer. In room X of the

Archaeological Museum in Iráklion, the works of art and craft dating from this period are on view and their uniformity is there for all to see, despite traces of Minoan influence.

The greater political picture is known in general: the deadly feuds between Greek tribes may have led to the brutalisation and weakening of the Minoan kingdom. The vagabonds, sea robbers and plunderers to whom the destruction of the cities and palaces of Hattuscha and Ugarit, Mycenae and Tyrins, Pylos and Thebes is attributed, may also have included Cretan and Mycenaean

adventurers (Achaeans, Pelasgers) as indicated in Egyptian inscriptions from the time of Ramses III (1196–1166 BC). But the Trojan War is dated at this period of Mycenaean decline too. The legends of the journeys of the Argonauts and the return of the Heraclidae indicate mass movements of peoples. Thucydides writes: "After this war (against Troy) the Hellenes moved and went to live elsewhere, and so there was no peace in the land and no power was gained. The late return of the warriors from Troy brought much strife. The conquered felt the need to leave and to found new cities."

Left, this golden double axe was found in the cave of Arkalochri. **Right,** the poppy goddess from Sazi is believed to be the goddess of fertility and healing.

At this time members of another Greek tribe, the Dorians from the north, migrated to Crete. Eteorcretans (the "real" Cretans), Pelasgers, Kydonians (West Cretans) and the Dorians made up a multilingual mix of peoples, among whom in the ensuing centuries, the Dorians were dominant.

The original inhabitants fled to remote and inaccessible parts of the island, there to guard their own cultural identity. They preserved their own ancient customs and forms of expression, although showing some Mycenaean influence (AMI XI, cabinets

which lie before the turn of the millennium, cultural schisms are evident with traces of Minoan customs in the regional development of the new Dorian "three-class system" (see Homer, *Odyssey*, XIX, 171). The newcomers and their warriors became the new ruling class; the burghers were guaranteed specific rights by a binding legislation. Then there was a third group of non-Dorians which seems to have constituted an oppressed servants' class.

Slowly, a political system of "Spartan" strength was formed on Crete. The towns

148, 154). Above all they kept their own original language.

By the end of this Post Palatial period, the Minoan dream of peaceful coexistence in a flourishing culture was lost. But the efforts of archaeologists, who have painstakingly unearthed traces of this civilisation, have revealed that Minoan culture did in fact remain unconquered and that, above all, its influence on the historical consciousness in the present century can easily be traced.

Geometric Period (1000–700 BC): Even in sub-Minoan times (1100–1000 BC) and in the Protogeometric period, the beginnings of

were heavily fortified and youths eligible for military service were trained. Tougher and more reliable weapons were produced with the use of iron, which now superseded bronze. Burial of the dead was replaced by urn cremation. The somewhat clumsy Protogeometric ceramic works are displayed in the Archaeological Museum in Iráklion, Room XI. With the development of the early Geometric Style which followed, starkly stylised figures, differing from those of the mainland, were created (AMI, cabinets 146, 155). In the later, mature Geometric phase there was a resurgence of original creativity, although the works cannot compare with the Attic amphoras or the Olympic bronze sculptures of the same period. The impression of a provincial, reactionary place poor in ideas slowly receded, and a period of isolation drew to a close for Crete. As a Dorian port of transshipment and centre of maritime trade, it was no longer cut off from the neighbouring Mediterranean cultures.

Archaic Epoch (700–550 BC): In the following Homeric and post-Homeric century and a half, Crete, as part of the Greek world, was drawn into the upheaval and radical change

In the realm of art, it can be seen that the years of relative isolation were over and that the stereotyped repetition of circular and rectangular ornamentation and uniform geometric figures was at an end. In the visual arts, Homeric myths were presented in a more varied and lively way, freeing them from the constraints of the ornamental and decorative style and breathing new life into long-buried creative ability.

Perhaps Crete had already been stimulated artistically by the completely different cultures of Syria or Assyria, for there was much

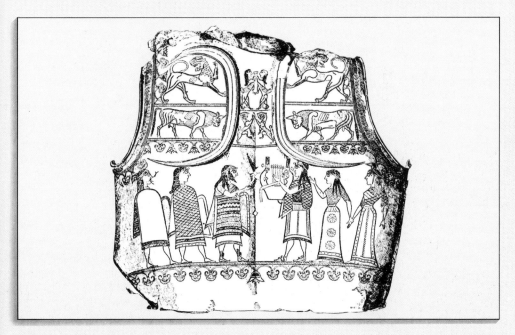

which characterised this period of strife, poverty and over-population. A colonisation movement led to the formation of almost 1,500 city-states, some of which were tiny. This movement of peoples stimulated the region, both politically and economically. The high turnover of goods through the new trading centres of Ionian Asia Minor, and throughout the Levant, brought about an economic upsurge.

Left, the little horses of the pyxis are from the Geometric epoch. **Above**, graphic imitation of Mycenaean armour.

trade between those countries, or perhaps its location had attracted foreign artists to settle, enriching the artistic creativity on the island. Whatever the reason, for the last time in its long history, Crete developed its own form of artistic expression: the Daedalic Style. Among the numerous workshops on the islands in the Aegean and on the mainland, the school of Daedalus and his pupils was considered of decisive importance in the renewal of Greek sculpture. And the name lives on, giving lasting renown to that style and legendary time.

In the grotto long associated with the birth

of Zeus, unique bronze shields and tympana (sound cymbals) were discovered first by Cretan shepherds and later in 1885 by Fabricius, Halbherr and Aerakis as a result of systematic excavation. Because of their oriental relief work, they were ascribed to functions in the cult of Zeus. Legend has it that a warlike noise was made while dancing to drown the cries of the infant Zeus hidden in the grotto, in order to save him from being swallowed by his father Kronos.

The bronze work demonstrates a transformation of oriental form and content. From

Athena. Notable too are the Sphyrelata from Dréros near Neápolis – three cult figures which depict Apollo, Leto and Artemis. Hammered bronze once covered their wooden cores like a skin, but the cores have long since rotted away. Although damaged, the 80-cm (31½-in) high central figure is impressive with her oriental cap, as are the goddesses adorned with early Daedalic hair ornaments (AMI XIX, 210).

The oldest of the temples built in the archaic period with Minoan architectural elements have been excavated near Priniás

the oriental hero Gilgamesh, the hand of either a Cretan or an immigrant North Syrian master has fashioned a wonderful drawing of the Cretan Zeus (AMI XIX, cabinet 209).

The importance of early Cretan sculpture is apparent by the stone sculptures of the goddesses of Górtis, a town in the region of Festós, which was growing more powerful (AMI XIX). This may be a representation of Artemis and Leto, in Minoan-Dorian oriental style; the statuette with a helmet (AMI XVII, cabinet 193) which was found at Górtis in a holy place on the Acropolis, is generally taken to represent the goddess

on the eastern foothills of the Ida Mountains. The unique late Daedalic portal sculptures of two goddesses seated opposite one another clearly reflect traces of Egyptian and Syrian/Phoenician iconography.

The picture of the Archaic epoch may be completed by a visit to the Dorian city of Lató in the district of Mirabéllo, which was founded at this time. With its streets lined with houses and its ground plans of the stores, particularly the agora, or meeting place, and the show staircase area, it gives a significant insight into the early history of Greek city life and theatre. Looking at the old steps, reminiscent of the arenas of Festós, Gourniá or Agía Triáda, one can sense the *joie de vivre* of the Minoans across the ages which Homer so vividly describes:

> *Glowing youths there and much acclaimed young women danced around, hand in hand.*
> *Soft clothes covered the youths, light as oil's soft glow, and the maidens were veiled in linen.*
> *Every dancing girl was adorned with a lovely garland, and the youths had golden daggers at their sides in silver belts...*
> *Many were those crowded around the lovely dancers, rejoicing with all their hearts...*
> –Homer, *Iliad*, XVIII, 5593/604

As the Archaic epoch drew to a close, Crete sank back into the obscurity of an island province.

Classical Hellenistic Period (550–67 BC): During this time, the political and cultural focus was finally established on the mainland. Attica became the new centre of Greece. Athens, which rivalled Sparta, had been waging war for centuries – and not only against the threatening enemy of Persia. With the birth of Greece from the Aegean (Gaitanides), Crete was relegated to the cultural and political sidelines. Although tradition and poetry enabled the island to keep its high artistic reputation, there was no new outstanding creativity in the field of art during this period.

There is, however, one extraordinary document which must be mentioned: a stone inscription which affords the visitor a glimpse into the ancient Cretan legal system. "King Minos" was renowned for his wisdom, although he was also known as a stern lawmaker and judge. It is said that the legendary Spartan lawmaker Lykurg studied on Crete. Even Solon enriched early Greek legislation from Cretan law. So, for the an-cients, Crete was also an island with a high reputation in the field of law.

In 1884, Federico Halbherr – soon to be assisted by Ernst Fabricius – found the great inscription of Górtis. Standing in the mill canal of Déka, they deciphered a total of 17,000 signs carved in broadstone which was the legal script of the rising Cretan town of Górtis.

This settlement on the Messará plain had long lain in the shadow of the older royal residence of Festós, but now the city was on its way to becoming the centre of this fertile

region. With its two trading ports of Mátala and Levín in the south, it was able to outstrip Festós, and possibly the other cities of the island too. There are 12 columns each with 52 lines expertly carved in the stone in a special "printed carving" in the language of an old Dorian dialect. The lines follow a so-called "ox turn", that is, the lines turn like the ox when ploughing (*Bustrophedón*). They do not simply follow each other but alternate and reverse with the letters set in the mirror image. In the early Greek alphabet, the letters Phi, Chi, Psi, Zeta, Eta and Omega are missing. The 20 tablets of law, each about 70

Left, remains of the once lively stage in Agía Triáda. **Right**, the caves of Mátala, so often inhabited in times of need.

cm (27½ in) wide and about 170 cm (67 in) high, make up the longest Greek inscription ever found and reflect a hitherto unknown and very ancient set of laws. The inscription is generally dated at about the first half of the 5th century.

There is no clear separation of the different branches of the law. The work deals with civil and criminal law, substantive and procedural law, and deals with the punishment for adultery and claims following a death. Different sanctions were imposed for both free and unfree burghers (by the latter one

Reference to the old laws showed interesting developments in the new laws. In this period, influenced by the Dorians, there are no longer any indications of a matriarchal society, and the rights of women are hardly better than those of slaves.

Interesting information is also provided on the methods of giving evidence: "If the case concerns a slave (or any other possession) and each party maintains that he is the owner then, if a witness testifies, the judge will rule in accordance with that evidence; but if witnesses support the claims of both

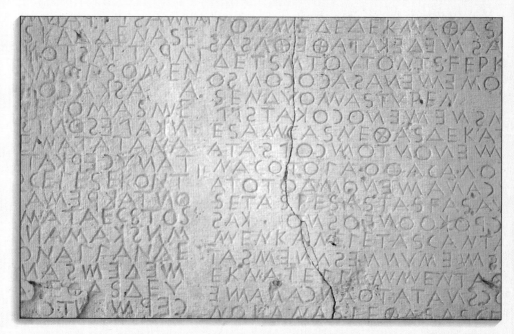

assumes the descendants of the old suppressed Minoan peoples are meant). Here is an example: "Whoever assaults a free male or female, must pay one hundred strate… If a slave assaults a free male or female, he must pay double… Whoever assaults his own slave, must pay two strate…"

Even the rights of possession of the slaves' children had been dealt with: the child of an unmarried slave woman was allocated to her father's master; the child of a married slave woman, to her husband's master.

It was correctly assumed that this body of laws was of more than regional importance.

parties, or of neither, then the judge must rule in accordance with his conscience under oath." (I, 16–24).

Not much took place on or around Crete at this time. Górtis had almost attained its goal of becoming the main city, and in the changeable Cretan city-state history there were many often short-lived agreements and contracts. Sometimes they backed the wrong horse, as when they supported the Persian fleet in the sea battle against Alexander the Great in Issos (333 BC). He remained unvanquished. The Hellenic events which influenced world history, from the death of

Alexander the Great (323 BC) to the death of Caesar (44 BC) were only followed from a distance on the island of Crete.

Roman Occupation (67 BC–AD 337): For almost two thousand years, Crete was occupied by unbidden intruders and their hostile armies, who saw the island as a breadbasket or as an important strategic naval base. However, throughout the period, the Cretans always put up a strong resistance.

The new Mediterranean power of Rome (and later world power) was the dominating factor in Cretan life for the first 400 years. In the Mediterranean and whose bases were on Crete with the support of the islanders. The Roman General Gnaeus Pompeius the Great swept them off the sea with 500 ships and 120,000 soldiers.

Ruins and archaeological finds give evidence of a Roman way of life, but also reflect the restraints imposed on the foreign rulers by the Cretans, and the compromises they were obliged to make after many years of suppression and rebellion. That the island experienced a modest flowering is indicated by the theatres and temples, villas and water

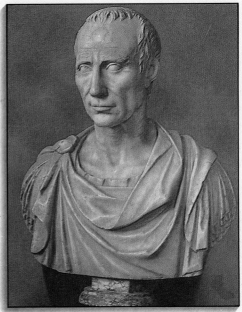

the year 67 BC the Praetor Quintus Caecilius Metellus and his troops landed near Haniá and, after several years of resistance, conquered the island which then became another Roman province (Crete-Cyrere). As Górtis had been friendly to the Romans, helping them in their occupation, the town was made the island's capital as a reward.

One of the first things the Romans did was to eradicate the hordes of pirates terrorising

Left, the law carved in stone at Górtis. Above, Gaius Julius Caesar, 100–44 BC (right) raised eyebrows when his face was put on a coin (left).

systems, especially in Górtis and the new garrison city of Knossós.

Crete also played a part in the early history of Christianity: St Paul, whose companion Titus became the first bishop of Crete, stopped at Kalí Liménes on his way into captivity in Rome in AD 59. As the new religion spread, the island had its martyrs, such as the "Holy Ten" (Agii Déka) who were beheaded in AD 250 for refusing to worship the Roman gods. With the decline of Roman imperial power, Pax Romana – the long reign of Roman stability – and the suppression of piracy came to an end.

45

Byzantines (AD 337–826): Crete maintained its non-central role during the rule of the Byzantines, who dominated this Mediterranean region during the 4th century after the fall of the Roman Empire. On 11 May 330 the old city of Byzantium was renamed Constantinople, after Rome's first Christian emporer, Constantine, and it became the capital of the new Eastern Empire with a state system which was to last for a thousand years. Crete was administered from there and was left to its shadowy existence.

Christianity was allowed to flourish on the

island. Many churches were built, of which the most important architecturally and from the point of view of ecclesiastical history is perhaps the domed basilica of Holy Titus in Górtis. This dates from the 6th century and was probably built on the site of a more ancient building near the Roman odeon and theatre.

Crete, which between the 4th and 6th centuries can be assumed to be politically stable, and the rest of the Aegean remained unaffected by assaults by Germanic tribes which were the first convulsions to shake the Byzantium Empire. But, in AD 623, the island was disturbed by the Slav migrations and from the mid 7th century, Crete was the scene of Arab attempts to move northwards to conquer Constantinople, the cultural and political centre of the world at that time. After decades of fighting for supremacy, the Byzantines lost Crete along with Sicily in 827. Both islands were ceded to the Arabs.

Arabs (AD 826–961): The ports of Crete soon became used by the Saracen pirates, who made life dangerous throughout the whole Aegean up to the Dardanelles. This was a permanent feature of life under the Arabs whose rigid exercise of power was to last for more than a century. However, worse was to come with the complete destruction of all Christian monuments on the island and the gruesome pursuit and persecution of Cretan Christians. Once again many islanders retreated to their hide-outs in the mountains.

In AD 828, the Arabs set up their headquarters in the fortress el-Khandak, near the present-day city of Iráklion and the old city of Górtis was irrevocably destroyed. Finally in 961, after several unsuccessful attempts, the Byzantine army, led by Nikefóros Fókas retook Crete. As the Byzantines began to display their power once again, Crete's rule was returned to Constantinople.

Return of the Byzantines (AD 961–1204): The retaking of the island was extremely bloody, even by the standards of those days, and Saracen heads were used as catapult ammunition against the city of El Khandak. The siege lasted for months, and was not helped by a great famine, but nevertheless it culminated in the eventual storming of the city. Thanks to the retaking of Crete and of Aleppo in 926, Fókas was made emperor two years later.

By then Crete was a relatively independent military and administrative region. Its location led to a certain isolation and agriculture soon went back to the feudal system. Merchants from Constantinople and allied neighbouring lands came to Crete, reinvigorating the sea trade, which was mainly controlled by Genoese families. As life became more stable, both politically and culturally – architecture and fresco painting experienced a revival – so the power of Constantinople declined. This was demonstrated by the big landowners being exempted of paying tax and the emergence of a bureaucracy. According to tradition, an attempt to gain autonomy took place at the time of the Byzantine defensive action against the Seljuks (1090–92), but it ended with the arrival of the imperial sailing fleet, commanded by Johannes Dukas.

Byzantine art was dated from the dominant period of Constantinople (up to 1202–

Venetian Rule (1204–1669): The historical background to the change of ruler which heralded the decline of the Byzantine Empire was the sacking of Constantinople by the Fourth Crusade. Venice acquired Crete through a contract of purchase from the Genoese owners (a gift of the last Byzantine Emperor Alexios III Angelos).

The Venetians were able to make good use of the island to widen their maritime interests. By means of only a few representatives stationed on Crete, these new strong and dictatorial rulers managed to put down 14

04). The Byzantine church buildings of Miriokéfala (Panagía Church, 11th–12th century) with its many frescoes was constructed during the period of the reconquest of Crete. Byzantine art treasures from the following Venetian epoch are more numerous, but equally admirable, in Assómatos (Arhánes, Church of the Archangel Michael, 14th century) or in Kritsá (Panagía-i-Será, 13th–14th centuries).

Left, view of the excavation site of Górtis. **Above**, stone-cold structure: monument to Byzantine rule at Moni Arkádi.

major uprisings and a rebellion during the ensuing four and a half centuries, while at the same time expanding the economy. The island of Crete was completely transformed and brought in line with Venetian ideas. Place names were changed – Crete took the name of Candia as did the capital Iráklion. Building began, in order to change the face of the island – not entirely to its detriment, it must be admitted.

In some parts of the island, the Cretans were able to escape Venetian political influences. In other parts, the islanders rose up against the nobles of the ruling class and proclaimed a "Republic of St Titus". Finally, a concession for religious tolerance of the Eastern Christians ensured the solidarity of the people, but the gruesome end of the uprising in 1363–64 was inevitable.

Only after the final fall of Constantinople in 1453 to the Ottoman Turks did Byzantine artists and learned men come to Crete. They were to enrich this Greek- and Byzantine-influenced island considerably. Some ships and volunteers had, in fact, taken part in the defence of Constantinople against the Turks. Now this coming together of the Latin early

Bursa (Brusa) made in 1326 to the most important power in the Eastern Mediterranean with Constantinople as their final prize in 1453. As they pushed westwards, the Ottomans encountered fierce resistance (Battle for Vienna 1683). Their conquest of the island was brutal, and succeeded despite the resistance led by Francesco Morosini. There were persistent attempts by the islanders to break free.

For the Turks, Crete was not only a source of tax revenue but, more crucially, it was a base of great military importance, so that

Renaissance spirit and the Greek Orthodox antique heritage was to bring forth its own results. This was most clearly demonstrated in the new capital Candia (Iráklion) where features still visible today, such as the Morosini Fountain, the Loggia and the Agios Márkos Basilica, reflect this new culture. The Ottoman Turks took the island in 1669 after three harsh years of siege, leaving a count of about 150,000 dead.

Turkish Occupation (1669–1898): By the time the Turks had conquered Crete, their Ottoman Empire had grown from a band of clans with their first conquest of the town

even when the islanders refused their economic cooperation and the towns grew desolate, the retention of this island, so dearly paid for, still seemed justified.

In Cretan lore the famous attempted uprising of 1770 has never been forgotten. Before the Cretan Dhaskalojánnis could organise a coalition with Russia (the enemy of the Turks, during the Russo-Turkish War of 1768–74), he was tricked and executed by the Sultan.

But Crete remained an inspiration to revolt for the other Aegean islands, and the numerous battles constantly necessary to safeguard conquered territory slowly wore down the Ottoman Empire. Gradually a Greek national consciousness was born. In 1821 the Greek mainland and some of the islands rebelled. The Peloponnése was free.

In the winter of 1824–25, Mohammed Ali, viceroy of Egypt and the new commander in chief of the occupational fleet, landed on Crete, which had been given to him by the Turks as a reward for his punitive expedition against the Greeks. Once again the island was conquered. Meanwhile, other great European powers had decided to try to inter-

now chafing under the rule of a Bavarian king's son (Prince Otto). But there was still no peace on Crete, and in 1841 the British took it away from Egypt and returned it to Turkey. In 1869 the Paris Conference extended autonomy to Crete but it was too late for the hundreds of Cretans who, three years earlier, had blown themselves to bits by exploding a cache of arms in the monastery of Arkádi, rather than be captured by the Turks.

To this day, Crete celebrates its own National Day on 8 November. Freedom or death – for decades this was the only honour-

vene and deal with this centre of conflict. The result was that on 6 July 1827, an armistice was arranged between Russia, Great Britain and France in which Greece (without Crete) was guaranteed autonomy, although still under Turkish sovereignty.

It was not until 1830, after continued acts of war, that a peace settlement came into force. In 1832, Greece became a kingdom,

Far left, icon of Mary, the Holy Mother of Jesus. **Left**, Turkish Cretans. **Above**, an old Cretan tells the story of the Turkish occupation of Crete with a couple of visual aids.

able maxim for survival through times of rebellion and heroism when retaliation was part of everyday life.

In 1897, an attempt by the mainland to win back the island failed. Then in the following year Crete acquired "autonomous status" under Ottoman supremacy, with the full support of the great powers. The high commission of Prince George became the party responsible for the island's administration. An almost incidental event, when some British soldiers were killed, finally led to the end of the Turkish presence on Crete and in 1899 the first Cretan government was sworn in.

Life on Crete during the 20th century has essentially been influenced by three main political events. First, union with the mainland of Greece (*enosis*) aroused passions and no foreign interference was acceptable. During World War II, the people were suppressed by German troops who occupied the island; finally, there was the terror perpetrated during the years 1967–74 by the colonels who siezed power in Athens.

At the beginning of the century, Crete was

still under international protection. True autonomy and the *enosis* which everyone had awaited for so long still had to be fought for. The struggle for independence was led by the Cretan Elefthérios Venizélos. He was head of the liberal party and later Minister of Justice and Foreign Affairs in the relatively powerless Cretan national government of Prince George. His goal was finally achieved on 30 May 1913, after the abdication of Prince George (1906), the dissolution of the high commission (1908) and, finally, the withdrawal of international forces from the island (1909). Venizélos' attempt to occupy

the Turkish capital and to found a new Byzantium ended miserably in bloody failure. Crete was obliged to take 13,000 Greeks from Asia Minor in exchange for 11,000 Cretan Turks (and over 1.55 million Greeks who were living in Turkey were made to leave the country).

More drastic for the islanders was the occupation by German troops during the war. On 20 May 1941, German parachutists and mountain infantrymen landed near Haniá, where they attempted to provide security for further airborne contingents. This risky operation resulted in far more casualties than the Germans expected, because the British, who were defending the island, had been preparing for the invasion. The Germans left Crete on 2 November 1944, although the last units did not leave western Crete until after the war. During the occupation, the island was ravaged with hundreds of men and women falling victim to the cruelty of the Nazis.

When the Cretan Resistance fighters had initiated guerrilla actions against the German occupational forces, the latter retaliated by destroying whole villages and arbitrarily shooting Cretan civilians. German orders were "10 Cretans for every German shot". In some mountain villages, the male population was wiped out. Today, young Germans who know the history of the island can only marvel at the great hospitality now shown them by the Greeks.

The long occupation and terror did not succeed in breaking the resistance of the Cretans. On the contrary, the island became the very centre of Greek resistance. Many of the actions taken by the Cretan people were courageous ones. They paid for them in blood during the rigorous punishments inflicted by German occupying forces.

The older people still remember these incidents vividly, particularly the surprise action by partisans which caused the capitulation of the German headquarters in October 1944. But even this led to a terrible revenge, and the mountain village of Anógia was completely destroyed. The effects of such persistent resistance, which brought so much grief and sorrow, were still being felt long after the war and later, the official recognition of this was of great importance.

It was not until 1945 that the last troops departed from Crete, leaving burnt villages, bombed out cities and destroyed roads behind them. The island was in economic ruins.

The last important chapter of the struggle for freedom lies in the recent past, and the bloody civil war that followed World War II when, backed by the Allies, the post-war

tained in the Greek parliament until 1963.

On 21 April 1967, a group of right-wing colonels staged a *coup d'état* against the elected government, and destroyed the liberal politics of the centrist coalition under George Papandréou, establishing a military dictatorship. Any opposition was rigorously suppressed, detention camps were set up, and the regime supported the foreign policy of the American protecting power.

Student unrest in 1973 and the Junta's involvement in Cyprus in 1974 resulted in the final downfall of the dictatorship. In

authorities went to battle against the left-wing groups that had emerged from the wartime Resistance.

In 1947, Greece became a republic with parliamentary democracy, with Crete as one of its 10 administrative provinces. Because of Greece's strategic importance on the eastern flank of NATO and what the Pentagon and the CIA continued to see as a communist threat, conservative majorities were main-

Left and above, monuments to the freedom fight of the Cretans. Venizélos was in the forefront during the fight for independence.

1981 PASOK, the socialist party led by George Papandreau's son, Andréas, came to power on the promise of freeing the country from US influence.

British troops are still stationed on the island and the US, who replaced Britain as the "protective power" in 1952, has military bases at Timbaka in the Messará plain and Goúves near Iráklion remain. They show that, however beautiful the island may be to visitors, however much apparently off the beaten track it seems, its strategic importance is as relevant to its people today as it has ever been.

Crete, an island of sunshine equidistant from Asia, Africa and Europe, has become a major tourist attraction. What's more, its popularity continues to grow, a trend not likely to change for some years yet.

The many battles fought over Crete serve to reinforce the historical importance of this central point of the Mediterranean. It is still a very important place today. In the old days, it was a necessary base from which the safety of trading routes could be ensured, whereas nowadays its strategic military importance which precedence. With its air force and rocket bases and the fleet in Soúda Bay, Crete is now one of the most vital NATO bases in Europe.

Here on the island of Crete, about 4,000 years ago, the first great European civilisation developed. It was named the Minoan civilisation, after the mythical king Minos, son of Zeus and Europa. Numerous excavations have yielded a great deal of information about this period, but much of the life of the Minoans still remains obscure. What is certain is that the Minoan palaces and places of worship constitute some of the main attractions of the island. Even Homer (c. 800 BC) was full of admiration as the *Odyssey* shows:

Crete is a land set in the dark billowing seas,
Fertile and charming and surrounded by water. There live
Numerous people, and their cities are ninety,
People of many races and many languages! There live
Achais, Kydones and native Cretans,
Dorians of three different groups, and noble Pelasgers,
Their royal city is Knossós, where Minos ruled,
Who spoke nine years long with Zeus, the great god.

But even for Homer the Minoan epoch was ancient history and shrouded in that same mystery which captures and fascinates visitors to Knossós to this day.

Explorers assume that the 90 cities referred to had about 1.2 million inhabitants. Today there are only about half a million people who live on the island, but the mixture is still as colourful. The appearance of Crete has, however, changed dramatically. Ancient authors tell of huge cypress and pine forests, but centuries of plunder have denuded the island, leaving bare limestone scenery. Only further inland, mainly in the west, are there any wooded areas.

Geography and Economy: There are four high mountain ranges which form the backbone of the island: the Lefká Ori in the west with Páchne at 2,452 metres (8,045 ft); the central Ida or Psilorítis Mountains with Mount Ida at 2,456 metres (8,057 ft); the Díkti Mountains with its highest peak 2,148 metres (7,047 ft) in the east are the Sitía Mountains with the highest peak, Aféndis Stavoménos reaching 1,476 metres (4,843 ft). Then there are the lower ranges such as the Asteroússia Mountains in the south, so that 51 percent of Crete is mountainous and another 26 percent is hilly.

The remaining 23 percent of flat land is devoted to agriculture, which next to tourism is the main industry on the island. Vegetables, olives, vineyards and citrus fruit are cultivated. On the Messará Plain, with its vast expanse of about 140 sq km (54 sq miles), and in other smaller flat areas, production has been increased by the introduction of greenhouses enabling the farmers to reap more than one harvest per year.

The fertile high plains of Lassíthi, Omalós, Nída and Askífou provide not only a sharp contrast to the limestone mountains, but offer the only ground where potatoes and cereals can be grown, although the bulk of these still has to be imported.

Organisation and Population: Crete is divided into four administrative districts and the four capital cities of these districts lie on the north coast. It is quite impossible to say which is the most typical city, as with Knossós or Kydonia in ancient times, for the four are completely different from one another. Each has its own character: Iráklion with its oriental colour and confusion epitomises the choleric, effervescent temperament; Haniá by contrast is sanguine. Réthimnon has a melancholy aspect, while Agios Nikólaos is phlegmatic and opulent.

As the best beaches are on the northern coast, it is here that the tourists congregate. Almost 50 percent of all holiday makers are to be found on the 70-km (43-mile) stretch

populous region. Of course other districts have their own attractions: Haniá with its 126,000 inhabitants is full of contrast; Lassíthi with 70,000 people in a large area, is the least densely populated, and Réthimnon with 62,000 people, is the smallest and most mountainous district.

Climate and Weather: Blue skies and a glorious view over fields, mountains and sea: most brochures picture Crete as having eternal summer weather. In fact, there are three climatic zones on the island. The north has a typical Mediterranean climate, the interior

Crete and Southern Greece

between Iráklion and Agios Nikólaos, which is home to the current tourist capital of the same name.

Iráklion, with its namesake capital city, is the colossus of the districts. About 244,000 people live here, almost half the total population of the island. Here too more ancient sites are found than on the rest of the island districts put together, which indicates that even in the early days this was the most

has mountain weather and the south is subtropical, with desert climate at times. There are only two seasons, the dry season from April to October with July and August as the hottest months, and the cooler season from November to March, with the rainiest months being from November to February. While there is no real autumn, spring arrives briskly in April and May. The short spring has beautiful, clear weather without the intense heat of summer.

These climactic changes do, of course, have an effect on the choice of holiday period. The summer months are the best for beach holidays, as the sometimes almost unbearable heat precludes walking and sightseeing. The cool, sunny weather in April is a good time to explore the south coast and the glorious flowers which bloom in profusion are a sight to behold. The sea is warm right up until October, but by autumn the colours have faded and the fields after the harvest are empty and brown.

Then there are the unpredictable winds, which can change suddenly. The hot, dry south winds which often carry sand from the Sahara can be felt even in the north. The

strict laws for the Spartans, and today the island is a sad reflection of unlawfulness. No one knows to whom the island belongs, least of all the Cretans, who in the past, and in recent times have shed so much blood trying to free themselves from the yoke of Islam, but in vain. The valiant sons of this classic isle fight this national battle bravely, and at the head of the warriors, as in Ireland, Poland and Tirol and elsewhere in similar struggles, are enthusiastic priests for whom the fight for freedom of the land is consecrated to God. The capital city, Candia, and the impor-

northwesterly winds, however, cool down the air in the baking summer heat. However, if you go out boating, you really must pay special attention to the extremely change-able nature of the winds on the waters around the island.

Tourism: About 100 years ago, according to the *Illustrated Manual of Geography and Ethnology*, this was the sight which greeted the traveller arriving by sea: "In the distance the jagged mountains of the isle of Crete appeared, with the highest peak the Ida, where Cretan Zeus was born. From these people, the Cretan Dorians, Lykurg took his

tant port of Canea have little attraction for us today as things stand, we'll leave them be-hind, and sail to the island of Milo, where there is peace."

This impression seems to have lasted for a long time. Up until the 1950s, travellers would pass Crete by. In 1953, for example, only 450 visitors were counted. Since then the numbers have steadily increased and today more than 1.5 million visit the island each year.

In accordance with Arthur Koestler's re-mark that "tourists are more easily milked than cows" (here it's sheep and goats, of course) the revenue from tourism has almost equalled that of agriculture, traditionally the most important branch of the economy. This change has brought with it a range of problems, some direct, others less so. It's quicker to earn money as a waiter than as a farmer, so many young people are leaving the villages, which then suffer a rise in the ratio of old people. In the long run, this could bring about the decline of the rural economy.

There has definitely been a decline in local traditions, most notably from the tourists' point of view, with regard to hospitality.

often to the detriment of the local cuisine.

Prosperity alone has altered things too and brought modern Western standards into conflict with local traditional values. While the difference in the standard of living between those people directly involved in the tourist trade and those who are not have, in some cases, led to social divisiveness. This is happening today, not just in the coastal areas, but also within the villages and towns and even in quite isolated mountain settlements.

There are also other quite unexpected difficulties. As most tourists don't just come for

In fact the legendary Cretan hospitality in olden days was only offered to certain foreigners, who were to a some extent "the minority passing through". Nowadays, if one arrives alone, particularly in the interior, or visits older folks, everything is still as it used to be. However, certain things, particularly in the gastronomic field, have changed. Food has had to match international tastes,

Left, pupils from the Music School of Réthimnon acquainting themselves with Cretan folk music. **Above**, viticulture is one of the most important sources of income.

the Minoans or the climate, but want to experience something of the "real" Crete, they are irritated that their money has had the effect of changing the country in a way which is actually not in their interest at all.

Motorways, of great benefit to everyone, are seldom criticised, but when village communities tear down their old houses, which were uninhabitable by our standards, and rebuild themselves villages in the finest concrete, then one can understand the public's irritation, for we want everything to stay nice and picturesque. At least on holiday one wants to enjoy unspoiled beauty.

Many places are financially far better off than before, but this new competitive thinking often leads to quarrels. In Paleóhora, which has for years been prone to such bickering, a rather bitter joke used to go around that the Cretans were going to leave their little town to the tourists and retreat into the mountains.

Despite what one sees in Hersónissos or Mália, Crete is in no real danger of being spoiled. Regular visitors will see immense changes: a remote village which has suddenly popped up, or another daring dream of

climate and natural beauty, is a boon to the tourists. One just has to try to ensure that the development is kept within limits, thus preserving the intrinsic charm and loveliness of the island so that it can still be considered a blessing to everyone.

The Church: Almost all Cretans are adherents of the GreekOrthodox Church, which has always played a special role on the island. During the long periods of foreign domination, the Church was much more than just a community of believers. It was a social institution, running schools and hospitals;

the Cretan planners come true. This trend of thought led Ierápetra, perhaps with an envious eye on the sophistication of the French Riviera, to build a promenade of overly grand proportions.

But it would be a mistake to see only the negative side of tourism on Crete. There are no natural resources on the island and, apart from a few food and textile factories, no industry either. Thus jobs are extremely scarce here. It is noticeable just how many Greeks speak English. All in all, one has to admit that tourism is as much a blessing to the island, as Crete, with its Mediterranean

most important, it was the focus of unity and resistance to oppression.

In a novel by P. Prevelákis, the following dialogue takes place between a worker and a monk. The two are locked in an argument with each other:

"Worker: And to think I took you for a holy man.

Monk: Here one is a man first, and only then holy."

This original and somewhat profane interpretation of Christian teaching (think of "turning the other cheek") is typically Cretan. The struggle of the people against the various foreign rulers over the centuries has always been closely bound up with the Church. The many attacks on the island's 34 monasteries are a clear indication of just where the enemy suspected the centres of resistance to be.

Just how seriously the Cretans took their maxim "freedom or death" was never more clearly demonstrated than at the monastery of Arkádi. Although there have been similar struggles and battle cries elsewhere (in Germany, for example, in the ballad of *Pidder Ling* by Detlev v. Liliencron, 1883, the cry

has also been criticism of the attitude of the Church during the Turkish occupation, including charges of co-operation.

Civil marriage was introduced in 1983, and many of the younger Cretans now prefer this alternative. But among the older folk, and particularly in more remote areas, the influence and standing of the Church are as great as ever. Of course, none of this is a uniquely Cretan phenomenon.

Politics: It could be said, as an analogy to what the monk said, that "here one is first a Cretan, and only then a Greek". It is true that

was "rather dead than slave"), nowhere has the duration of suppression equalled that which has taken place on Crete over the centuries. Thus the bonds between Church and people became particularly strong.

But nowadays the influence of religion is waning. The younger generation is not prepared to grant the Church its traditional influence. Church greed is criticised. There

Left, the Lassíthi Plateau is the centre of agriculture. **Above**, tourism makes money ever important both as a means of payment and as a status symbol on Crete.

the Cretans have always worked towards *enosis*, union with Greece, but for reasons of security, not because of any deep feeling of solidarity. There's a saying, "The English are megalomaniacs: they think they are the best in the world. The Irish are more modest – they merely feel themselves superior to the English."

Those sentiments, so neatly expressed, could apply equally well to the relationship between the Cretans and the Greeks, who are not megalomaniacs. Cretans put aside their feelings of superiority and cheer loyally when football teams from Athens or

Thessaloniki are beating teams from other European countries.

Fundamental to this feeling of superiority is the longing for freedom. Anything which appears to a Cretan as a curtailment of liberty is rejected. The course of their history has forced the people to become experts at discerning enemy intentions. It's no wonder that at Greek election time, the results from the administrative district of Crete are always markedly different from those returned by the rest of the country.

When a referendum on the abolition of the

ate, self-sacrificing and hospitable, then one can see the resemblance of these traits to the climate. But of course, there's another side to the coin.

When studying the Cretan character, one could be forgiven for thinking that the words "Cretan" and "critical" were related, or even had exactly the same meaning. (Etymologically however, there is no connection: critical comes from the verb *krínein*, to separate.) Cretans are definitely highly critical. As they are interested in any kind of politics, the main target of their criticism is clear. But not

monarchy was held in 1974, only 69 percent of the Greeks voted for abolition, whereas 91 percent of the Cretan population returned a vote against the monarchy. And where else would ordinary people go into the streets armed, to protest against the removal of art treasures from their museums? That's what happened in 1979 in Iráklion when the then Prime Minister Karamanlís wanted to loan part of the Minoan collection abroad.

The Cretan Character: There's an interesting theory that, in time, human nature takes on the characteristics of the weather. When one hears that Cretans are brave, proud, passion-

far behind is their propensity for criticising each other. Cretans are proud to be Cretans, and this is evident in their criticism of other groups and nationalities. But internally, this critical attitude leads to a kind of hierarchy of superiority. The educated feel superior to the uneducated, the city dwellers to the farmers, those who live in the mountains to the fishermen, the rich to the poor, which again makes Crete rather like the rest of the world.

Over two thousand years ago, Epimenides remarked that "all Cretans are liars, lazybones and bad hats". As Epimenides himself was a Cretan, the saying takes on another dimension. What might just have been an objective truth becomes something more. The philosopher would not have made such a remark casually. At the time, Crete was ruled by the Dorians, and one can imagine that his remark was meant to sow the seeds of doubt in the minds of the rulers, making them feel that there was nothing in either the character or action of the Cretans which they could take at face value.

It was only after St Paul had quoted this phrase of Epimenides (Epistle of Paul to Titus, 1:12) adding "This witness is true" that the remark took on the gravity of a judgement. So how do the Cretans stand these days as regards their attitude to the truth? All things considered, the following picture emerges: Cretans are given to showing off and making up stories. They talk a lot, promise a lot, and the next day they've forgotten it all, or it doesn't matter any more. And whether from necessity or for fun, they do tell lies. Reliability is just not their strong point. They are undisciplined and seldom finish what they start. If you arrange something with a Cretan, you can be pretty sure it won't come off.

An old saying on the island goes: "He who doesn't cheat stays poor." The author D. McNeil Doren, who lived on Crete for a long time, wrote of a Cretan girlfriend who completely changed character when he entered her shop to buy something. Having just helped him as a friend, she immediately tried to diddle him as a customer. This strange phenomenon is apparently quite common, as Cretans try to find out in their own way just how clever someone is.

So, feeling disillusioned, you go to the beach and cast your longing eyes at a succulent grape and the next minute it's yours. Or, in the evening, you ask the waiter at a café or hotel bar the name of a particular song that is being sung on television and the next morning there's the cassette at the reception desk, as a gift for you.

Left, in Iráklion Cretans and non-Cretans alike spend hours in the cafés. **Right**, iced coffee (known as frappé) is refreshing on hot days.

Generosity and indifference, spontaneity and calculation. How can these attributes be so intertwined? It's probably best simply to accept the Cretans, rather than to try to understand them. Perhaps they really are like the weather – where out of a clear blue sky, a sudden squall can blow up, or without warning, the temperature change – and who can honestly say that they have ever understood the weather?

Once Again – the Minoans: The singularity of Crete was accurately summed up by Henry Miller when he wrote in 1940:

"Greece is that which everyone knows, even if they have never been there... Crete is something else. Crete is a cradle, an instrument, a test tube in which a volcanic experiment is taking place." One could add the paradox, Crete is that which no one knows, however many times he has been there.

While architecture, politics, philosophy and religion all have clear-cut contours in Greece, on Crete so much is still lost in the mists of time. If you are looking for well-preserved monuments like the Parthenon temples, you will probably be disappointed. For on Crete there are only fragments, but these don't pose limits on the imagination.

Despite many successful excavations, there is still so much which is unknown about the Minoan civilisation, and so much which may never be known. Was there in fact a monarchical system? If so, then what kind of monarchy was it that literally dared to place itself in the midst of the people, as is so clearly evident in Káto Zákros? What was the function of the buildings we refer to as palaces, and what was their relation to each other? If one assumes a matriarchy, then were the supposed kings actually priests, and the priestesses perhaps queens? So many questions still remain unanswered.

This mystery, together with the lack of clear-cut facts, is in itself an attraction. It's not that everyone can make up their own exact picture of the Minoans, but the relative absence of hard facts gives an unusual leeway for personal theories.

The Cretan authority J. Gaitanides went one step further when he asserted that Crete was a continent. Such excess must surely have been influenced by the Cretan love of exaggeration. But what else can one call the sites of the Minoan culture, rising like huge monoliths out of the surrounding wilderness? Even later periods of foreign rule concentrate such a quantity of historical events on the island as are normally only found on whole continents. Last but not least, a world of consummate independence has been created by the fiercely individualistic Cretan people. In a word: the man is right! And you cannot really get to know a continent in one brief visit.

A Practical Start: It's best to be mobile on the island of Crete. The public bus service is good, and you can reach quite remote places on buses, but they are rather slow. So it is much better to hire a car, although more expensive. As you can move freely in a car it's easy, particularly in mountain areas, to underestimate the distances. Only the New Road along the north coast is worthy of motorway status. However, there are other well-built stretches of road along which you can make quick progress, for example, from Iráklion in the Agía Varvára direction.

But perhaps when you are exploring the island you should allow enough time for time itself to become unimportant – and simply enjoy the holiday. Or how about riding on a motorbike or moped? It will carry you – although not quite as safely – to your destination with the refreshing Cretan wind blowing in your face.

There are bicycles too for hire in certain places. Or if you want to enjoy the scenery more intensely, why not try shanks's pony? It pays to plan your days. If you have only a little time, but want to see a lot, there's a danger of missing the essential nature of the island, while ruining your holiday. The maxim of "better to enjoy the beach than traipse around the monuments in boredom" has turned many a Crete visitor into a Crete lover. Antique monuments have the enormous advantage that they won't walk away. If you visit them, don't try to cram in too many facts and figures. Just remember that under the bright Cretan sun, everything changes. It's best to travel light – that goes for your mind as well as for your luggage!

Festivals: The Minoans loved celebrations, if H.G. Wunderlich is to be believed. He was inspired by a mural to describe a harvest festival. As he saw it, the people had gathered in the palace courtyard, the women dressed in their best and their dark hair elaborately styled. The sign for the beginning of the tournament was about to be given by the priestess with the holy snakes held high in her hands. Seven young men and women were to perform a breakneck leap over the bull. Then the people would go outside until the evening, when they would all reassemble in the theatre to watch the dances of the girls.

Cretans today like nothing more than a celebration. Any excuse will do. Most festivals are in honour of the saints, and on their name days, a service is held in the church dedicated to the saint, which is followed by a public festival. (See Travel Tips, pages 232–233.)

The most important festival of all is still a wedding. Before the roads were properly built, wedding celebrations often lasted a

week. As travel was difficult, a wedding would be a good opportunity for people to get together and to enjoy each other's company for a while.

At the beginning of the century, a traditional wedding would be conducted as follows: First, an "inviter" chosen by the relatives of both the bride and bridegroom, would go to the villages where the couple came from, to announce the good news, and to invite the guests.

The wedding itself would always be held on a Sunday. On the Saturday afternoon, This was an opportunity for many tears to be shed, as the wedding also meant that the bride would leave her parents' home for ever. Then the *pastiká* would be sung (*mantinádes* especially composed for the occasion, and all about the bride). The bridegroom was not allowed to hear these songs, and they had to be finished by the time he and his relatives and friends arrived to fetch the bride and her party to the church.

After the wedding service, the dance for the bridal veil was usually held immediately outside the church. All the male relatives of

some of the guests would carry the trousseau, which had been on view for a few days, from the bride's house to that of the groom. *Balotés* were sung, often the impromptu *mantinádes* (two- or four-line strophic songs with a chorus).

On Saturday evening, the villagers from the place where the couple were to make their home would bring symbolic gifts, the *kaniskiá*, which mainly consisted of meat, cheese, oil and wine. Poorer people often brought bread, potatoes and onions.

On the Sunday morning, the bride dressed in all her finery would receive the guests. the couple would dance with the bride. The last to dance would receive the veil, which meant that he too would soon be married. Then the procession, led by a lyre player, would go to the bridegroom's house, and again *pastiká* would be sung. This time the subject of the songs would be wider with plenty of good wishes and practical advice for the couple.

In the groom's house, the bride's mother-in-law would give the bride honey and nuts, *melokário*, as a welcoming gift. Before the bride crossed the threshold, she would dip her finger into the honey, and make a cross on the door. This ritual was performed to bring good luck to the household.

Before the guests sat down at the tables laden with good things, everyone sang a prayer like song in which the mothers-in-law were wished strength to accept their new son and daughter-in-law. Then to the sound of gunshots, the festivities would begin, which would continue for a good three or four days. A great deal of crockery would be broken during the proceedings. Nowadays, this old-fashioned kind of wedding is only celebrated in the more isolated villages.

the most important. Following the winter carnival season, Lent is traditionally a sombre time of fasting and church-going; however, many Greeks don't take it so seriously these days. Orthodox households adhere to strict dietary rules which become more and more rigorous as Easter approaches. During Holy Week, meat and eggs are forbidden; even cooking oil is not allowed. Only on Wednesday may one use oil for cooking.

After Midnight Mass on Easter Day, there is a traditional procession, which is the climax of the Greek religious year. Churches

A christening is another very important occasion for a feast, although this event is less lavish than a wedding. The celebrations always take place at night, and often everything is over just after midnight. Here too, special songs have to be sung, and the health of the child is toasted with wine and *rakí* –a grape-crush brandy.

Out of all the Church festivals, Easter is

Left, a group of Orthodox Greeks present bread as an offering to St George. **Above**, even in this modern day and age, traditional weddings do take place.

are packed to bursting with the faithful, all of whom have brought along candles with which to "carry home the light" of the Resurrection. Outside in the churchyard, a funeral pyre is erected and an enormous effigy of Judas Iscariot is burnt. Then they all make up for their recent deprivations, and family meals turn into festivals of music, song and dance, with traditional Easter roast lamb, tripe soup and red eggs.

Harvest festivals, too, such as the Orange Festival in Skinés, the Wine Festival in Réthimnon and the Sultana Festival in Sitía are relaxed and joyful occasions.

In the beginning is chaos. From chaos, Gaea arises, bringing heaven (Ouranos), the sea (Pontos) and the mountains (Ourea) to the world. For lack of any other male, Gaea weds her son Uranus, and with him begets the Titans. Soon Uranus has set himself up as ruler of the world. But he fears that his children might challenge his power, and so forbids Gaea to have any more children. But Gaea joins forces with her youngest son, Cronus, who without hesitation castrates Uranus and takes his place. Then Cronus marries his sister Rhea, and begets many children by her.

But now the same fear assails Cronus as once plagued his father: he fears for his power. As he does not want to forgo the pleasures of procreation, he decides to swallow the newborn infants. This fate befalls Hestia, Demeter, Hera, Hades and Poseidon. Rhea goes to the more experienced Gaea for advice. When another child is born, Rhea wraps a stone up in swaddling clothes, and gives it to Cronus to eat. While Cronus is lulled into a false sense of security, Rhea gives birth to a son Zeus, in the Díkti Cave. He is fed by the three nymphs Amaltheia, Adrasteie and Io, and later moves to the Ida Cave, where he spends his youth.

When Zeus finds out that some of his siblings are in Cronus' stomach, he becomes cup-bearer to his father, and slips the old god an emetic. Soon afterwards his brothers and sisters are born for the second time. They acknowledge Zeus as their leader and overthrow and ban Cronus.

Once Zeus becomes the most powerful among the gods, he decides on Olympus as their home, and establishes a state and territories. This arrangement has the advantage of leaving Zeus free to pursue his main pleasure in life, which is love. Being a god, he can take on any form he chooses. One day he falls in love with Europa, the beautiful

The Sun God in zodiac circle and the Earth Mother with her children, the Four Seasons (Roman floor mosaic from Sassoferrato).

Phoenician princess. Disguised as a bull, he approaches the Phoenician coast. Europa leaps onto his back. He immediately jumps into the sea and swims to Crete, going ashore in the Bay of Mátala. Then, under the evergreen plane tree, he either reveals himself to Europa as a god and seduces the princess, or turns himself into an eagle and rapes her. Three sons are born: Minos, Rhadamanthys and Sarpedon. Soon Zeus finds other amorous pursuits. Europa marries the Cretan king Astarios who adopts her sons.

Minos is the only son who keeps up his

Wishing to discourage other aspirants to the Cretan throne by a show of power, Minos asks Poseidon for a miracle: a white bull is to emerge from the waves. Poseidon grants him his wish but the bull is so beautiful that Minos cannot bring himself to kill it, and offers a different one to Poseidon. However, Poseidon is not deceived and punishes him by making Pasiphae, Minos' wife, fall in love with the bull. In her anguish, Pasiphae confides in the court engineer Daedalus.

He ingeniously constructs a model of a cow. Pasiphae then hides herself inside the

relationship with his father. He spends nine years in the Díkti Cave, learning the art of leadership from Zeus.

Armed with tablets of law, Minos returns to humankind, banishes his brothers, and becomes the sole ruler of Crete. Even the critical historian Thucydides was impressed by the unanimity of opinion handed down by tradition, which portrays Minos as a wise man. It was not until later that contradictions appeared and he was seen as a power hungry tyrant, a shameless wooer of women – Briómartis threw herself into the sea to escape him and was saved by fishermen's nets.

model, which is immediately mounted by the bull. Thus the Minotaur is born half man half beast. Minos is beside himself with fury, and wants to kill the monster. But Ariadne, his daughter, begs for mercy for her half brother.

The white bull, saved from sacrificial offering, gains fame as an exceptionally strong and dangerous Cretan bull. Later, Heracles, who in a fit of mental disturbance killed his children, is ordered by the Delphic Oracle to perform 12 heroic deeds, one of which is to capture the Cretan bull. Heracles succeeds, and takes the bull to the Peloponnese, where it does much damage.

At this time, Androgeus, the son of King Minos, has just won the pentathlon in the Panathenian Games. While out hunting the bull, Androgeus is ambushed and murdered by a jealous rival. As soon as he hears of this, Minos sends his fleet against Athens. After a long struggle, the Athenians surrender.

As recompense for his son's murder, Minos demands the sacrifice of six youths and six maidens each year. He then orders Daedalus to construct a labyrinth below the Palace of Knossós where the Minotaur must live. Whoever enters it is faced with two

adne. She reciprocates his feelings, and promises to help him. Once the deed is done, they will marry and flee to Athens. Actually Dionysos has a claim to Ariadne, and she herself has no idea just how she can help Theseus. She turns to Daedalus for advice, and he suggests that she should give Theseus a ball of thread. Theseus fastens the thread at the beginning of the labyrinth, feels his way to the end, kills the Minotaur and, with the aid of the thread, returns to daylight and flees with Ariadne.

While they are resting on Naxos,

adversaries: the confusing labyrinth and the monster itself.

One day Theseus, the son of the King of Athens, is chosen as a sacrifice. It is more likely, however, that Theseus took it upon himself to go to Crete to fight the Minotaur. As he leaves, he hoists a black flag on his ship. If his mission is successful, Theseus is to hoist a white flag on his return.

On Crete, Theseus falls in love with Ari-

Left, figurines of the mythological bull in sale. **Above**, a modern representation of the figure of the Earth Mother.

Dionysos appears, demanding his rights. He abducts Ariadne to Lemnos, where she later bears him four sons. Theseus is in such despair at the loss of his love, that he forgets the agreed-upon sign on his journey homeward. When Aegeus sees the ship returning with a black flag aloft, he assumes that Theseus has been killed by the Minotaur. Despondent, he throws himself into the sea, and that's why it's called the Aegean.

Later, Minos discovers that it was Daedalus who helped Ariadne and Theseus to flee. As punishment, he locks Daedalus and his son Icarus in the labyrinth. But Daedalus easily finds his way out. His only problem is how to escape from the island. He makes wings for himself and Icarus. Daedalus warns his son not to fly too high, for the sun will melt his wings, nor too low for the damp sea air will weigh down the feathers. Icarus ignores the warning and flies higher and higher. The wax melts and Icarus falls into the sea. Hence the name Icarian Sea for that part of the Mediterranean.

Daedalus is a different kind of father from Aegeus. He does not commit suicide from grief, but flies as planned to Sicily. There he goes to the court of King Kokalos and, as a man of ideas, is received with open arms.

Minos has in no way forgotten the shameful deception. Eager for vengeance, he sets out to search for Daedalus. To find him, Minos thinks up a trick: he takes a spiral-formed shell and offers a big reward to anyone who manages to pull a thread through the shell.

During his travels, Minos goes to Sicily. One day he arrives at the court of King Kokalos and sets his task. Kokalos takes the shell and says he can pull the thread through. Kokalos goes to Daedalus. Now it is clear Minos has the measure of his erstwhile court engineer. In his vanity Daedalus is of course determined to solve the problem. He ties the thread to an ant, bores a hole in the shell, and lets the ant creep through the shell attracted by a trail of honey.

When Kokalos shows him the shell, with the thread pulled through, Minos knows he has reached his goal, and demands the surrender of Daedalus. Kokalos agrees, but before carrying out his promise, he offers to hold a feast in honour of his illustrious guest. Now Minos' end is drawing near. While taking his bath to prepare for the grand feast, he is murdered by the daughters of King Kokalos, who pour boiling water over him. Thus Minos, the son of Zeus, meets his end in a Sicilian bath. He disappears from the scene as suddenly as the civilisation which bore his name.

Inner picture in an Attic clay bowl from Duris (about 470 BC), Athena and Heracles.

SUPERSTITION

The atomic physicist Niels Bohr was just putting a horseshoe up in his house when a friend arrived. "What are you doing that for?" he asked, amazed. "Surely you're not superstitious?" "Of course I'm not," answered Bohr, "but I've heard it works all the same."

It is generally thought that superstition is a relic of the distant past, of pre-Christian times, when every natural phenomenon had its own god or "prime mover". But just as Christmas was "created" in 336 by the Church to counterbalance the winter solstice, so probably the early, disparate gods have been incorporated in our one almighty God. When, from time to time, one of these emerges from obscurity, and throws into relief the underlying disunity of the Christian faith, we call it superstition.

Apart from the summer solstice, other heathen customs have been so completely integrated into orthodox belief and practice, that people are in fact quite unaware of their origin. The plea for deliverance from suffering and infirmity must be one of the most ancient expressions of religion. It was for this purpose that several thousand years ago different parts of the body were fashioned in clay and set up in the holy places. Votive offerings were linked to this, as the gods did nothing for nothing. The process has hardly changed, except that nowadays the sacrificial offering is money, and light metal plaques are used instead of clay. In Hrissoskalítissa there are many such votive offerings.

A popular dictionary defines superstition as "belief in unnatural processes, as opposed to valid religious and scientific concepts." Just think about a "miracle" in this context. There belief and superstition are inextricably linked; in fact the one defines the other. For a

A grotesque tree root, believed to work miracle and protect the inhabitants of the shore of Préveli.

miracle is by definition that which is not explicable in terms of "valid religious and scientific concepts" or, in other words, concepts which have arisen from experience of life and an interpretation of the laws of nature. Belief and superstition are in fact very closely linked, but not always quite as closely as on Crete. However, people here don't think they are superstitious at all, despite "clear indications to the contrary".

An example of this close link between belief and superstition would be the peasant woman who can instantly calm a screaming child. Exercising her God-given gift without any kind of hypnosis, she simply uses a belt and a secret ritual. Whether the "girdle of the mother goddess" has anything to do with it, she won't say.

Here are more examples of what would elsewhere be called superstition:

1. On the first day of the quarter and, in some areas, also on the first day of the month, it is most important to note who first crosses your path. If the first person is bad, that will bring bad luck. So on those days, a family member who is – of course – a good person is sent out onto the road to test the ground. Without this precaution, no superstitious person would set foot outside the door.

2. If an unexpected guest arrives, someone creeps outside the door and spills salt on the ground. This is supposed to ensure the speedy departure of the guest.

3. At Epiphany, after Mass, believers take home candles lit from the holy flame and replace the cross burnt on the door lintel. This protects the house from bad luck and evil spirits the whole year.

4. Kazantzákis in *Zorba the Greek* refers to a "Mara" who is supposed to be the spirit of evil and a cunning pimp.

5. Black cats and broken mirrors have no meaning on Crete, but it is considered lucky to own a black hen.

tive
ferings:
presentations
afflictions
ured as a
sult of
ayer.

Modern Cretan literature is stamped by the influence of the writers Níkos Kazantzákis and Pantelís Prevelákis. Kazantzákis was born on 18 February 1883 in Varvári. The first play written by this qualified lawyer was performed in Athens in 1906. He spent the next few years in Paris studying political science and philosophy (under Henri Bergson). In 1915 he was a volunteer in the Balkan War and, four years later, Venizélos appointed him Minister of Welfare.

On leaving politics, Kazantzákis travelled to England, Spain, Russia, Japan and China. These journeys inspired him to write a series of critical travel books. In addition, he wrote lyrics, stories, novels and tragic plays with predominantly historical or religious themes, as well as philosophical essays and epic poems such as the *Odyssey*, which appeared in 1938. In 1945 he returned to politics and took a ministerial position in Soufoulis' cabinet, but soon resigned because of inter-party quarrels.

International fame came to Kazantzákis with his later works, particularly through his novel *Zorba the Greek*. However, this work has often been misunderstood. Many believe that the character of Zorba was heavily influenced by Nietzsche and is a superhuman creation, incorporating in part a second side of Kazantzákis' character, much embellished and with delusions of grandeur. In fact, although the novel cannot be regarded as a factual account, Zorba is supposed to be modelled on a man with whom Kazantzákis lived and worked on a Cretan beach for six months in 1917.

A further misunderstanding arises from the fact that Alexis Zorba is more widely known through the somewhat shallow film of the book than through the original. He is often considered to be the archetypal noble Cretan. But Zorba is, in fact, not a Cretan at all, but a Macedonian. Zorba, a Greek from

Preceding pages: upholding tradition. **Left,** Anthony Quinn and Alan Bates in the Michael Cacoyannis film *Zorba the Greek*.

the mainland, brings a breath of freedom to the Cretans caught up in their ghostly traditions. Even on Crete, Zorba only became known through the making of the film, and it is said that those who saw the film were shocked at the representation of earlier conditions on the island.

In the novel, Zorba, the man of action, comes face to face with the intellectual ditherer, Kazantzákis. Zorba stands at the centre of life, accepting things as they are. He has no inclination to improve the world. Taken in isolation, this is a conservative standpoint,

Here we come to another misunderstanding: the book is no mere adventure story, but a philosophical novel dealing with existential questions, questions of life and death. As in all Kazantzákis' works, the central theme is that of the relationship of man with God.

There's no doubt, however, that in his indisputable love for his homeland, Níkos Kazantzákis himself is the archetypal Cretan. He is always aware of the special nature of the island, and of its past. "Being a Cretan is a duty," he says. This conduct, almost that of a representative, is strongly reminiscent

which could well arouse criticism. But, on the other hand, Zorba does in fact alter the world around him – even if unintentionally. He is a kind of "mystical realist", who views things in daily life always as new and wonderful. He does not separate this sense of wonder – as would a believer or an intellectual – from reality; for him it is the substance of reality itself. This infatuation is infectious. In contrast, there is the "boss" full of questions, doubts and problems. He makes grandiose plans, none of which ever come near to being put into practice. He fails to "come alive".

of Thomas Mann, a similarity which extends beyond their wide education and range of interests to certain physiognomic similarities. It is certainly in no small measure due to this whole-hearted patriotism that Kazantzákis (despite the criticism) embodied in his works that he became and has remained so popular on Crete.

However, in the depiction of his contemporaries, particularly of former friends, Kazantzákis is sometimes very severe. If someone has surrendered to fate, become complacent and stopped fighting, Kazantzákis' contempt and despair is plain. In his autobiography, *Report to El Greco*, he describes a small rural scene: a bluebird has just flown past and Kazantzákis wishes to know what kind of bird it is. The peasant he asks replies, "Why do you want to know? You can't eat it." To mollify the reader, Kazantzákis adds, "I was no misanthrope; I always loved people, but from a distance…"

Almost as well-known as *Zorba the Greek* is *Freedom or Death* (1953), an exceedingly pessimistic depiction of the uprising of 1889 against the Turks. Here a different characterisation of God is given: "If you are a wolf,

works on the Index – the Vatican's list of forbidden books.

What is amazing is not so much the fact of the Church's initiative, but the timing. As early as 1928, in his book *Askitikí*, Kazantzákis had expressed what he saw as insurmountable contradictions in the so-called message of salvation: it is not God who saves man, but man who must save God.

In his novel of 1948, *Christ Recrucified,* Kazan-tzákis takes up Dostoyevsky's dark vision that the Crucifixion of Christ is extremely necessary to the Church and that it

eat; if you are a lamb, let yourself be eaten! And who is God? He is the Great Wolf – who eats both lambs and wolves and all their bones!" Certain passages in this book and many parts of the later novel, *The Last Temptation of Christ*, have offended the Church. However when the Vatican announced that it intended to excommunicate Kazantzákis, there was such an uproar in the literary world, that it was decided simply to put both

Far left, Giorgis Zorba, model for the novel. **Left**, Dimitsana with Prevelákis. **Above**, hundreds paid their last respects to Kazantzákis.

may need to be repeated throughout eternity.

With the filming of the novel *The Last Temptation of Christ* by Martin Scorsese more than 30 years after it had been put on the Index, the Church's inability to come to terms with Kazantzákis is remarkable. The objections raised today sound like a parody of the earlier criticism. Kazantzákis brought out the human side of this exceptional being – Jesus Christ – and portrayed him as "the animal that questions", a man who thinks but who also has natural desires. For anyone even partially free of prejudice, it is clear that neither in the novel nor in the film, is

Jesus disparaged. Scorcese has interpreted the novel entirely as the author intended.

The opinion that the mystery of the Passion is lessened by this interpretation echoes the same false argument as those who maintain that modern scientists have eliminated the wonder from religion. They ignore the fact that the more the scientists discover about nature, the more wonderful it becomes. Great thinkers, notably Einstein and Heisenberg, have made penetrating comments on this subject.

Kazantzákis was nominated for the Nobel

NIKOS KAZANTZAKHS

Prize for Literature in 1955 by Albert Schweitzer, among other eminent persons, but the Church managed to prevent this honour being bestowed upon him.

From 1950 onwards, Nikós Kazantzákis and his wife lived in Antibes on the French Riviera. He died on 26 October 1957 in Freiburg in Breisgau. His coffin was brought to Iráklion where it was received by enormous crowds and he was buried in the Martinengo Bastion of the old city wall in southern Iráklion. In the background is the striking profile of the Joúchtas. Inscribed on the tombstone are the words of Kazantzákis:

"I hope for nothing. I fear nothing. I am free."

It is often maintained that Kazantzákis was posthumously "banned" to the Martinengo Bastion and that he was denied burial in consecrated ground. This is certainly not true, it is a custom on Crete to allocate special burial places to prominent citizens. Also when he died, he received a proper funeral service and in 1977 a memorial Mass was celebrated for him.

Pantelís Prevelákis: It was surely an omen that he was born in Réthimnon on 18 February 1909 – 26 years to the day after Níkos Kazantzákis. Prevelákis studied philology in Paris and Thessaloníki and, from 1939 to 1975, was professor of Art History at the Academy of Arts in Athens. All his life he remained in close contact with his birthplace. This fascination can still be understood today, for in no other Cretan city is the "geological layering" of time so clearly in evidence as it is here.

So perhaps it is no wonder that Prevelákis became known as an author of "historical dimensions". For the interpretation of the changes wrought by time, he invented a new category, that of "Mythistory", a mixture of historical interpretation and subjective mythological impressions.

In 1938 his first effort in this direction, *Chronicle of a City,* appeared to great acclaim. Later novels received a varied reception by critics and readers. There was, however, widespread agreement that the historical and the subjective mythical did not complement one another and in the end should be treated as separate entities.

While Kazantzákis' international fame lives on, Prevelákis was soon eclipsed after his death in March 1986. Bookshops and librarians no longer remember his name. But while not enjoying the same level of recognition, Prevelákis is nevertheless an interesting and gripping writer.

Reading works by these two native sons is essential if you wish to gain an understanding of Crete before your visit.

Left, Kazantzákis – still revered in Crete. **Right**, taking after the legendary Alexis Zorba.

Archaeologists and modern adventurers only began to discover the secrets of Crete, the birthplace of European civilisation, less than a century ago. Yet for thousands of years this sunny island, the fifth largest in the Mediterranean and just 320 km (199 miles) from the shore of Africa, has been casting its spell over foreign invaders.

In recent times there has been a different kind of invasion of Crete. Searching for the origins of our culture and also for a kind of lost paradise, visitors of different kinds have attempted to take possession of the island. This time things are different. The intention of the new "invaders" is peaceful, and their aim is to benefit mankind by safeguarding the birthplace of European civilisation.

What began as a matter of scientific interest revealed a glorious culture which shattered the historical notions about the development of the Occident. The joy of life and the love of peace evident in the Minoan epoch, as well as the superior place women used to hold during that time, were extraordinary revelations to the world.

And in the 1960s, it was this ancient philosophy and the natural purity of the Cretans' simple way of life that beckoned to the disillusioned youth of the industrialised nations, tired of a materialistic, Western lifestyle. Attracted by the world of Zorba, they saw Crete as a place where dreams came true and settled in small communities where they enjoyed a carefree, happy lifestyle in idyllic surroundings.

The invaders of today usually land in Iráklion, disembarking from countless ferries and charter flights. Tourism has left its mark on Crete in many ways. There is now an average of eight flights

Preceding pages: calmness of the sea revealed through a hotel window white and blue, the Greek national colours; storm over Iráklion.

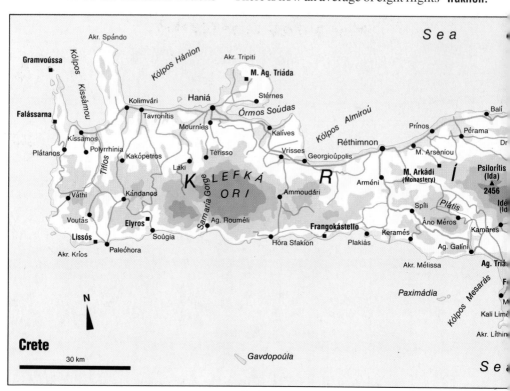

daily from Athens to Iráklion, four from Athens to Haniá and thousands arrive each year on ferries from Piraeus.

Concrete and asphalt have altered what not so long ago was the unspoilt charm of the island. But if you take the time and make the effort, the world of the Minoans and of Zorba is still there, far from the madding crowd. Off the beaten track a fascinating and unique island is waiting to be explored.

To help you on your journey of discovery, the following chapters have been compiled to offer inspiration as well as practical advice, starting with Iráklion. If you wish to avoid the heat, dust and tourist rabble, then you should attempt a cool, quiet visit to the two excellent museums of archaeology and history of Iráklion. Here you will gain some insight into the turbulent history of Crete's largest city.

From Iráklion, move on to Knossós, the most important excavation site on Crete. More Minoan palaces can be found in Arhánes, Mália, Agii Déka and Festós, as you follow the road south.

From Réthimnon you can follow a trail of discovery to numerous old Cretan monasteries before continuing westwards to the city of Haniá. The highlight of the journey through this part of the island is a visit to the spectacular Samariá Gorge.

Then it's eastward, back to the tourist centres, the bustle and the liveliness of the beach resort of Agios Nikólaos, and on to southern, coastal Ierápetra and Sitía. For those interested in art, there is another fascinating Minoan palace located in Káto Zákros.

Lastly, a visit to the Lassíthi Plateau, the centre of Cretan agriculture, and the Díkti Cave, the birthplace of Zeus, where the tour comes to an end.

Detailed information on travel, accomodation and dining can be found in Travel Tips on pages 250-254.

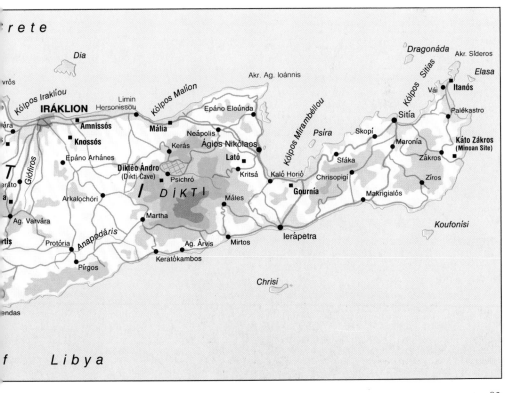

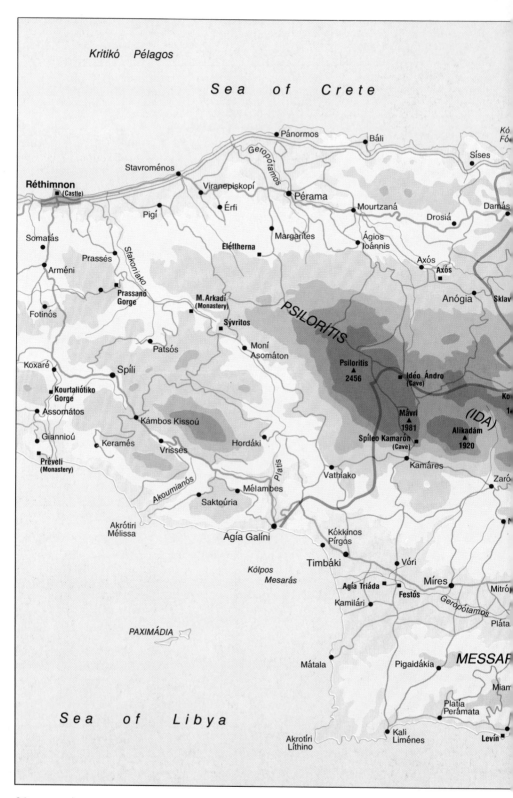

Kritikó Pélagos

Sea of Crete

Pánormos
Báli
Kó
Fó

Síses

Stavroménos
Geropótamos

Viranepiskopí
Réthimnon
■ (Castle)

Pigí
Érfi
Pérama
Mourtzaná
Damás

Drosiá

Somatás
Margarítes
Ágios
Ioánnis

Prassés
Eléftherna ■
Axós

Arméni
Stakoniako
Axós ■

Prassanó
Gorge ■
M. Arkadí
(Monastery) ■
PSILORÍTIS
Anógia
Sklav

Fotinós
Sývritos ■

Patsós
Moní
Asomáton
Psiloritis
▲ 2456
Idéo Ándro ■
(Cave)

Koxaré
Spíli
Ko
1

Kourtaliótiko
Gorge ■
Mávri
▲ 1981
(IDA)

Assomátos
Kámbos Kissoú
Alikadám
▲ 1920

Giannioú
Keramés
Spíleo Kamarón ■
(Cave)

Préveli ■
(Monastery)
Vrissés
Hordáki
Kamáres
Zaró

Akoumianós
Platis
Vathíako

Saktoúria
Mélambes

Akrótiri
Mélissa
Agía Galíni
Kókkinos
Pírgos

Kólpos
Mesarás
Timbáki
Vóri

Míres
Mitró

PAXIMÁDIA
Agía Triáda ■
Festós ■
Geropótamos

Kamilári
Pláta.

MESSAR

Mátala
Pigaidákia
Miam

Platía
Perámata

Sea of Libya

Akrótiri
Líthino
Kali
Liménes
Levín ■

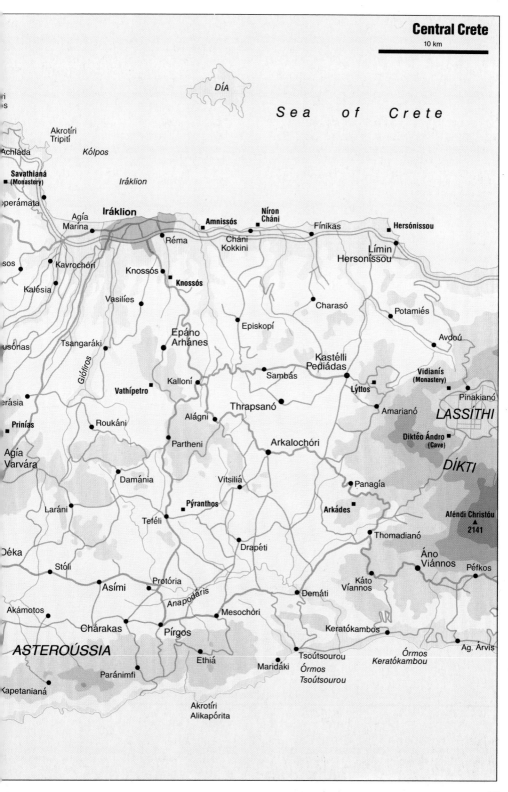

DÍA

Sea of Crete

Akrotíri
Tripití

Achláda

Kólpos

Savathianá
■ (Monastery)

Iráklion

perámata

Agía
Marína

Iráklion

Amnissós

Níron
Cháni

Fínikas

Hersónissou

Réma

Cháni
Kokkini

Límin
Hersoníssou

sos

Kavrochóri

Knossós

Kalésia

Knossós

Charasó

Potamiés

Vasilíes

Episkopí

Avdoú

usónas

Tsangaráki

Epáno
Arhánes

Kastélli
Pediádas

Vidianís
(Monastery)

Giófiros

Kalloní

Sambás

Lýttos

Pinakianó

Vathípetro

Thrapsanó

Amarianó

LASSÍTHI

erásia

Prinías

Roukáni

Alágni

Arkalochóri

Diktéo Ándro ■
(Cave)

Agía
Varvára

Partheni

Vitsiliá

Panagía

DÍKTI

Damánia

Pýranthos

Arkádes

Aféndi Christóu
▲
2141

Laráni

Teféli

Drapéti

Thomadianó

Áno
Viánnos

Péfkos

Déka

Stóli

Protória

Demáti

Káto
Víannos

Asími

Anapodáris

Mesochóri

Akámotos

Chárakas

Pírgos

Keratókambos

Ag. Árvis

ASTEROÚSSIA

Ethiá

Maridáki

Tsoútsourou

Órmos
Keratókambou

Paránimfi

Órmos
Tsoútsourou

Kapetanianá

Akrotíri
Alikapórita

IRÁKLION

There was a city named Iráklion on Crete as early as the Minoan epoch. Greek mythology tells that it was here that Heracles performed the seventh of his 12 deeds: the slaying of the fire-breathing Cretan bull. The Greeks probably named the city Herakleion or Herakleia, in honour of their hero. In the following period, under the Romans and Byzantines, this region was only sparsely populated. It was not until after the conquest of Crete by the Saracens in AD 827 that Iráklion once again gained importance when it was expanded and fortified. The new name El Khandak, which meant "castle with moat", described the architectural alterations of the city.

In 961 Nikefóros Fokás reconquered Crete for the Byzantine Empire. By doing so, he completely destroyed El Khandak, which was later rebuilt and named Chandax.

The Venetians took Crete without bloodshed in 1204. They bought the island, but it took them until 1210 to supplant the Genoese. Chandax became Candia, and not long afterwards the whole island was given that name. During the four centuries of Venetian rule, Candia became a centre of culture. In practice this meant that the new rulers lived in luxury in the main city, while the native Greek inhabitants were stripped of their land and possessions and reduced to slavery.

After 1536, the Veronese fortifications engineer Michele Sanmicheli built a great fortress around the city, which withstood the attacks of the Turks for 21 years. But eventually the Venetians could hold out no longer, and in 1669 the Turks took Crete. Once again the city of Candia changed its name. This time it was called Megálo Kástro, meaning great fort, but again its

influence waned. The Turks selected Haniá as their centre of activity, and in 1850 its status was elevated to that of the island's new capital. Even today, Haniá retains its Turkish character.

When the Turks finally left Crete in 1898, Megálo Kástro once again became Herakleion – or Iráklion in modern Greek. After the annexation to Greece, Iráklion took on the aspect of a metropolis. In World War II the city suffered heavy bombing by the Germans and British. But it was not until 1972 that Iráklion once again became the capital city of Crete.

Many travellers have the same problem with the city of Iráklion as they do with Greek cuisine. They are disappointed before ever really giving it a chance. However, there's no denying that Iráklion is difficult to fall in love with at first sight. Particularly in the city centre, it seems to be exactly what the tourist is trying to escape – filth, noise

and nothing but traffic and ugliness. But if you explore behind the scenes, you'll discover the true nature of the city. It has, in fact, a lot that is pleasant to offer; not least its people, who manage to combine metropolitan open-mindedness with unspoilt warmth.

A city tour could begin at the **market place**, where the unusual oriental atmosphere makes a visit an interesting experience. It is located on 1866 Street, to the south of **Nikefóros Fokás Square,** and is quite small. It is usually incredibly crowded, as locals as well as tourists come to do their shopping here. Although the prices are not the lowest, the quality is high. You can buy fruit, sweets, bread, fish and drinks as well as clothes, reproductions of antique works of art and souvenirs.

Halfway down the market street, **Fotioú Street** leads off to the left. This used to be the place to enjoy the relaxed atmosphere of little *tavérnes,* but these days everything is cool and profit orientated. The food is still good, but far too expensive. The market street leads to **Kornáros Square** with its lovely Turkish well house and the **Bembo Fountain**. The headless Roman statue was brought from Ierápetra by Z. Bembo.

If you turn to the right just before the end of the market street, you will find yourself at the city's handicraft centre. Here the quaint shops are huddled together as they were 100 years ago in the time of the guilds.

There's plenty of life in **Eleftherías Square** and plenty of traffic too. This semicircular area to the south of Fokás Square is lined with expensive cafés and restaurants where culture enthusiasts can relax and enjoy a drink after visiting the Archaeological Museum.

On **Dedálou Street**, one of the few pedestrian precincts in the city, there are shops to suit every taste. This street leads to **Venizélou Square** which, with

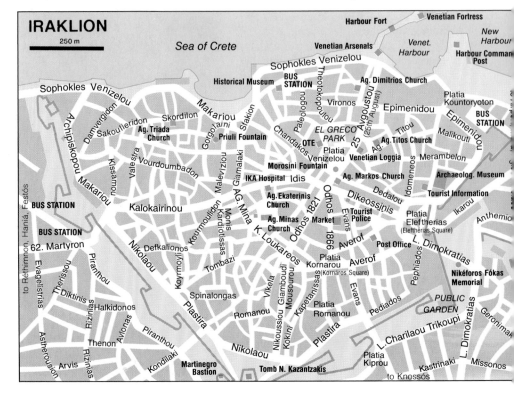

its huge traffic junction, is clearly the epicentre of Iráklion. Here in the evenings, the youth of the city gather, and as most of the stores stay open for business until late in the evening, there are always crowds of shoppers whatever the season.

The **Morosini Fountain** was built by the Venetian governor Francesco Morosini in 1628, at the end of a 15-km (nine-mile) long water pipe. This aqueduct (parts of which can be seen behind Knossós above the motorway) brought water to the city from Mount Joúchtas. The four water-spouting lions' heads are the emblem of the city, but few notice that the fountain is decorated as well with ancient mythological scenes.

Hándakos Street leads due north from the fountain. The first part of the street is also a pedestrian precinct. Here cafés and restaurants stretch for about 50 metres (55 yards).

On the eastern side of Venizélou

Square is **Agios Márkos Basilica**. This church with three aisles is the oldest Venetian basilica on Crete and impressively illustrates the eventful history of the island. It was built in 1239 in honour of the patron saint of Venice and restored several times after earthquakes in 1303 and 1508. From 1669 to 1915, it served as a mosque; later it was used as a warehouse, then as the branch of a bank and finally as a cinema. After renovation to its original Venetian style in 1961, it is now an exhibition centre for icons and copies of frescoes from Byzantine churches on Crete.

If you keep right after Agios Márkos Basilica, you reach the Venetian **Loggia**. This two-storey building was also built by Francesco Morosini, 1626–28, and was a club (*loge*) for the Venetian aristocracy. In World War II the Loggia was so badly damaged that the authorities decided to pull it down and rebuild it in the original style. Behind is the

leftheriás
quare.

present Town Hall, which used to be the **Armeria** – the Venetian armour.

Agios Títos Church, dedicated to Titus, the patron saint of Crete and its first bishop, was the seat of the Archbishop of Crete for many years. It was after the expulsion of the Saracens that the bishopric was moved from distant Górtis to Chandax (Iráklion) and this basilica was built. As the metropolitan church, it was spared by the Turks for a long time, but eventually it was turned into a mosque.

The earthquake of 1856 damaged the church so much that the renovation project of 1972 almost amounted to one of rebuilding. During these changes elements of Ottoman style were incorporated. In many ways Agios Títos is an unusual church. Among its treasures, the iconostasis and the skull of St Titus in a golden vessel are of particular note.

After crossing **25th August (25 Augústou) Street**, you can go down to the Venetian Port, where nowadays there are not many fishing boats but plenty of private luxury yachts. On the right are the enormous cylindrical vaults of the so-called **Arsenal**, which are now mainly used as shipyards and docks. A breakwater leads to the impressive harbour fort of **Koules**.

If you turn southwest from the Morosini Fountain away from the harbour and carry straight on, passing through 1821 Street, you reach a square with three churches. The largest of these is **Agios Mínas Cathedral** (1862–95). However, apart from its huge dimensions and the fact that it is the metropolitan seat, it has nothing special to offer. Nearby is the little **Agios Mínas Church** noted for its remarkable iconostasis, which is not always on show, as the church is usually locked. In the northeast corner of the square is **Agía Ekateríni Church**, which was built in the year 1555 as part of the "Convent

The church of Agios Titos.

School of Mount Sinai". This unusual school produced among others the writers V. Kornáros and G. Hortátzis and the painter El Greco. During Turkish rule Agía Ekateríni Church was also turned into a mosque.

Today the church is used as an exhibition hall for Christian art. The greatest treasures are the six icons of Michaíl Damaskinós, painted in 1580 for the Vrondissi Monastery.

From here you can cross Markopoúlou Street and carry on in a southerly direction to see the grave of novelist Níkos Kazantzákis in the **Martinengo Bastion**. It is not easy to find, but the way there leads through fascinating little lanes and alleyways; you may need to ask for directions now and then.

The **Archaeological Museum** of Iráklion is as controversial as the "restored" site of Knossos. Some say it is the most beautiful museum in the world; others maintain that it is quite the

opposite. Here in one single museum is the ultimate documentation of the Minoan civilisation. The presentation of the exhibits does, however, leave much to be desired.

A major design fault of the museum is the poor ventilation in the building, and visitors sink down on benches outside completely exhausted after their visit. Although going round the museum can be as strenuous as a 5-km (3-mile) jog, it is still a must for the tourist.

Here one can see traces of a culture which made a substantial contribution to Crete being labelled the "Cradle of European civilisation". If one studies the Minoan culture closely, one can conclude that this civilisation marked a high point of achievement from which there seems to have been a steady decline right into modern times.

The **Historical Museum**, which chronicles the Post Minoan epoch up to the present day, is also worth a visit.

arbour
tivity.

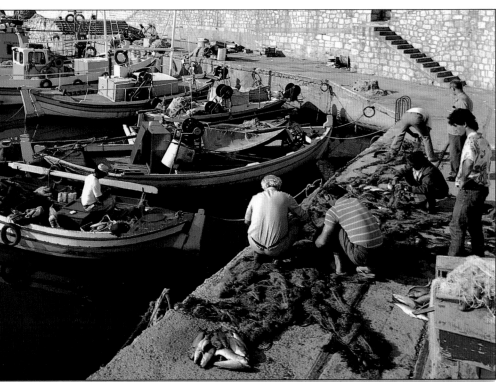

KNOSSÓS

The **Palace of Knossós** lies 5 km (3 miles) south of Iráklion. The best way to get there is by turning into Demokratías Street from the south side of Eleftherías Square, and then driving straight on.

The site of the palace must have been popular even in Neolithic times, as the layer of rubble beneath the palace, lying almost 6.5 metres (21 ft) deep, indicates dense and continued settlement. Where the west wing stands today was the location of an older palace, built like the early palaces of Festós and Mália in about 200 BC. This was probably destroyed by the earthquake of 170 BC. Other later palaces were built around 1600 BC and these were larger and more beautiful than the earlier ones.

In the Palace of Knossós the architectural apogee of the "Golden Age" of Minoan culture can be seen. The site of the palace extends over 2 hectares (5 acres). It's believed that there were 1,300 rooms arranged on four storeys and that about 80,000 people once lived here.

In around 1450 BC all the palaces were destroyed by another natural catastrophe, caused by the eruption of the volcano of Santorini. Only the Palace of Knossós was rebuilt, possibly by Mycenaean invaders. But in 1400 it too disappeared and with it the whole Minoan civilisation. Whether this was due to another earthquake or battle is unclear.

Part of the palace, if not all of it, has the Greek designation of Labyrinth. If it is accepted that the word "labyrinth" derives from the Anatolian "*labrys*", then its meaning would be "House of the Double Axe".

At Knossós several such artefacts were found in the so-called "Shrine of the Double Axe", and the holy sign of the double axe was scored into pillars and on votive objects – as at other Cre-

tan palaces. Of the 90 towns mentioned in Homer's *Odyssey*, Knossós is named "the Great", in the sense of "the most famous". That Knossós was great in size as well was established in Roman times by the geographer Strabo. The 30 stages, by means of which he calculated the diameter of the city, indicate a distance of almost 6 km (nearly 4 miles).

In all the credit and controversy surrounding the archaeologist Arthur Evans, the discoverer of Knossós (see page 110), Mínos Kalokerinós, the Greek archaeologist, is usually forgotten. This merchant from Iráklion, whose hobby was archaeology, completed a total of 12 excavations, which revealed large parts of the west wing and six storehouses. Then his activities were halted by the Turkish governor, who forbade further digging.

Kalokerinós had been inspired to undertake his excavations by Heinrich Schliemann's success. He had tried to

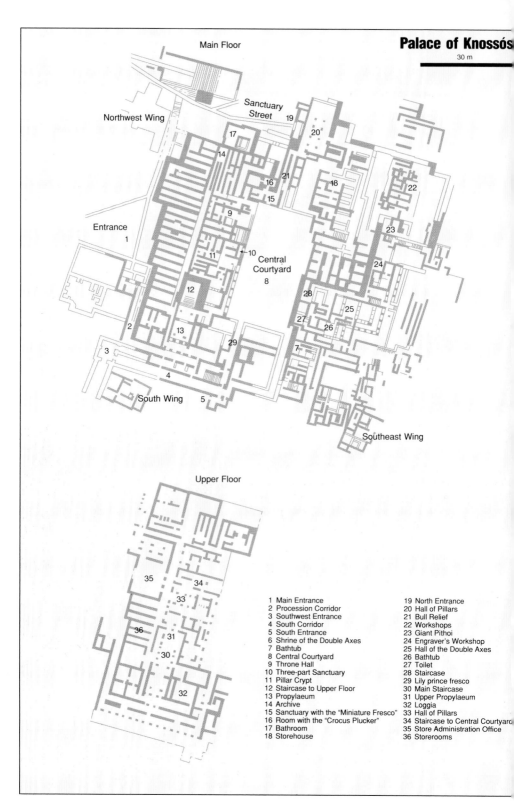

Palace of Knossós

30 m

Main Floor

Sanctuary Street

Northwest Wing

Entrance

Central Courtyard

South Wing

Southeast Wing

Upper Floor

1 Main Entrance
2 Procession Corridor
3 Southwest Entrance
4 South Corridor
5 South Entrance
6 Shrine of the Double Axes
7 Bathtub
8 Central Courtyard
9 Throne Hall
10 Three-part Sanctuary
11 Pillar Crypt
12 Staircase to Upper Floor
13 Propylaeum
14 Archive
15 Sanctuary with the "Miniature Fresco"
16 Room with the "Crocus Plucker"
17 Bathroom
18 Storehouse

19 North Entrance
20 Hall of Pillars
21 Bull Relief
22 Workshops
23 Giant Pithoi
24 Engraver's Workshop
25 Hall of the Double Axes
26 Bathtub
27 Toilet
28 Staircase
29 Lily prince fresco
30 Main Staircase
31 Upper Propylaeum
32 Loggia
33 Hall of Pillars
34 Staircase to Central Courtyard
35 Store Administration Office
36 Storerooms

buy the site and was planning to excavate the Palace of Knossós "…in a week, using a hundred workers". However, the Turkish owners declined the offer, luckily, for what would have become of Knossós had Schliemann been able to put his plan into action?

So it was extremely fortunate that Arthur Evans was in charge of the excavations. He was highly ambitious and had plenty of time to devote to his project. Of the 90 years of his life, 35 were spent at Knossós, and several more were devoted to the study of Minoan civilisation.

While considering the wonders he worked at Knossós, it is often forgotten that he never did achieve his initial aim to decipher the ancient Cretan script. Linear-B was not deciphered until six years after his death and disagreement about it persists to this day. Despite some wilful and misguided interpretations (for example "Megaron of the Queen", "Prince with the Feather Crown", etc.) and falsifications (the "Bath of the Queen" – a vessel without a drainage hole, found far from the bathroom), the value of Arthur Evans' achievements is indisputable.

The main objections raised against his work are usually to do with his use of colour and concrete. Evans used colour to mark the reconstructed areas, and he used concrete only after much reflection after trying out all the other materials available. Another criticism is that Evans used concrete although he knew that it too would not last for ever. Indeed, parts of the concrete have weathered badly.

Whatever else may be said, had Evans not used concrete, the Palace of Knossós would have been destroyed in the earthquake of 1926. And apart from that it would be much the poorer to look at, something not to be forgotten in all the controversy.

ging up
past at
ánes.

THE GENTLEMAN WHO DISCOVERED KING MINOS

When Arthur Evans was eight, his father John caught him playing in the garden. He was burying a broken doll, complete with clothes, like an offering. When they were covered over, he inscribed on a tombstone everything he had buried. But his father did not find the behaviour in any way strange, for the boy was only emulating him.

John Evans was a papermaker, a successful businessman who was to leave his son a fortune. But he was also an explorer, who at his own expense undertook excavations in France, attempting to trace the origins of man. The subsequent trailblazing books he wrote on geology and anthropology made him one of the most well-known research scientists of his day.

Arthur, who was born in 1851, took after his father physically, too. He was short-sighted and was only 1.57 metres (5ft 2in) tall, earning him the nickname "Little Evans". He also had the same vitality and stamina as his father, and he shared his love of adventure and his wide-ranging interests. But it was not immediately evident that the young Arthur would one day become one of the most important archaeological explorers of all time.

By the time Arthur left Harrow school, his father was the owner of several paper factories. It was assumed that Arthur would succeed him, but he declined, continuing his history studies at Oxford University.

He was 20 years old when the world's press heralded Heinrich Schliemann's discovery of what was alleged to be ancient Troy. The young student was fascinated. Frustrated with the narrow scope of the academic syllabus, he had already begun his own research and soon published an essay on numismatics. He interrupted his studies to make frequent trips to the Balkans and, at 25, his first book was published: *On Foot through Bosnia and Herzegovina*, a politically engaged and critical account of his journey. Arthur Evans supported the Panslav freedom movement and also helped in an organisation for refugees. As a special correspondent for the *Manchester Guardian*, he reported from the areas of crisis on the opposition to Turkish tyranny.

All his life, Evans was moved by the needs of others. However, he was extremely reserved in his relationships with those close to him, even his own relatives. He was 26 when he met Margaret Freeman, the daughter of an English historian. As secretary to her father, she had amassed an immense amount of knowledge and was a proficient linguist. Arthur was impressed with the calm composure of this young woman, and Margaret liked the energetic, humorous young man who was three years younger than herself and they were married in the autumn of 1878.

In 1882, reporting again from the Balkans for the *Manchester Guardian*, Arthur was imprisoned in Ragusa, present-day Dubrovnik, for his political activities. Margaret and his family stood by him and managed to secure his release after a few weeks. He returned to England and, with the publication of a second book on the Balkans, was regarded as an authority on the history and contemporary situation of that region. He wrote for several specialised magazines, worked on a book on the city of Ragusa and became an expert on the subject of Greek and Roman coins.

A journey to Greece with his wife brought him into contact with Heinrich Schliemann, who by then was 61. The young couple listened in fascination to Schliemann's tales, and visited the excavation sites at Mycenae, Orchomenos and Tiryns. From that time on, Arthur Evans turned his attention to the Minoan civilisation.

In Oxford, Evans was offered the post of curator of the Ashmolean Museum. He was only 33, and was extremely happy to accept the position. In his introductory talk as the new director, he declared that ethnology and archaeology had "to a large extent, the same

Right, memorial to Arthur Evans.

goal: that of throwing light upon the laws of evolution which underlie the forms of human art." The museum, in Evans's estimation, should not be a "curiosity shop" but rather a centre of archaeological research. In a short time he doubled the number of exhibits and ordered a new heating system to ensure the best possible conditions for their preservation. The new curator, however, was often absent, away on travels pursuing his own interests.

In Greece, he scrutinised the gold objects Schliemann had found. There were diadems,

themselves from Turkish rule and once again Evans offered his services in aiding a people in need. In fact, it is thanks to his social and political engagements on their behalf that the Cretans granted him permission to dig at the site of the still-buried Knossós.

In 1900, Evans began his excavations on Crete. On the second day, he found some fresco fragments. Exactly a week later, the first sensational discovery was made. Clay bars covered in signs revealed the existence of a prehistoric script. In just a few days, more than 100 such clay tablets had been

signet rings and goblets decorated with motifs quite different from those of classical Greece. The many octopus drawings, for example, led him to believe that there was a pre-Grecian, Mycenaean culture, the origins of which were not to be found anywhere on the Greek mainland.

Four years before starting to dig at Knossós, Evans announced that the golden age of Crete lay "far beyond the limits" of the Olympic historical period, regarded as the beginning of the time of the Greeks.

While Evans was making his pronouncements, the Cretans were attempting to free

uncovered, the oldest ever indications of a European civilisation.

At the beginning of April there was another amazing discovery. On the floor of one of the halls, the fragment of a fresco of a life-sized figure was revealed and according to Evans it was "the most notable figure of the Mycenaean period". The archaeologist telegraphed his father, and John Evans was able to share in his son's triumph.

At first, Evans did not use the concept "Minoan". But a few days later, a throne was found made of delicately veined gypsum – alabaster. He announced his findings in an article in *The Times* and it was then that he made the connection between Knossós and the legendary King Minos. In August of the same year, the highpoint of the excavations was reached with the discovery of a coloured stucco relief: this was a glorious representation of a bull.

The discoverer's theory became a certainty. Out of the obscure past, a unique culture, the oldest European civilisation, had appeared. Evans called it the Minoan civilisation, with Minos as its ruler, like a Pharaoh, "…or whichever historical personage is

kingly city is Knossós, where Minos ruled, who nine years long spoke with Zeus, the great god." Elsewhere, in the *Iliad*, Minos is referred to as the "Protector of Crete". Evans cited this, as well as the legend of the Minotaur, for bulls' horns indicated the places of worship in the palace.

A mural, which has since become well known, was a particular mystery to Evans. He called it the "Bullfighter Fresco", as two women and a man appeared to be executing daring acrobatics on the bull's back. Evans travelled to Spain and talked to bullfighters

the origin of the name". He was thus well aware of the dubiousness of the nomenclature. He knew that mythological events and figures could not easily be translated into history, even if Schliemann had been remarkably successful in his findings based on the poems of Homer. However, when other written evidence was lacking, then archaeology had to fall back on mythology. In the 19th book of the *Odyssey*, Homer put these words into the mouth of his hero: "Their

Left and **above**, photographs of the excavation work from Evans's extensive archives.

in order to find out if such feats were possible. The experts said no. It would be impossible to hang on to the horns and vault up and over a galloping bull. But Evans was unconvinced, and held to his belief that the mural depicted an actual event, not merely a myth. He concluded that the myth of the Minotaur, to whom young Athenians were sacrificed, might refer to gruesome spectacles which had in fact taken place at Minoan Knossós.

The excavations were in their third year. After heavy rainfall, parts of a royal villa were revealed outside the palace boundaries. But inside the palace, too, there were more sensational discoveries. Evans came upon a treasure chamber, in which there were petals of gold foil, glass beads, goblets, vases and ivory carvings as well as a glazed figure of a snake goddess. In ancient times, the snake was a symbol of rebirth and immortality, and of the reincarnation of dead ancestors. The snake goddess therefore emphasised the prominent position that was held by women in Minoan civilisation.

The same interpretation applies to a temple fresco depicting a crowd of some 500 people. The front seats are occupied by

might have had an effect on the health of the people. The doctors he consulted reassured him that it was all right.

In the living area of the palace, Evans discovered rooms which, because of the "feminine charm" of the murals and their luxurious appointments and comfort, he identified as "*megaron* of the Queen" a *megaron* being the main room of a house.

Special significance was accorded the symbol which appeared even more often than the bull on the palace walls, and surpassed all other symbols in its frequency in

ladies in elegant clothes, apparently spectators waiting for a special display or ceremony, perhaps even "bull vaulters".

Then the spade revealed part of a wall decoration, which when put together and completed showed an elegant young man with a kind of crown on his head. Evans did not hesitate to interpret this as the figure of a priest-king. He was sure that after finding Europe's oldest throne, he had now discovered Europe's oldest crown.

The tight belt at the waist became the hottest European fashion for both men and women. Evans wondered if this strait-lacing

relief work: the Cretan double axe. According to feminist theory, it is evidence of a gynaecocratic epoch in history, a sign of matriarchal rule.

The sign of the double axe was found everywhere, on walls of caves or temples, whether scratched on or drawn. Other discoveries seemed to reveal further goddesses and evidence of the elevated position of women. This was not a phenomenon unique to Minoan civilisation, for similar conditions were evident in paleolithic Europe and, in the Neolithic period, in Anatolia and Umbria. The Egyptian matriarchal succession to the throne was another indication of a gynaecocratic epoch that extended throughout the whole of the ancient world.

However, traditional archaeology has been extremely hesitant about accepting these findings. It has not denied the extraordinary peacefulness, the dominance of "feminine taste" in Minoan culture, nor has it overlooked the favoured role played by women in public, as well as in the religious hierarchy, with the "great goddess of the earth" at the head. But scholars have stressed that a matriarchal principle in religion and

The "crown" which Arthur Evans identified on the head of the "youth" is at first sight evidence against this. But the headdress is no longer thought to be a crown, and the "prince with a crown of feathers" is not taken as an indication that there were male rulers.

It would be presumptuous to maintain that this question has been settled once and for all, but archaeological circumstantial evidence does seem to tip the scales in favour of priestess-queens.

Arthur Evans's male contemporaries, however, were aghast at the prospect of hav-

society does not necessarily imply the existence of female rulers and queens.

There is a difference of opinion here, and agreement cannot be reached by imagining a male and female regent on Minoan Crete, for in the throne room of Knossós there is clearly only room for one elevated Minoan. That this person could have been a priestess is a theory taken extremely seriously by scholars today and the theory is being carefully researched.

Left and above, parts of the interior decoration of the Minoans in the Palace of Knossós: frescoes of fabulous animals, and a pillared arcade.

ing to share history with women. The idea was greeted with amazement, and even with condescension. Here, for example, is the opinion of Sir Galahad, writing in the 1930s about the frescoes of Knossós: "Women, women, nothing but women, just like on the Riviera, overdressed, permed, in high heels, a naked young man or two around... no sign of any venerable old men. There's no place for them in a female realm... men are in subordinate positions, pages, cup-bearers, flautists, field workers or sailors... not one king, priest or hero. What was at first automatically taken to be a male ruler, on a half flaked fresco, turned out to be a woman, too. Women are queens, priestesses, goddesses, rulers – never serving girls."

Arthur Evans was one of the first archaeologists to call upon building experts to help him in his work. With the aid of Theodor Fyfe, excavation and reconstruction went hand in hand. Evans spared neither cost nor effort in rebuilding the old walls. His aim was to "conserve something of the inner life of the ancient palace holy place".

The Swiss painter Emile Gilliéron was commissioned to restore the frescoes. Some

The results of this work were impressive. Most visitors feel that the Palace of Knossós gives them an insight into history which no other excavation site can equal. Others speak of the "film set of Knossós" and criticise Evans for his over-enthusiastic restoration and improvement of his discovery. But the majority of scholars are in agreement with Evans that reconstruction was necessary at the Palace of Knossós to stop it becoming a mere heap of rubble.

The Cretan writer Níkos Kazantzákis described the vivid impression it made: "The

consisted of no more than a few fragments, and were in need of considerable restoration. But Evans was constantly seeking reference points and analogies. He hit on a plan of producing replicas which resembled the originals as closely as possible to decorate the palace walls just as they would have done in Minoan times.

All work was undertaken in accordance with the principle that the new additions should be clearly differentiated from the old. The supporting bars and concrete copies of pillars were purposefully made completely different in colour from the old walls.

palace, half decayed, half rebuilt, was still radiant after all those thousands of years and once again delighted in the sunshine of Crete. This palace does not offer the symmetry and geometrical architecture of Greece. Here fantasy reigns, and the free expression of man's creativity. This palace grew like a living organism, like a tree…"

At an archaeological congress in Athens in 1905, Evans presented the chronology of the Minoan period. This was based on the stratigraphic method, layer digging. There were in those days no laboratory tests to determine dates precisely, such as the analysis of trace elements in vessel clay with the aid of neutron activation. Evans had to rely on his geological experience and on favourable circumstances. Fortunately, the layers of earth had remained almost undisturbed over the centuries and, at important spots, archaeological finds which came to light could be accurately dated.

In one fell swoop numerous historical works on ancient Greece became obsolete, as the dating structure submitted by Evans altered everything. Modern research techniques have since confirmed the accuracy of

he left his son enabled Arthur to finance and complete his grandiose plans himself. The way in which he brought the buried past back to its former glory would today be an almost impossible achievement.

Modern archaeology is changing from a science based primarily on evidence gleaned from field research to one based on laboratory examination. The methods are are increasingly exacting and expensive. Growing demands are confronted with shrinking means. The urbanisation process destroys sites, and archaeologists often can-

Evans's chronology. His sensational findings drew numerous archaeologists to Crete. The results of their efforts are still visible today in the many excavation sites, such as those at Festós, Mália and Káto Zákros. In all, it took six years before the Palace of Knossós area was revealed. At times as many as 100 people were at work on the site.

In 1908 Evans's father died. The fortune

Left, excavation site at Arhánes. **Above**, Sandy Mcgillwin, Director of the British School in Knossós, studies the drawings of important burial finds.

not undertake thorough excavation projects.

In 1911 Evans was knighted. Sir Arthur Evans became president of the Greek Society and was elected honorary professor of archaeology at Oxford University. Another 20 years of sporadic excavation and research followed until the work at Knossós was finally deemed complete. In the meantime he drew up what was probably the best account of an archaeological discovery ever written. By the time of his death at the age of 90, he had crowned his life's monumental achievements with four volumes entitled *The Palace of Minos*.

AROUND IRÁKLION

From Iráklion, there is a 14- km (8½-mile) road which passes through Knossós. After 10 km (6 miles), the road branches off, and here one must keep right. The last part of your journey takes you through a lush vine-growing area. **Arhánes**, a small town of over 3,500 inhabitants, is the centre of Cretan wine production. The 1,200 or so vintners have united in a co-operative, and dessert grapes, *Rosáki,* are grown here too.

Like almost any region where wine is produced, Arhánes has a friendly and inviting atmosphere. Whether or not you are interested in the Minoans, it is pleasant to spend a few days here. In the late afternoon, life begins in the cafés and *tavérnes* around the main square of the town. The men meet over the popular *távli* (Greek backgammon, played to slightly different rules) or card games. One can just mingle with the locals, and get to know something of what Crete is really all about.

In and around Arhánes there are various excavation sites. The first is to be found in the town itself and is not difficult to find. Just after entering the town, you will see a secondary school on the right – you can't miss it. Then you go on down the main street for about 200 metres (219 yd) until you come to a sign "To the Palace". Here you drive about 100 metres (110yd) uphill to the left, then turn right and you will soon arrive at the the site. The signpost is now revealed as a gross exaggeration. It may well have led to the expectation of a Knossós-like construction, but there's nothing like a palace here.

The building, which dates from about 1500 BC and has only been partially excavated, is not very impressive. There is nothing very remarkable to see here in the dozen or so rooms, apart from the bases of two pillars. Experts are divided as to whether this is in fact a palace or merely a mansion. There seems to be no chance of finding out either, as excavations have been stopped out of consideration for residents in the surrounding area.

The second site, the **Necropolis** of Fourni, is reached by a small road which branches off just by the secondary school. As the road is only suitable for cars for a short distance, it is advisable to leave your car in the town. After a 15–20-minute climb up the slopes of the **Fourni** hills, you will find yourself in front of the gate of the excavation site, which is usually locked. It is therefore essential to obtain the key from one of the cafés in the main square before attempting to visit the site.

In fact, the site isofficially open on Mondays, Fridays and Saturdays, from 9am until dusk. Anyone asking for the key should, in point of fact, be accompanied there by a guide. These guides

Preceding pages: Massara Plain and the Ida mountains. Below, vintner in the castles of Arhánes.

are supposed to sit in the cafés waiting to show interested persons around; their wages are paid by the state, although they have no objection to the odd tip. All this applies equally to the mansion site of Vathípetro.

The Necropolis of Fourni, which was in use from early Minoan to Mycenaean times, and thus for more than 1,000 years, is held by experts to be the most important of such sites on Crete, if not in the entire Aegean.

Orientation: The entrance is on the eastern side. The slope on the left faces south; Tholos A is on the right, and so faces north.

Of the more than 20 round graves, some are particularly interesting: Tholos D (a little to the left towards the edge, a woman's grave with jewellery burial offerings, Mycenaean); Tholos E (a little higher up, a communal grave from the Prepalatial era, 31 sarcophagi, 2 *pithoi*); Tholos C (a terrace higher, a communal grave of a Cycladic group, idols and amulets of obsidian); Tholos B (formerly two-storey layout of the Prepalatial period, a communal grave, fresco decoration); Tholos A (about 45 metres to the north, a woman's grave – perhaps that of a queen or priestess-queen – with many jewellery burial offerings, vessels, bull and horse skulls, late Minoan-Mycenaean). The finds are displayed in the Museum of Iráklion (I and VI).

The third excavation site is that of a temple on the hill of **Anemóspilia**, a rarity of the first order among the many interesting finds on Crete. The well preserved temple dates from the time of the old palaces. It is to be found on the north slope of Mount Joúchtas, southwest of Arhánes. This was a most important find as, until it was discovered, it was still a matter of conjecture whether temples had existed at all in Minoan times. Then there was an amazing discovery: it

appeared that a human sacrifice was in the process of being made when a huge earthquake (around 1700 BC) interrupted the procedure.

The temple consisted of an anteroom and three long main rooms of equal size. In the middle of the main rooms stood a wooden image of a deity with clay feet, which were, ironically, the only part to have been preserved complete. In the anteroom there were 150 vessels, of which some were inscribed with script (Linear-A). In many of the pots, it was possible to detect traces of the contents: fruit, cereals, honey and wine.

Also in the anteroom, skeletal remains of a human were found, and two further skeletons in another of the main rooms. They were later identified as a man and a woman. The man was adorned in such a way as to indicate the possibility that he could have played a main role in some event, perhaps as a sacrificial priest. On the stone altar, the

remains of another person were found. He was lying on his right side, the lower legs bent at an acute angle – presumably tied at the upper thighs. Next to his chest lay a 40-cm (16-cm) long sword or knife, with which he had probably just been killed.

Forensic medical examinations have revealed further astonishing details. The woman was 28 years old, the adorned man 30, and the sacrificial victim, 18. Although the woman was suffering from a blood disease, the difference in colour between the upper and lower sides of the skeleton indicated that the sacrificial victim had bled to death during a blazing fire.

It is possible that the following may have taken place: the ceremony was almost over when the earthquake began or intensified. A helper, who was just about to carry a vessel containing the blood of the sacrifice from the side room into the main room where the image of the deity stood, was killed by falling masonry. The priest and the woman were killed instantly by the quake right next to the sacrificial victim. The flames of the torches of the temple eventually set the place on fire. The fire made it possible to establish that the young man was not killed by falling debris, but died from loss of blood, and thus was considered to have been a human sacrifice.

This find and the results of subsequent examinations are worthy of note, but it is still surprising when reference is made to a "sensational human sacrifice", even though such occurrences were not rare in the religions and myths of the Mediterranean area. For example, there were the famous sacrifices which involved Abraham, Agamemnon and Idomeneus. Nevertheless some of the conclusions drawn from this episode are odd.

It is generally supposed that the Minoans, possibly having had some indication of the imminent earthquake,

Hospitable Cretan from a small village in the Ida Mountains.

resorted to human sacrifice in order to attempt to avert the catastrophe at the last minute. At the same time, archaeologists believe that this was the first and only human sacrifice undertaken by the Minoans. However, the accuracy of this assumption is questionable.

If the Minoans wanted to prevent the catastrophe with a human sacrifice, surely it would follow that they would do this each time there were indications of a strong earthquake making it unlikely that this was an isolated incident. Archaeologist Iannis Sakelarakis, the *ephor* in charge of Arhanes, made himself unpopular in the Greek archaeological world for reporting such findings, and the "evidence" is still being hotly debated.

There is so much which is still unexplained. It is possible, for example, that the building was not in fact a temple, but a store for the hilltop sanctuary on Mount Joúchtas. Some experts think

that the sacrificial sword or knife was actually the tip of a spear. It is also not certain that a priest was present. However, on the sarcophagus of Agía Triáda a priestess is illustrated in connection with the sacrifice of an animal.

Mount Joúchtas, 811 metres (2,661 ft) high, lies to the west of Arhánes. It can easily be reached by car. The fourth excavation site, a Minoan hilltop sanctuary, is up on the northern summit, along with a radio and weather station. Unfortunately the site is not on view to the public, but that is unimportant. The main attraction here is the glorious view of Iráklion right to the sea. This is the mountain you see before you at Knossós as you look south, so even for the Minoans this was no ordinary place.

The significance of this mountain is heightened when one realises that it is in one of these caves that Zeus is believed to have been buried. The mountain is thought to reflect as, whether observed

**e path to
e Ida Cave,
eltered
om the sun
y clouds.**

from the west or east, it resembles the profile of a reclining head. Popular belief has it that it is the face of the sleeping or dead Zeus.

On the southern summit, reached via a gravel path along the saddle, is the **Aféndi Church** which is a combination of four different, chapels. On 6 August the Transfiguration of Christ is celebrated up here. In cloudy, windy weather this place has an aura of fascination and mystery.

South of Arhánes 3 km (1¾ miles) is the Minoan mansion of **Vathípetro**. The way to this important excavation site is well marked. The mansion was built around 1580 BC and only inhabited for about 30 years. It is assumed that a larger palace-like structure was to have been built here, and that an earthquake put paid to the plan. In one of the secluded houses, there are many large storage vessels (*pithoi*) and a winepress. One can assume, therefore, that

the vineyards of this area have a very long history.

Old Road to Tílissos: If you take the fast road for this short stretch westwards, you make your journey unnecessarily complicated, for at the other end there are numerous little crossroads without any signposts. It is much easier to take the old road from Iráklion towards Réthimnon. Ignore the turning to Rogdiá, and 4 km (2½ miles) further on, take the turning to Anógia. After 3 km (1¾ miles), you arrive at **Tílissos**. On this stretch you pass a somewhat dilapidated but impressive building with three cupolas, in which there is a workshop today. Here in earlier times travellers would spend the night if they did not manage to enter Megálo Kástro (Iráklion) before the gates were closed.

Tílissos is a small town on the eastern flanks of the Ida Mountains. The north wind blows through its lovely gardens. Here it is not fruit and flowers which are

Excavated mansions in Tílissos.

grown, but olives and vineyards which provide a living for the people of Tílissos. Despite the presence of the Minoan mansions which have been discovered here, the place is still unspoiled and is not on the tourist trail. This is probably because the town is not far from Iráklion, and visitors tend to return to their hotels there and in the surrounding area after visiting the site.

Apart from the excavation site, there really is nothing else here, but an evening among the friendly people of Tílissos gives you the chance to experience a side of Crete no longer found in the tourist centres. Here, you have the chance to enjoy the pleasures of the island and the hospitality of the locals.

To reach the site, just follow the signs. (Oh, if only Zeus had willed that every site in Crete were so well signed!) The mansions erected on the foundations of older buildings were inhabited between 1600 and 1450 BC. These, like the great palaces, seem to have been destroyed by the catastrophe of 1450 BC. It is particularly interesting to note that these detached houses, of two or possibly more storeys, were built earthquake proof. A water supply system is clearly recognisable too.

Of the many finds, three enormous bronze kettles are the most remarkable. They stood in one of the three store rooms of House C, and are quite out of proportion for this dwelling place, unless the houses were much taller, and had far more rooms than has been postulated. It is, however, quite certain that these kettles were not simply used for family cooking. The largest has a diameter of almost 1.5 metres, and weighs over 50 kg (110 lb). Most probably they were used for soldiers, perhaps to prepare food for the guards of the mountain pass. The kettles and other finds, amphorae, *pithoi*, vases, double axes and the bronze statue of a praying figure are

ourful
ations
for sale.

125

exhibited in the Archaeological Museum of Iráklion, Room VII (standing alone and in cabinet 89).

If you make your way to the neighbouring *tavérna,* and are interested in unusual knitwear, you might like to take a beautiful jumper home as a souvenir knitted by members of a family there. Although much of their work is geared to tourists nowadays, every now and then they produce something truly original. Prices vary according to your bargaining skills.

Mountain village: There are a number of wonderful trips from Iráklion into the surrounding area to the northwest, such as to the mountain village of **Rogdiá**, 16 km (9¾ miles) away. The best approach is to take the old road, and turn off after 7 km (4¼ miles) at the signpost for Rogdiá. This stretch goes past one of the few industrial areas of Crete, which seems particularly hideous, lying as it does in such a wide expanse of unspoiled countryside. Some say it is a cement works, but the inhabitants of Rogdiá refer to it as a refinery. After a short breezy drive along a coastal road, with a wonderful view out over the sea, you reach Rogdiá, which lies about 300 metres (984 ft) above sea level.

It is a village which, apart from the ruins of a Venetian palace and a church, is well worth visiting for its own sake and its friendly café opposite the palace.

Below the village one can see the remains of a Venetian fortress built in 1206, the **Paleókastro**. In this castle, the conditions for handing Crete over to the Turks were negotiated.

Rogdiá is a wonderful starting point for walks into the surrounding countryside. There are few people here in the vineyards, and very often there is a gentle breeze blowing. But it is better to take a car if you wish to visit the monastery of **Savathianá**, especially in the summer months, even if you have heard that it is only a quarter of an hour away. The truth is that the 5-km (3 miles) stretch involves a climb of 120 metres (394 ft), and is in fact surprisingly exhausting. Many an unwary tourist has regretted taking that Cretan quarter of an hour at face value.

Although it does not lie in a bare landscape, the convent of Savathianá has the appearance of an oasis in the desert. It was built in a watery gully and the well-tended vegetation flourishes, so the white buildings are almost hidden by lush growth. You walk past glorious flower beds to the church of Agios Sávas, a building which is actually incorporated into the mountainside.

There is a remarkable collection of icons, as well as other treasures displayed near the entrance of the church. After a visit inside, you will be invited into a cosy room for coffee, quince jam and *tsikoudiá.* It is most pleasant to chat with the nuns, who sell woven cloth, embroidery, postcards and reproductions of icons. And what about that

The convent of Savathian

excellent Schnapps? The little nun looks quite put out – that's not for sale.

El Greco's birthplace: From Rogdiá it is about 12 km (7½ miles) to **Fódele** either straight up north on small roads, or back towards Réthimnon and onwards via the motorway. The village lies among orange groves, and proudly announces itself as the birthplace of the painter Doménikos Theotokópoulos (1541–1614), better known as El Greco, who later lived in Toledo in Spain.

As El Greco never clearly stated in which Cretan village he was born, there was much dispute among villages as to where, precisely, he came from. But Fódele presented the most credible documentation and, in 1934, it finally emerged as the victor in the dispute over this native son.

Fódele is a secretive place. As you enter the village, you have the impression that the whole place is asleep, but you soon realise that there are hundreds of people already there. They are eating and drinking in a *tavérna,* which, of course, is named El Greco's. Yes, it was definitely worth the fight. Without its famous son, the village would certainly not be on the map.

The birthplace of the painter has been completely renovated, and is to be found to the north of Fódele in the isolated village of Lumbiniés, where the little 13th-century Panagia Church with its well preserved frescoes is worth a visit too. Sadly, there are no original El Grecos on Crete (there is one on Syros), so the visitor must make do with the photographs and copies housed in the church at Fódele.

On the return journey to Iráklion, it is worth making a detour to the Bay of **Agía Pelagía** where the bathing facilities are good and the *tavérna* offers a warm welcome.

Zorba Momentoes: Mirtiá is reached via Knossós, and then past the restau-

e
zantzákis
seum is
Mirtiá.

rant at Spiliá. About 1.5 km (¾ mile) after that, take a left turn through the vine-growing valley of Arhánes. The wine-producing village of Mirtiá gives an impression of flourishing prosperity, as one would expect from a place with such a product as its mainstay.

The **Kazantzákis Museum** is in the centre of the village. Looking at the pictures of its inauguration, one can only marvel at the international "community" of the writer Níkos Kazantzákis (see Literature, page 81).

In the museum there are many of the writer's personal possessions as well as expositions on him and his work. Of course *Zorba the Greek* is prominently featured in the exhibition and has pride of place among the various theatre productions. There are busts, oil paintings and sketches, among them some horrendous attempts to portray the "heroic thinker" Kazantzákis as well as all sorts of meaningless trifles, which would be totally insignificant if they belonged to anyone else. There is even a tin of sweets, with bits of cinnamon sticks and a mint inside.

When there is no film or television crew at work there, the museum is quite quiet. For Kazantzákis fans a visit signifies respect for the author. The rather high entrance fee and cost of a brochure are understandable if one realises that the museum is completely self-financing; there are no subsidies at all.

Pottery town: The way from Mirtiá to **Thrapsanó** seems quite straightforward on a map. If only it were. A detailed description of directions would be just as confusing as the journey itself, so it is best to ask directions along the way. Everyone is aware of the problem and they all know exactly what you want when you ask for Trápsano instead of Thrapsanó. The trick is to believe people when they seem to be directing you the wrong way – they really do know the area better than you do. The roads are not in fact that complicated; they are simply wrongly drawn on the map. If you manage to find Thrapsanó from Mirtiá on your first attempt, you really have achieved the impossible.

The best pottery of Thrapsanó is to be found just before you reach the village as you come from Mirtiá. Large pots are made here. If you want to get to know the village, leave your car outside, for it has hardly changed over the centuries, and its cobbled streets were not designed for today's vehicles. Around the centre, which lies in a slightly elevated position, are many interesting potteries, where you can buy all kinds of arts and crafts, with tasteful work displayed right next to the most awful kitsch.

You really should visit the pottery at the edge of the village. Here Ioánnis Moutzákis and his wife and son work with a few helpers. There are 15 potter's wheels for large pots (*pithoi*). The clay from the surrounding area is sieved again and again to obtain as high a **Pottery today...**

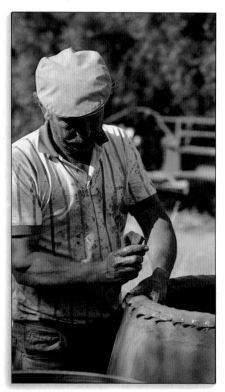

standard of purity as possible. After the first watering and kneading, the clay is kept under cloths until used. The axles of the wheels are set in the ground, and the wheels themselves are just above the ground. A boy down in a ditch turns the wheel while the master forms the pot on the wheel above.

It really is worth a trip to Crete just to see this process. When the pots are the right height, they are left to rest for a while, then they must regularly have water poured over them to prevent cracks forming. When the pots are finally dry, the master goes from wheel to wheel taking the clay strips which have been needed by the perspiring boys. He then expertly forms the rolled rims, the last part of the pots.

Meanwhile the fire for smaller objects has been prepared. A huge heap of sawdust is put in front of the oven mouth. The fire is lit and one of the helpers throws one handful of sawdust

after another through the stoke hole. This simple process gives an almost constant oven temperature, which ensures the quality of the pottery. It gets extremely warm just watching, even quite a distance away from the oven. The sawdust thrower is almost roasted, and there is a change of shift every 20 minutes. In summer, when the temperature is up in the high 30s, the quantity of drinks that are consumed by the helpers is immeasurable.

Even if you show no inclination to buy anything, you will be served coffee and *rakí*, and the master will give you his card. He speaks in the regional dialect so that *rakí* is pronounced *ratschi*, and his name becomes Ioánnis Moutzátasch. He loves his work so much that he never takes a holiday. What, not even on Sunday, on *Kiriaki*? Well, no, he does take "Tschiriatschi" off. His speech is so infectious that one is tempted to recount a visit to the

Kazantzátsch Museum, which is always a good subject of conversation, simply to get him talking.

Knossós's Port: The Bay of Karterós lies 7 km (4 miles) to the east and offers the best bathing in the Iráklion area. The beach is divided into four parts, and only the first two can really be recommended. These are Florida Beach and EOT Beach where you have to pay to go on. The area then gets more run down further on where the noise of aeroplanes taking off and landing is terrible.

Behind Amnissós Beach, which is the third part, lie the ruins of the famous old city of **Amnissós** which was once the port for Knossós, and also played a major part in ancient mythology. Idomeneus and his soldiers left from here with 80 ships to sail for Troy and Theseus landed here with the young Athenians who were to be sacrificed to the Minotaur. Homer mentions Amnissós in the 19th Book of the *Odyssey*.

As Amnissós lies in an unfavourable position buffeted by the north wind, one assumes that the place was chosen for its proximity to the Eileithyía Cave, and not for its pleasant location. Excavations on the hill of Amnissós by S. Marinatos have revealed some interesting details.

Apart from the harbour and various houses, a large well was also discovered. On the north side, a house appeared from beneath a layer of pumice stone, the so-called "House of the Harbour Master," and because of this discovery, the "volcano catastrophe theory" was reinforced. It had been assumed that lava and ash once covered Crete, but this has since been refuted.

On the eastern side, the "Villa of the Lilies" was discovered, named after the lilies on a fresco which are now exhibited in the Museum of Iráklion, Room XIV. The function and arrangement of the house are still unclear. The open side

The excavated Palace of Mália.

of the courtyard faces the sea, and small storerooms were found. The obviously more recent buildings on the hilltop date from a Venetian fort, which was destroyed by the Turks.

The **Eileithyía Cave** is reached along the old road past the turning for Episkopi. After a short distance, the cave entrance can be seen on the left, below the road.

Eileithyía was the Cretan goddess of fertility and birth, daughter of Zeus and Hera and sometimes equated with Hera or Artemis. The special significance of the cave is that it was a place of worship for a period of over 3,500 years.

The cave, which is 63 metres (207 ft) long, and at the back almost 12 metres (39 ft) wide, contains stalactites (among them a stalagmite in the shape of a phallus) which are a clear indication that cult rites were practised here (AMI, I, 1). Unfortunately, the cave has been locked for some time now, and can only be visited with permission from the museum administration in Iráklion.

On the old road, further to the east 14 km (8½ miles) away, lies the village of **Kókkini Háni**. Here in 1912, Arthur Evans and M. Xanthoudidis excavated the Minoan mansion of **Nirou Háni**, in which enormous bronze double axes were discovered (AMI, VII, standing alone) as well as many vessels, altars and lamps (AMI, VII, 89). It is supposed that these objects were intended for export, to be shipped not from Amnissós but from here. Remains of the harbour can be made out near the Knossós Beach Hotel.

Along the road after 3 km (1¾ miles), there is a turning to **Goúves** which you can take to **Skotinó**, 5 km (3 miles) further on. Then it is a further 1.5 km (¾ mile) to the **Cave of Skotinó**. The speleologist Paul Faure worked here for a long time. The cave is appreciably bigger than the Eileithyía Cave but no

old ction of lia does part for rism.

less important. Ceramic finds from the Minoan era right up to Roman times indicate a long, unbroken period of utilisation as a place of worship. Briómartis, the Cretan Artemis, was worshipped here.

The old road continues for 26 km (16 miles) to **Límin Hersonissou**, which used to be a little coastal village but which is now completely swamped by tourists and new hotels. There is nothing to differentiate it now from the countless other beach resorts all over the world.

The inhabitants, however, are pleased with the development and the holiday-makers, most of whom are on package tours. In the evenings, the road along the beach is full of life. Bathing along the coast here is excellent but the beach is overcrowded in high season as would be expected.

At 30 km (18½ miles) is the resort of **Stális** and at 34 km (21 miles) is **Mália**, which has for some time now been divided into two parts. On the right is the old part of the town, relatively untouched, and on the left, towards the sea, is an amusement street. This is presumably modelled on the Italian pattern, where there is one *tavérna*, café, bar and disco after another, each trying to drown out its neighbour. For those looking for a nerve-shattering experience, this is the place to visit.

However, for those in search of peace and relaxation, Mália is definitely to be avoided but the division of the town makes it rather interesting; all the visitor needs to do is just cross the road and he or she is in a different century. Attempts are being made to rectify this. Although the place has lost none of its natural beauty, this rapid development has meant that it is always congested.

To the east, about 3 km (1¾ miles) away, you reach the Palace of Mália, which is the third largest of the Minoan

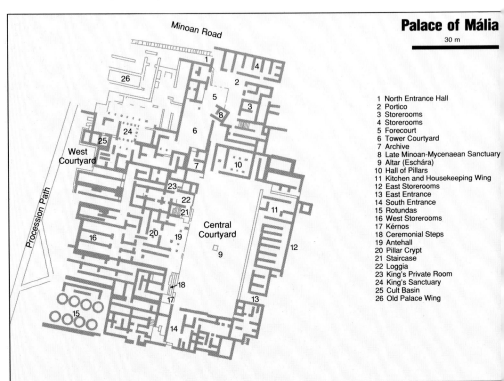

Palace of Mália

30 m

1 North Entrance Hall
2 Portico
3 Storerooms
4 Storerooms
5 Forecourt
6 Tower Courtyard
7 Archive
8 Late Minoan-Mycenaean Sanctuary
9 Altar (Eschára)
10 Hall of Pillars
11 Kitchen and Housekeeping Wing
12 East Storerooms
13 East Entrance
14 South Entrance
15 Rotundas
16 West Storerooms
17 Kérnos
18 Ceremonial Steps
19 Antehall
20 Pillar Crypt
21 Staircase
22 Loggia
23 King's Private Room
24 King's Sanctuary
25 Cult Basin
26 Old Palace Wing

palaces. According to myth, this was the palace of King Sarpedon, brother of Minos and Rhadamanthys.

It was built around 2000 BC, renovated in about 1650 BC and finally destroyed in 1450 BC. Like the other palaces, it has a rectangular courtyard which lies in a north-south direction measuring 50 metres by 22 metres (164 ft by 72 ft) and comprises several sacral rooms, storerooms, pillared rooms and some royal apartments as well as kitchen quarters.

In the so-called "Loggia" a sceptre and a sword were found (AMI, IV, 47, 52) but no frescoes were discovered. Near the southwest side of the courtyard on a paved gallery, you will find the famous **Kérnos**. This is a round stone with a diameter of 90 cm (3 ft) and which has been the subject of many and various interpretations.

The stone has 34 evenly-spaced small hollows around the edge and a large hollow in the centre. It was thought for a while to be a kind of gaming board, but that theory has now been discredited. Some say it is more likely to have been a sacrificial stone. But none of the interpretations is certain, and as the stone still lies in its usual place, you can form your own impression.

The Palace of Mália is not as impressive as that of the Palace of Knossós, but its location on the seashore does provide a new perspective on the Minoans and their lifestyle.

Later, when you have visited Festós and Káto Zákros, the question uppermost in your mind may well be: which is the more pronounced – the differences between the palaces, or their similarities? It is fascinating to compare and contrast these historic sites as an amateur archaeologist, while you explore the relics of an ancient but, at the same time, advanced Minoan civilisation on the island of Crete.

xurious
tels line
e coast
Mália.

FROM IRÁKLION TO THE SEA OF LIBYA

The village of **Agía Varvára** with its open spaces and wide streets, lies almost 29 km (18 miles) from Iráklion. During the months of June and July, even before you reach the village, you will be greeted by an interesting sight. You will see the local children holding up strange-looking clusters for sale. These are bunches of cherries, beautifully bound on sticks. As Cretan cherries are very popular, and because the sellers take no heed of road safety while plying their wares, traffic jams often build up. Nevertheless, do try one of these delicious cherry sticks before driving on.

The square in front of the small Church of Elias is geographically the centre of the island, thus metaphorically the navel of the Cretan world and that's why it is named Omphalos, which means navel. And that's really all there is worth saying about Agía Varvára

A small road which branches off to the left, almost back in the direction of Iráklion, leads to **Priniás**, which is about 7 km (4 miles) away, and the site of ancient **Rizinia**. There was a settlement here in Minoan times, and its most important period was during the 6th and 7th centuries BC. It was the work of two Italian archaeologists in particular which revealed the ruins of two temples, the famous knight fresco in the style of Daedalus, many sculptures (Briómartis among others) and artefacts (AMI, XIX).

After this detour, it's back to Agía Varvára, where the road forks right in the direction of **Panasós** and **Gérgeri**. Whereas Panasós is beautiful to look at, Gérgeri, with its hordes of happy children, makes a livelier impression. There is a 15th-century Panagia Church in the village cemetery. Unfortunately not

much of the fresco decoration remains. The church was built in Byzantine style, and the church tower, set at a distance from the church itself, looks quite incongruous. Behind Gérgeri there are huge octopus-like agaves, or century trees, some of which reach a height of 10 metres (23 ft), their graceful, sturdy limbs curving delicately upwards, loaded with seed pods.

The contrasts continue, and after the restraint of **Nivritos**, you come to **Zarós,** which is large and noisy, with about 2,000 inhabitants. The spring water here is so exquisite that even in ancient times, the city of Górtis went to the expense of building an aqueduct to obtain it. There is one *tavérna* after another along the short stretch of main road, and they certainly don't just sell water. Just before you leave the village the road forks, and you go to the right.

The Monastery of Vrondíssi: Just 4 km (2½ miles) after Gérgeri, also on the

Left, church bells ring on the way to the Sea of Libya. Right, baking for Easter.

right, there is a road up into the mountains. A little further on, you will find yourself in front of the Monastery of **Vrondíssi**. The forecourt alone makes the journey worthwhile, but it is merely an introduction. On each side of the entrance to the monastery is an enormous plane tree.

Apparently, the trunk of one was once hit by lightning and is now hollow. There is room inside for a small one-man kitchen from which coffee is served. In the corner, behind this "Plane Tree Café", is a Venetian fountain. Adam and Eve stand over the four sources of paradise, symbolised by four bearded heads. Unfortunately, the sculptures have been badly damaged, and one can only guess at the former beauty of the fountain. But it is still lovely, nevertheless.

On the right side of the square, under the other plane tree, long tables and benches have been set up, looking for all the world as if the feeding of the five thousand was about to take place. They are simply there for the Feast of St Thomas, which is celebrated on the first Sunday after Easter, and then there are only just enough seats for everyone. There is, however, a large guesthouse opposite the entrance to the monastery, which provides hospitality to anyone unable to find space under the trees.

It is not known exactly when the Monastery of Vrondíssi was built. Although the dates 1630–39 are inscribed in the building, they may be not be correct. According to experts, the monastery must have been at least 250 years older, and could have belonged to the monastery at Valsamónero, which is much larger.

One nave of the church is dedicated to St Anthony and the other to St Thomas. In front of the church stands a belltower in Venetian style. The inside, particularly the southern nave, is decorated

Evening calm by the beach at Iráklion.

with frescoes and icons. In fact these icons are from the church in Agios Fanoúrios, which is all that is left of the enormous monastery complex of Valsamónero. The works of art were brought here for reasons of safety, as there has been a considerable increase in church robberies.

The six Cretan icons by the painter Damaskinós, for which the Monastery of Vrondíssi was so famous, have since 1800 been kept in the Ekateríni Church in Iráklion. They were brought there to be saved from the ravages of the Turks. The decision proved to be the right one as in 1821 the Turks destroyed everything they could find in the monastery, including the extensive library.

A glorious gateway leads to a beautifully paved inner courtyard. Yet a strange odour emits from a shed at the far end of the yard. It is the smell of cheese being produced in the time honoured method, using a goat or sheep skin. But the other side of the yard is fragrant with the scent of pines, palms and orange trees, and the view of the valley from there is glorious.

The right-hand corner near the entrance, under a pergola, is where the solitary monk who still lives here has his home. The monastery is an impressive sight, particularly when the sky is overcast or in rainy weather. Take your time here and try the excellent coffee made by the man in the Plane Tree Café.

As you go on to **Vorizia**, down on the left, below the road you will see a row of dilapidated houses. This is all that remains of the village of Vorizia, destroyed by the Germans in World War II. A row of houses built very close, as if for comfort, became the new village.

At the end of the village, a 3-km (1¾-mile) long road leads to the Monastery of **Valsamónero**. The keys for the church of **Agios Fanoúrios** have to be procured from the Greek Orthodox

ntacles
ng out
dry.

priest or the custodian, the *fílakas,* in Vorizia. The Byzantine frescoes here show a specifically Cretan style of representation, and it is even suggested that they may have been the work of El Greco or of Mikhail Damaskinós. Although this theory is not supported by art historians, it is difficult to see how either of the two masters of art could have improved upon the beautiful originals.

Ida Mountain Walks: The small village of **Kamáres** lies 3 km (1¾ miles) past Vorizia, and is a good starting point for walks in the Ida Mountains or for climbing Mount Psilorítis. Mountain guides are available on request. And to give your mountain climb more of a purpose, the famous **Kamáres Cave**, one of the main cultural attractions of the island is at the top – a good 4-hour climb away.

The cave is 1,525 metres (5,000 ft) up, and has a depth of about 80 metres (263 ft). The huge entrance, about 40 metres (181 ft) wide and 20 metres (90 ft) high, can be seen from a long way off, even from as far away as Festós. In Minoan times the cave was used for living in as well as for burial purposes, and the Goddess of Fertility was worshipped here.

The clay vessels, the Kamáres ceramics found in the cave, were produced in the workshops of the palaces of Festós and Agía Triáda. It was not until Kamáres ceramics were found in graves of the Middle Empire of Ancient Egypt, that the dates could be accurately assessed. A selection of pottery is on show in the Archaeological Museum in Iráklion, room III. They are characteristically thin, and brightly coloured, particularly in white, yellow and orange on a dark background.

Not far on from Agía Varvára is the **Vourvoulitis Pass**. There, from a height of 620 metres (2,034 ft), you will have your first view over the Messará

Steps at the Temple of Apollo Pythi in Górtis.

Plain right to the Asteroúsia Mountains in the south, between the plain and the Sea of Libya. Even in summer, when lorries full of melons and tomatoes pass by, a cold north wind can make one hurry on.

Saintly Spot: About 44 km (27 miles) from Iráklion, 15 km (9 miles) to the south of Agiá Varvára, is the village of **Agii Déka**, or the "Saintly 10". Here 10 Cretan bishops were put to death by the sword under rule of the Roman Caesar Gaius Decius (249–251). All of them had refused to take part in the consecration of a heathen temple. The stone which served as execution block has been preserved in the church. The 10 martyrs, later canonised, have been buried in a chapel on the western edge of the village.

Górtis: Only 1 km (½ mile) west of Agii Déka is the extensive site of ancient Górtis. From the road the imposing grandeur of the **Basilica of Titus**, one of the most impressive buildings on Crete, is clearly visible. It was built in the 6th century in memory of Titus, pupil of St Paul and later the first bishop of Crete. The church had to be renovated in the 10th and 14th centuries. The three-naved church which we see today is mainly the result of work undertaken at the beginning of this century. The only service held in the basilica these days is in memory of St Titus, and it takes place on 23 December. It is not easy to imagine the former glory of this place, as the traffic thunders past on the Mires road nearby.

A better sense of history can be experienced near the Odeon, which can be reached from the basilica, over the Agorá and then a little to the north. The **Odeon** is a 1st-century Roman rotunda. The famous inscription of Greek law is at the rear of the pillared entrance. For the Romans, who hardly understood the dialect, it served no civic function, but

ep in ught.

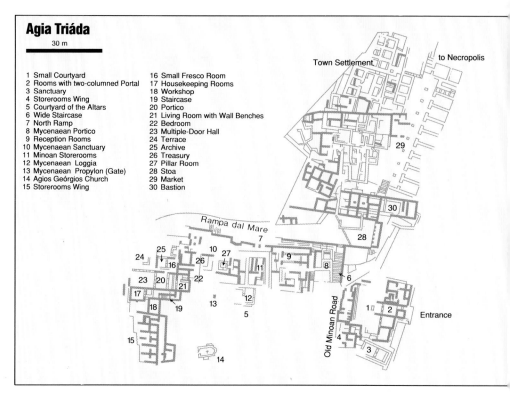

Agia Triáda

30 m

1 Small Courtyard
2 Rooms with two-columned Portal
3 Sanctuary
4 Storerooms Wing
5 Courtyard of the Altars
6 Wide Staircase
7 North Ramp
8 Mycenaean Portico
9 Reception Rooms
10 Mycenaean Sanctuary
11 Minoan Storerooms
12 Mycenaean Loggia
13 Mycenaean Propylon (Gate)
14 Agios Geórgios Church
15 Storerooms Wing

16 Small Fresco Room
17 Housekeeping Rooms
18 Workshop
19 Staircase
20 Portico
21 Living Room with Wall Benches
22 Bedroom
23 Multiple-Door Hall
24 Terrace
25 Archive
26 Treasury
27 Pillar Room
28 Stoa
29 Market
30 Bastion

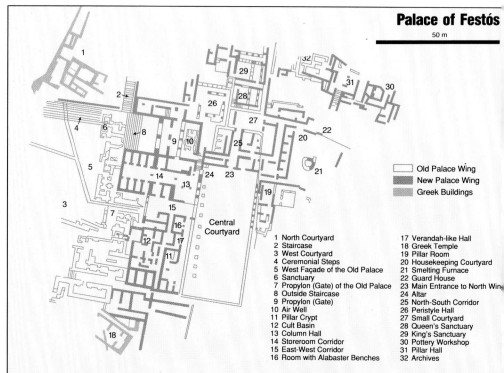

Palace of Festós

50 m

Old Palace Wing
New Palace Wing
Greek Buildings

1 North Courtyard
2 Staircase
3 West Courtyard
4 Ceremonial Steps
5 West Façade of the Old Palace
6 Sanctuary
7 Propylon (Gate) of the Old Palace
8 Outside Staircase
9 Propylon (Gate)
10 Air Well
11 Pillar Crypt
12 Cult Basin
13 Column Hall
14 Storeroom Corridor
15 East-West Corridor
16 Room with Alabaster Benches

17 Verandah-like Hall
18 Greek Temple
19 Pillar Room
20 Housekeeping Courtyard
21 Smelting Furnace
22 Guard House
23 Main Entrance to North Wing
24 Altar
25 North-South Corridor
26 Peristyle Hall
27 Small Courtyard
28 Queen's Sanctuary
29 King's Sanctuary
30 Pottery Workshop
31 Pillar Hall
32 Archives

was left there untouched for decoration. Opposite the Odeon is a small theatre.

There is a wonderful view of the whole Górtis area from the hill where an **Acropolis** once stood, but unfortunately the olive groves are too thick to appreciate it. However, the aqueduct which carried water here from Zarós, 15 km (9 miles) away can be seen clearly.

To explore the southern and larger part of historical Górtis, cross the main road and carry on along the asphalt road for about 250 metres (270 yd), then turn off to the left. Here, nestling close to each other, are a small theatre and the **Temple of Apollo Pythios**, which was built on the site of a Minoan building. On the outer walls there are inscriptions of Greek law which are older than the famed inscription of Górtis.

A little further to the north is the somewhat surprising temple in honour of Egyptian gods. They were worshipped on Crete for a while after the conquest of Egypt (AMI, XX). The highlight is the **Praetorium**, an extensive building complex which formed the palace from which the Roman Governor, the Praetor of Crete and Cyrene ruled. Everything in this imposing building seems to have been organised for efficiency. Even the ruins seem to reflect the builders' will to dominate. Minoan architecture, in contrast, seems ornate and harmonious in keeping with its peaceful, matriarchal culture.

Further south are the thermal springs, the amphitheatre, the cemetery and the stadium where chariot races were held. From a cultural and historical point of view this southern part of Górtis is considered rather unimportant. But whatever the experts say, for the visitor who really wants to understand life in a classical city, this site is unique.

Just by walking around and being receptive to everything that is "historical", you can learn so much more than from reading books or visiting a museum. Much of the ground is covered with fragments and potsherds which is against the law to take away. The visitor may find it hard to believe that this was once a centre of power, pride and battle. Nowadays, the atmosphere is peaceful and you can spend many happy hours just exploring and simply enjoying the atmosphere of the place and absorbing the sense of history.

Festós: On the way to Festós you pass **Mires**, the largest town of the Messará Plain, with more than 3,000 inhabitants. On Saturdays there is a big market here, a colourful, lively event. Mires is still comparatively untouched by tourism, as people do not seem to have realised the favourable location of the place. It is easy to reach Festós or Agía Triáda from there, and the whole of the glorious Messará Plain opens up towards Hárakas and Pirgos. as well as *tavérnes,* cafés and shops, there is a chemist, post office, OTE and even a branch of the Greek National Health Insurance.

own the eps of the alace of estós.

The **Palace of Festós** is almost 7 km (4 miles) from Mires – 62 km (38 miles) from Iráklion – and the excavation site is well-signposted 5 km ((3 miles) along the road.

Festós is most impressive but not, like Knossós, because of its reconstruction – it is the site which is spectacular here. The palace was built on a hill, 70 metres (239 ft) high, the summit of which had to be flattened to facilitate construction of the first palace. The panorama is breathtaking in any season, mountains to the north and south, the sea on the western horizon, and the seemingly endless fertile plain to the east.

In spring, its wonderful colours make it a particularly beautiful place. But in summer, the heat can be unbearable with the temperature reaching over 50 degrees, which makes you wonder what on earth made the Minoans choose such a place – an anvil in the sun.

However, their choice was certainly

not based on climatic criteria. For them the focal point was indeed something quite different. In the Ida Mountains to the north, to the right of a twin summit is a dark hole. It is the Kamáres Cave. The north-south axis of the palace points directly to this cave. Fragments of pottery found in the cave emphasise this relationship, for some of the wares were made in the palace.

In Festós one comes across another member of the mythological family of Zeus, Europa and her children. Rhadamanthys, the brother of Minos, is said to have ruled here, before being elected judge of the underworld.

Festós is mentioned in the *Iliad* too, King Idomeneus set out from here with his troops to support the Achaians in their struggle against Troy. As scientific research makes it seem ever more likely that the Trojan War actually did take place, mythology and history seem inextricably linked.

The site of Festós has been shown to have been inhabited from Neolithic times onward. The first palace was built in about 2000 BC, and it must have been heavily damaged by three strong earthquakes and fires. At the height of Minoan civilisation, the period between 1600 and 1500 BC, a new palace was built on the foundations of the old one. This palace too was completely destroyed soon afterwards in the catastrophe of 1450 BC.

Finds from the Geometric period and Hellenistic Epoch indicate that the area around the palace was also inhabited in post Minoan times. The prophet Epimenides was born in Festós in the 6th century BC. His most famous saying is, no doubt, "All Cretans are liars". But despite this artful paradox, it must not be forgotten that he was a serious thinker, who was even cited by Aristotle. In the 3rd century, before our time reckoning, Festós was forced to cede its position of superiority to Górtin.

The Palace of Festós is somewhat

Left, a flautist's welcome visitors to Festós. Right, the palace ruins

smaller than that of Knossós, but similar in layout. The separate sections, used for a variety of purposes, are grouped around a central courtyard measuring 46 metres (151 ft) long by 22 metres (72 ft) wide. Stonemasons' marks found in both Knossós and Festós indicate that some of the same craftsmen were at work in both palaces. There is also a great deal of evidence pointing to a close relationship between the two palaces as political and religious centres. The exact nature of the ties is, however, still not quite clear.

The famous Festós Disc, copies of which may be seen at every souvenir stall on the island, was not found inside the palace itself but in the so-called archives to the north of the site. It is not at all certain though whether the room was in fact used as the archives. It may have been a storeroom for the palace guards. This makes even a rough interpretation of the clay disc impossible

A brochure on Crete interprets the disc as merely a list of goods for export to the various countries with which Crete was trading at the time. This interpretation dates from 1982, and despite its overwhelming simplicity, it does not convince many people. In fact, it is completely discounted by the experts (AMI, III, cabinet 41).

In the cult basin, various ceramic vessels were found, among them the beaked can with grasses. They are exhibited in the Archaeological Museum of Iráklion (Room IV, cabinet 49). The melting furnace in the so-called production yard is one of the oldest such installations to be found in all Greece.

It is not true to say that the Italian excavators F. Halbherr (from 1900) and D. Levi (from 1952) did no reconstruction in the Palace of Festós. This impression is simply a result of comparing their work with that done at Knossós. Parts of the palace were rebuilt, but the

Festós, where the beautiful countryside beckons.

work was less ambitious, undertaken cautiously, and restricted to what was absolutely necessary.

Rooms are available in the tourist summer house at Festós, and it can be an unforgettable experience to spend the evening and the night in proximity to such an ancient palace. This encounter is definitely more interesting than the more usual tourist attractions.

In front of the car park in Festós there is a road which leads directly to the west, to the **Palace of Agía Triáda**. The route is a rather unusual one. You must go back onto the main road, then a short distance along towards Timbáki and left at the signpost.

A little further on, you will find yourself at the Geropótamos River, and depending on the time of year and the water level, you have to decide whether or not to cross. There is no bridge and in summer this is no problem. But if the water level is high, you might not want

to risk it. Once across the river, you should turn left at the next crossroads in the country lane, and on through the olive groves to the car park in Agía Triáda (Holy Trinity).

Since no name survived this place, it was called after the 14th-century church not far away, but that is all that remains of a village named for Father, Son and Holy Spirit.

Agía Triáda is not strictly speaking a palace, as it does not possess a central courtyard, which is the main feature of all other Cretan palaces. The rooms are set in two wings which are almost at right angles to each other. Royal Villa would probably have been a more appropriate label.

There is much evidence to suggest that Agía Triáda belonged to the Palace of Festós; it may have been the summer residence of the rulers. In Festós no frescoes or cult objects were found, whereas there was a surfeit in Agía

a Triáda, other nic sight ar Festós.

Triáda. The palace and villa were linked by a paved road.

The question then arises as to why, if the Minoan ruler wanted sea breezes, he or she didn't build nearer the seashore. The answer to that has been provided by the Italian archaeologists, who felt that there was enough evidence to indicate that, around 3,500 years ago, the sea was much nearer to Agía Triáda than it is now.

Of all the precious finds, the most important are the Harvester's Vase (AMI, VII), octopus and dolphin frescoes (AMI, XIV), steatite vases (AMI, IV), and the "Talents", 19 bronze bars, each weighing 29 kilos, from the sarcophagus of Agía Triáda (AMI, XIV) (see chapter on Cretan history).

Minoan Port: If you return to Festós and from there go on through **Agios Ioánnis** (St John) in the direction of Mátala, you will reach the excavation site of **Kómmos**. Just about 1 km (½ mile) after the village of Pitsidia, take a right turn onto a road which leads to the church. You have to continue for only another 500 metres (550 yd) along the shore to the north, to reach the site.

Kómmos, which was a port of Festós, has only been excavated since 1976, by Canadian archaeologists. The place was inhabited at the beginning of the middle Minoan period, around 1800 BC, and like Festós reached the height of its importance in the late Minoan epoch. The excavations are not yet far enough advanced for any extensive conclusions to be reached.

If the theory that the sea lay nearer Agía Triáda in those days is correct, then there must have been a bay here, with Kómmos being established on the southern side. Thus the western part of the Messará Plain must have been alluvial land. But don't let all this theorising stop you from enjoying the excellent bathing on this lovely beach.

Mátala beach seen from the caves.

Hippies'village: The fishing village of **Mátala** is only 7 km (4 miles) from Festós. Well-known during the 1960s for the invasion of the hippies, it now offers a surprise of its own. It is so famous that one would imagine it to be overcrowded and the beach totally overrun with tourists. Wrong. The fact is that Mátala has hardly changed at all. Of course it has spruced itself up a bit, has a few more *tavérnes* than it used to, but it has not lost its character.

The houses still make a strange matt impression in daylight. They look like a collection of old, temporarily inhabited gold prospectors' huts. And there's still a whiff of the freedom of the 1960s and 70s in the air, reminiscent of the old days of the flower children.

The atmosphere is relaxed, and no one pressures you to rent a room. There are still plenty of young people staying here, all enjoying the ambience of this laidback village. The place itself is beautiful, and the houses are grouped around the natural harbour and the steep cliffs rising up behind.

It is true that the caves were barred up a few years ago, but there are always climbers and they can be seen clambering up onto the narrow cornices. These caves, inhabited in Neolithic times, were taken over as living quarters again in the 1960s, when they provided comfortable but basic homes for the hippies. Later, the backpackers and hikers wanted to take up permanent residence there, but they were evicted mainly for reasons of hygiene. Many a crocodile tear was shed at the collapse of this last bastion of freedom.

In the evenings, if you sit in one of the restaurants opposite the cliff of caves, Mátala looks just like a ship about to set sail. It is a great place to relax as well as a good starting point for exploring the region and its towns, Kómmos, Festós, Agía Triáda and Górtis.

ach crowd
Mátala take
reak.

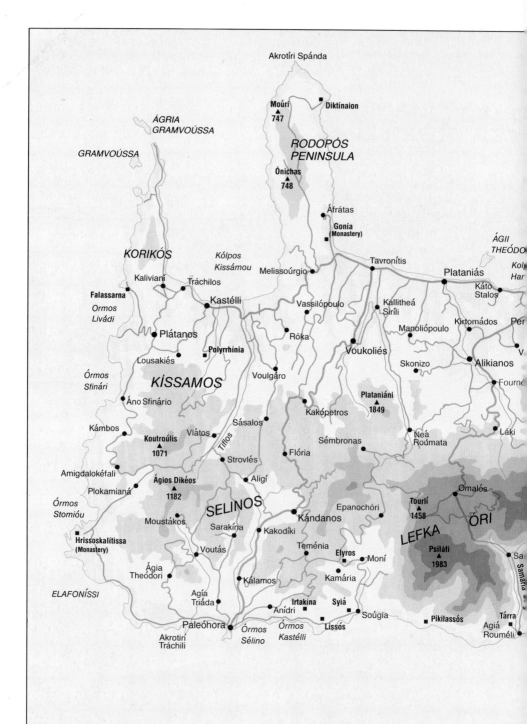

Akrotíri Spánda

Moúri ▲ ■ Diktínaion
747

ÁGRIA
GRAMVOÚSSA

GRAMVOÚSSA

RODOPÓS
PENINSULA

Ónichas ▲
748

Áfrátas ■

Goniá
(Monastery)

ÁGII
THEÓDO

KORIKÓS

Kólpos
Kissámou   Melissoúrgio ●   Tavronítis ●   **Plataniás** ●   Kol
Har

Kaliviani ●   Tráchilos ●   Vassilópoulo ●   **Kállitheá**   Káto
Stalos

Falassarna ■   **Kastélli**   **Siríli** ●   Kirtomádos ●   Per
Ormos
Livádi   Manoliópoulo ●   V

● **Plátanos**   Róka ●   **Voukoliés** ●

■ **Polyrrhínia**   Skonizo ●   ● **Alikianos**

Lousakiés ●

Órmos   Voulgáro ●   Fourné
Sfinári   **KÍSSAMOS**

● **Áno Sfinário**   **Plataniáni** ●   Láki
1849

Sásalos ●   Kakópetros ●

Kámbos ●   **Koutroúlis** Vlátos ●   Sémbronas ●   **Neá**
▲ 1071   Strovlés ●   Flória ●   **Roúmata** ●

Amigdalokéfali ●   **Ágios Dikéos** ●   Aligí ●   Omalós ●
Plokamianá ●   ▲ 1182   **SELINOS**   Epanochóri ●   **Tourlí**   **ÓRI**
Órmos   **Moustákos** ●   **Kándanos** ●   ▲ 1458   **LEFKA**
Stomíou   Sarakína ●   Kakodíki ●   **Psiláfi** ●   Sa
■   Voutás ●   Teménia ●   **Elyros** Moní ●   ▲ 1983
Hrissoskalítissa   **Ágia**   Kamária ●   Samána
(Monastery)   Theódori   Kálamos ●

ELAFONÍSSI   **Ágia**   **Irtakína** ■ **Syiá** ■   Tárra ■
Triáda ●   Anídri ■ ■   Soúgia ■   **Pikilassós** ■   Agiá
Paleóhora ●   *Órmos*   *Órmos*   **Lissós** ■   Rouméli
Akrotíri   *Sélino*   *Kastélli*
Tráchili

S e a   o f   L i b y a

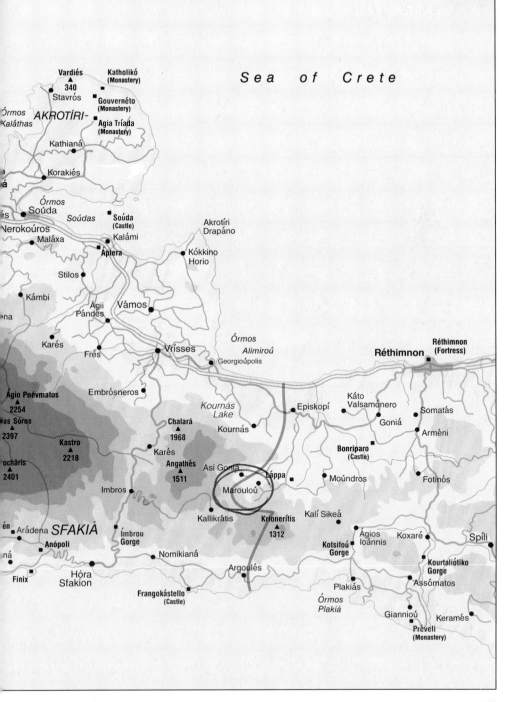

Sea of Crete

Vardiés
▲ 340
Stavrós
Katholikó
(Monastery)

Gouvernéto
(Monastery)

Órmos
Kaláthas

AKROTÍRI-

Agia Tríada
(Monastery)

Kathianá

Korakiés

Órmos
Soúda

Soúdas

Soúda
(Castle)

Akrotíri
Drapáno

Nerokoúros

Maláxa

Kalámi

Áptera

Kókkino
Horio

Stilos

Kámbi

Ágii
Pándes

Vámos

Karés

Frés

Vrísses

Órmos
Alimiroú
Georgioúpolis

Réthimnon

Réthimnon
(Fortress)

Ágio Pnévmatos
▲ 2254

Embrósneros

Kournás
Lake

Episkopí

Káto
Valsamónero

Somatás

as Sóros
▲ 2397

Chalará
▲ 1968

Kournás

Goniá

Arméni

Kastro
▲ 2218

Karés

Bonriparo
(Castle)

ocháris
▲ 2401

Angathés
▲ 1511

Asi Gonía

Láppa

Moúndros

Fotinós

Imbros

Marouloú

Kallikrátis

Krionerítis
▲ 1312

Kalí Sikeá

én
Arádena

SFAKIÁ

Ímbrou
Gorge

Ágios
Ioánnis

Koxaré

Spíli

Anópoli

Nomikianá

Kotsifoú
Gorge

ná

Argoulés

Kourtaliótiko
Gorge

Finix

Hóra
Sfakíon

Plakiás

Assómatos

Frangokástello
(Castle)

Órmos
Plakiá

Giannioú

Keramés

Préveli
(Monastery)

We
10 k

RÉTHIMNON AND SURROUNDINGS

The suburbs of Réthimnon are disappointing, with the usual monotony of concrete blocks. But if you leave the main road, and turn towards the sea, you will find yourself in the fascinating old part of the city of Réthimnon. The most interesting way in is through the beautiful Large Gate (Megáli Pórta) on the Square of the Four Martyrs. Many visitors are moved by this place, and as one of them, you might feel yourself transported back to the Middle Ages.

Réthimnon is a city of many contrasts, which is a result of the turbulent course of its history. The Fortezza, Venetian harbour and lighthouse, serve as reminders of the days of Venetian rule. Memories of the Turkish occupation linger in the mosques and minarets, two of which you can visit. To the east are the new parts of the city, with hotels and restaurants in profusion, as well as a number of interesting small shops selling everything from Cretan boats to lace. There is much to keep the visitor occupied in this fascinating city.

The area around Réthimnon was probably settled as early as the Late Minoan Era. A rock grave was found in the suburb of **Mastrabas**, and various archaeological finds are displayed in the Archaeological Museum of Réthimnon. However, no actual settlement of this period has so far been discovered. During the 3rd and 4th centuries BC a town named Réthimna flourished here. It was autonomous and had the right to mint its own coins. Where the Fortezza stands today was once the site of the Acropolis of Réthimnon with the Temple of Artemis and a shrine to the goddess Athena.

After Constantinople was conquered by the Crusaders, Crete fell to the Genoese Bonifatius of Monferat, who later sold the island to the Venetians. With or without the treaty of sale, it took the Venetians a further five years to rid themselves of the Genoese, who had established extensive trading contacts. Near the present day village of Monopári one can still see the remains of the Genoese Fort of **Bonriparo**. In 1229 the Venetians finally made the city more secure, concentrating on the western side of the little harbour. The more important fortifications were constructed during the period 1540–70, and the outer wall, parallel to today's Dimakópoulou Street and part of the "Great Gate", can still be seen. The architect was Michele Sanmicheli.

In 1573 work was begun on the "city within the city", as the Fortezza was often described. New buildings sprang up, and others were completed, such as the Rimondi Fountain, the churches of St Mary, St Mary Magdalene, St Francis and the Loggia, in which the

Archaeological Museum is housed (Arkadíou Street 220). The **Rimondi Fountain**, among other renovated fountains and wells, helped solve the city's water problems. The spelling Arimondi, which is often seen, is simply the result of adding the A of the first name Alvise to that of Rimondi. The lions' heads between the Corinthian pillars have unfortunately been ravaged by time, but the water still flows.

When the attacking Turks appeared outside the city in 1646, the inhabitants hesitated for too long before taking refuge in the unpopular Fortezza. Eventually they were forced to enter, but it soon became obvious that the fort could not withstand the Turkish onslaught. After a siege lasting 22 days, Husein Pasha took the city as well as the fort.

Réthimnon retained its position as administrative centre under the Turks, but its appearance was radically changed. All the Christian churches were given minarets and new names, thereby turning them into mosques. Thus St Mary's Church became the **Neratzés Pasha Mosque**, and St Mary Magdalene's became the **Angebút Pasha Mosque**, although now it is the Greek Orthodox Church of **Kiría Ton Angélon** (Our Lady of the Angels). Even the Venetian **Loggia** was not spared, and was also converted into a mosque. The Rimondi Fountain was given a traditional Turkish domed roof. Thus the Turkish rulers put their stamp on the way the city looked, a clear indication of their dominance.

The Turks wanted to change the Greek Orthodox inhabitants of Crete in the same way. They forced as many Cretans as they could to become Muslims. Some did convert, for reasons of practicality, but others remained steadfast despite reprisals. As a warning to others, four of those who resisted were hanged on the square which is today

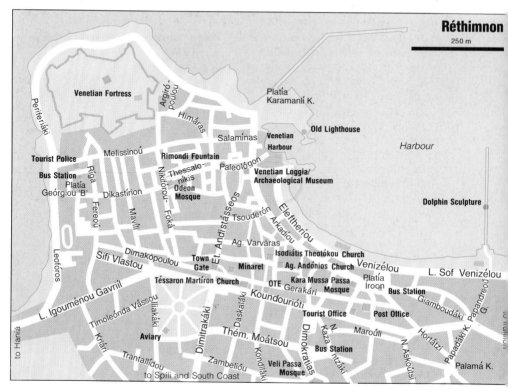

known as Platía Tessáron Martíron (Square of the Four Martyrs).

Tension between the two peoples came to a head in 1821, when the Turks unleashed a bloodbath among the Christians, and in 1828 there was even fighting outside the city gates. In 1866, long after the rest of Greece had attained independence, the Turks attacked Réthimnon. Thousands of Resistance fighters, women and children took shelter behind the walls of the Monastery of Arkádi but realising the hopelessness of their position and determined not to fall into Turkish hands, they blew themselves up.

It was another 32 years before Réthimnon was finally freed from Turkish rule. The city was not spared during World War II either. In May 1941, Réthimnon was attacked by German parachutists and became an occupied city.

A visit to the **Fortezza** is an absolute must. It is open all year round, and the view alone is an experience. You look out over the city, the mountains in the distance and the whole expanse of countryside reaching the sea. The Fortezza was built between 1573 and 1586 on the site of the old fortifications. The total circumference is 1,307 metres (4,288 ft). There are four bastions, and the building follows the natural contours of the hill.

The main gate in the east was the only link with the town, and was therefore built high and wide. The north and west gates were used for delivering supplies and for leaving the fort in the direction of the sea. Apart from barracks, warehouses, administrative buildings in the southern part of the fort and the powder and food stores in the northern part, the most interesting feature is the Venetian Cathedral at the centre of the edifice.

Here was yet another indication of the supposed unpopularity of the

Harbour lights at Réthimnon.

Fortezza. In 1585 the cathedral was to have become the seat of the bishop, but Bishop Carrara, with many a feeble excuse, refused to move there. It was briefly taken over by the Turks, who converted it and named it after Sultan Ibrahim. Apparently a minaret was added, but it later disappeared.

During the summer months, there is an enormous influx of visitors and the city of Réthimnon is completely geared up for tourism. The beach is right at the edge of the old city and extends to the east, although the bathing is better further away from the city. There is an open-air pool, too.

In March and April, a flower festival is held in the city park, which is just outside the old city. Better known is the flower market. People come from miles around to stock up on seeds and cuttings as this is an area of the island where there are many greenhouses.

The Wine Festival takes place in mid July. During this lively festival, the low entrance fee will give you free wine for the evening. After that there is the Music Week where dancers and groups from all over Greece come to perform. The proceeds of these events are used by the city administration to pay for necessary maintenance work.

The city and immediate environs make a prosperous impression, but in fact Réthimnon is actually the poorest of the four administrative regions in Crete. Unfortunately, the outlook for the city is not rosy either. The goal of a link to Athens (Piraeus) by ship is not attainable, nor is it possible for the city to participate in the trade and passenger transport between Soúda and Iráklion. So it loses out on a very profitable link. A badly designed breakwater has led to the silting up of the harbour, and as a result the big ships cannot berth there.

About a third of the city's population depends on earnings related to tourism, **"Fancy a coach tour?**

which, of course, is problematic in itself. But the real problem stems from the land itself. This is the most mountainous region in Crete, which makes life very difficult indeed for the farmers. The Amari Valley and the Nida Plain are fertile and prosperous, but olive growing, animal husbandry, milk production and flower and vegetable cultivation, mainly undertaken in greenhouses, are not very profitable at all.

It is not merely since the founding of the **Faculty of Philosophy** in 1977 that Réthimnon has had the reputation of being an intellectual city, although not much was possible under the constraints of military dictatorship. Many rich Cretans in the 14th and 15th centuries sent their offspring to Padua to study. They returned with new ideas, and it is thus that the ideas of the Italian Renaissance came to Crete. The "Cretan Renaissance" which followed in the 15th and 16th centuries produced literature of a high standard, and artists and intellectuals of Réthimnon played a prominent part. They included writers such as Geórgios Hortátzis with *Erophili*, M.T. Bounialís with *The Cretan War*, and probably the most admired of all, Vinzéntos Kornáros with the verse drama *Erotókritos*. Emánuel Tzánes Bounialís, one of the most highly regarded of all icon painters came from Crete. Such cultural expressions were forcibly interrupted for a long time by Turkish rule. Once again, in the 20th century, there is a great name in the literary world which is associated with the city, that of Pantelis Prevelákis.

Trips into the Surrounding Area: To reach **Argiroúpoli**, you can turn off the Réthimnon–Haniá motorway towards Episkopí. The village of Argiroúpoli, which is to the south of Episkopí, is of interest because it was built on the ruins of the Dorian settlement of **Láppa**, which was completely destroyed by the

e Fortezza
s much to
er to
dlorers.

Romans in 67 BC. However, it was rebuilt shortly afterwards by Octavius, later Augustus Caesar, who held the first census in the Roman world.

Near Argiroúpoli peasants found a burial site composed of five chambers. They believed it to have been the burial place of the five holy women who died as Christian martyrs during the Roman occupation. But archaeological research has indicated that the grave was in fact older.

Two children and two adults lie buried around a central room, which appears to have been used for sacrifices. The two statues of Artemis and Aphrodite found nearby are displayed in the Archaeological Museum of Haniá. Some mansions from Venetian times have also survived.

Argiroúpoli, as a centre of resistance, must have incurred the particular wrath of the Turks, for in 1867 it was subjected to an especially brutal campaign

of revenge. Houses were razed to the ground, orange and olive trees felled, and even the graves were disturbed and the remains of the dead strewn about all over the place.

Today, although seldom visited by tourists, the village is relatively prosperous. It lies between two rivers, and the water enables olives, maize, cereal and citrus fruits to grow well, while cattle graze in the lush meadows.

The village of **Miriokéfala** lies at a height of 500 metres (1,640 ft), up in the Lefká Ori. The "Monastery of the Panagía," founded in the year 1000 by John the Hermit, was burned down by the Turks in 1821. Only the church, with frescoes from the 11th and 12th centuries, withstood the fire. Miriokéfala is a good starting point for more ambitious tours of the Lefká Ori range, as the best mountain guides live here.

Agía Iríni (St Irene) is another destination in the immediate vicinity of Réthimnon. On the way south, you pass the dilapidated houses of the former settlement of **Mikrá Anógia**, which was once a fortress. Just before arriving in Agía Iríni, you will see the ruins of a monastery. There is a basilica with three naves and a reservoir hewn in the rocks. The next village is **Roussospíti**, where there are some well-preserved Venetian houses, a fountain and 15th-century murals in the church.

Kapediná is next, from which one can set out to climb the **Vríssinas** – 858 metres (2,815 ft) – to the south. In a wonderful position right at the summit is the Church of the Holy Spirit, **Agios Pnévmatos**. Every year at Whitsun, Mass is celebrated here, drawing believers from all over the region. In 1938 clay idols were found, indicating that there was a sanctuary here in Minoan times. And in 1973, pictures of bulls, eagles and goats were found in clefts of the rocks.

If you are interested in murals, return to Réthimnon via **Hromonastíri**. Near

Getting food ready for the lunch crowd

there is the Church of **Agios Eftíhios** with 11th-century murals, which are among the oldest in Crete, but unfortunately not very well preserved.

The road continues through the Gorge of **Míli**, with an abandoned village of the same name located in the middle. It is then only a stone's throw to **Missíria**, from where the bus for Réthimnon leaves.

There is another gorge near the village of **Prassés** on the way to Amári. You can only walk through the **Prassanó Gorge** in summer, as there is a gushing torrent in winter and in spring. The gorge was formed by the river **Plataniás** which flows into the sea east of Réthimnon. The walk through the gorge takes a good five hours. At their highest, the cliff walls just reach 150 metres (492 ft), nothing like the height of the imposing Samariá Gorge.

The beauty of the gorge lies in its lush vegetation – carob trees, plane trees and oleander grow here – as well as in its peaceful atmosphere, despite the proximity of Réthimnon. As yet, there has been little in the way of development here. The turning to **Mírthios**, where there are a couple of ruined houses dating from the 7th and 8th centuries, leads on to **Sellí** and **Karé**, where there are remains of a basilica with a lovely mosaic floor. Then it's back again to Réthimnon via Arméni.

Along the Coast: Réthimnon has been blessed with beautiful beaches. Nowadays this means one thing – the building of new hotels and the advent mass tourism. So often this spoils the character of a place. **Missíria** and **Adele**, on the longest sandy beach in Crete, stretching more than 15 km (9 miles) have managed to preserve a friendly atmosphere and a touch of elegance, although not much individuality.

Platanés and **Stavroménos** have retained more of their original character. Behind Stavroménos you drive through the fertile delta of the **Milopótamos**, a lush area of fruit and vegetable cultivation. The village of **Pánormos** has no beach and is thus quite unable to compete with its neighbours.

It has visibly deteriorated since Byzantine times when it was a bustling port for **Eléftherna**. All that remains of its former days of glory are ruins of the old harbour walls and parts of the Byzantine basilica. And all that has survived of the enormous Venetian castle, which one would have expected to survive the ravages of time, is its equally enormous name, Milopótamos.

To the east of Pánormos is the little village of **Balí**, set around a series of small coves, and considered by many to be the most beautiful place on Crete. The motorway has, of course, robbed Balí of some of its isolated charm. It is still a glorious spot, however.

Experts think this was the site of another ancient city, **Astáli**, the port of the city of **Axós**. The small village of Balí is

n on a
ny beach,
iohora

on the way to becoming the Kritsá of fishing villages. Despite the threateningly large streams of tourists who visit, the infrastructure has managed to cope, and so far no high-rise hotels have been built. But the place is too lovely to remain that way. The rather shabby gravel beach will not put people off much longer.

The Monastery of Agios Ioánnis situated in the northern foothills of the **Kouloúkonas** mountain is also well worth a visit.

Minoan Necropolis: If you enjoy walking and come prepared for the sun, you can reach **Arméni** in about two hours. Leave Réthimnon in a southerly direction going through the villages of Gállou and Somatás and you will come to the late Minoan necropolis of Arméni. It mainly comprises underground beehive and chamber tombs hacked out of the rocks. The larger ones can be reached by steps.

Many of the finds unearthed in this cemetery, dated at between 1350 and 1200 BC, are displayed in the Archaeological Museum of Haniá. There are clay idols and ceramic pots, but also tools, weapons and sarcophagi. They are richly decorated with religious motifs and among some of the most valuable finds on the whole island. They also indicate the spread of Minoan culture to the west of Crete.

One of the most impressive of the larger graves is probably that of a Minoan duke or king. The impressive entrance area, 13 metres (43 ft) long, leads down 7 metres (23 ft) to the grave itself, which is about 4.5 sq metres (48 sq ft) in area. The scarabs on the steps are reminiscent of Egypt. However, the burial chamber, despite the technical capabilities of the time, is not symmetrical. Nor was it designed according to any geometrical principles.

It is also quite impossible to fit the graves themselves into any kind of pattern or systematic arrangement. It has

been suggested that the graves had some kind of alignment, either north–south or some other formation, but none of these criteria accords with the facts. It seems that some completely different way of thinking was behind the arrangement here. There was also a settlement near the burial site, but that has not yet been found.

Strange insects, which cannot readily be identified as any known species, have been seen flying around the area. They are about 2 cm (1 in) long, seemingly multi-winged and have greenish yellow bodies which are thick and roundish. From their heads protrude large beak-like proboscises.

One way to return to Réthimnon is to take the route via **Methóhi Risváni**. This is a settlement where the house of Irfan Bey may be seen as well as some ruined churches. Perhaps the best view of Réthimnon, from anywhere, is from the hill of Evliyiás.

Below, still life in a *tavérna*. Right, peasant woman on her way to the Ida Mountains.

FROM RÉTHIMNON TO THE IDA MOUNTAINS

If you take the road southwards from Réthimnon, you reach the intersection at **Koxaré** and then the **Kourtaliótiko Gorge**. The motorway goes part of the way through the gorge, and it really is a good idea to stop here for a while. This gives you the opportunity to enjoy the island atmosphere. You just listen to the sound of water splashing, of birds singing and frogs croaking. A shepherd whistles to his goats while nimbly climbing up the steep slopes of the hills. The source of the river water is just near the entrance to the gorge. High up in the rocks there are five holes from which the water springs.

This is a miraculous phenomenon ascribed to Agios Nikólaos (St Nicholas). The five holes are said to symbolise the five fingers which he laid on the rock. The strange fact is that the river never dries up, not even during the hottest summer. A narrow path leads to a little chapel erected to commemorate the spring, which is known locally as the "Blessing of the Lord".

Just down the road, there is a dilapidated settlement. Although it does not look impressive, it is worth a visit. Above one of the doors is a plaque with the date 1795 on it. There is a stable too, with room for over 20 cattle, quite a few smaller rooms, most of them quite well kept, and some decorated with murals. A well house with a dome, dated 1865, has been constructed over the spring. Finally, on the church wall is a plaque commemorating the destruction of the village by the Turks in 1821.

These ruins are in fact all that remains of the Lower Monastery of Préveli, **Káto Préveli**. What is inconceivable is that the monastery was actually built here in the first place. Strategically, it is very badly positioned, and location was always an important consideration for those building a monastery on Crete. It is possible that the mountain used to look different, or that the construction of the road altered the place.

Whatever the case may be, the fact is that Upper Préveli, or **Písso Préveli**, was the more important structure, and this is what is generally meant when the Monastery of Préveli is mentioned. Its location is quite superb, 170 metres (558 ft) above sea level, facing southeast. It is not known when the monastery was built. And as the old monastery church, where one might have expected to find clues, was abruptly demolished in 1853 when the new one was built, there seems little chance of finding out more now. Some chroniclers believe that circumstantial evidence points to a construction date of about 980.

The whole place has a friendly atmosphere, in fact almost merry. There is a television antenna on the abbot's roof,

ft,
new
onastery
Préveli.
ght,
akiás.

and soft drinks are kept cool in a plastic bag in the inner room of the church, all of which adds to this light-hearted impression. But one must not be misled – Préveli was a centre of solidarity and national Resistance particularly during the years of oppression.

Although not of the same political significance as Arkádi, it was far more important in economic terms. In its heyday, the monastery was incredibly rich. Gifts, generous donations and transfers by means of which rich Cretans kept their possessions out of Turkish hands, brought huge areas of land under the protection of the monastery. The olive harvest brought in about 130,000 litres of oil per year. Then there were 80 tons of cereals, 120 tons of carob, as well as large amounts of fruit and vegetables. About 2,000 goats and sheep grazed in the meadows, and there were pigs, cattle and mules.

In addition, the monks kept bees and silkworms. Préveli was like a prosperous estate which invested in community projects and social progress. Churches, schools, hospitals and many other establishments were founded or aided with the money from Préveli. It is thus no wonder that one finds valuable icons here as well as an interesting library and an extensive museum.

The most important item in the monastery is a gold cross set with diamonds, in which a splinter of the cross of Jesus is reputed to be kept. It was a donation of the former abbot, Ephraim Prévelis (1755–75), a direct descendant of the founder of the monastery, Akákis Préveli. The cross is said to heal eye disorders, and is even supposed to have given the blind their sight. There are many tales concerning the powers of this miraculous cross.

One such tale relates to the German occupation during World War II. The Germans had heard of the conspiracies

Mountain road from Préveli to Plakiás.

and Resistance activities centred on Préveli. Many Britons and New Zealanders hid here and later managed to escape in Allied ships. As punishment for such opposition, the Germans wanted to weaken the economic power of the monastery. They chased animals away and robbed the monastery of its treasures. Among the articles stolen was the miraculous cross.

Three times the Germans attempted to take the cross to Germany, but each time they put it on board an aircraft, the engines, which up to then had been in perfect working order, failed. In the end the Germans did not merely give up, they actually returned the cross to the place where it belonged.

A little further westwards is the small palm-fringed beach of Préveli. As you come away from the monastery, turn right into a country lane a short way along the road. It is easy to find but not marked. In season, others are bound to

be looking for the place too, and if in doubt you can always ask the locals. The reward is that, after a detour of about a quarter of an hour, you arrive in a real tropical paradise.

From Koxaré to the West: Apart from the Monastery of Préveli, there are a few other interesting villages in the region of **Agios Vasiléos** (St Basil). They can be reached either on the broad road from **Koxaré** or from Préveli by way of **Lefkógia**. Further to the west at the crossroads of Préveli, Réthimnon and Frangokástello is the village of **Selliá** at an altitude of 300 metres (984 ft). To the north it is protected by the massif of **Psílis** and to the south the countryside stretches away to the Sea of Libya.

The better-known former fishing village of **Plakiás** belongs to the same municipality. Its mild climate, wonderful beach and proximity of the gorges of **Kotsifoú** and **Kourta-Liótiko** make it a a worthwhile stop on any itinarary.

sheltered
ve below
e Monastery
Préveli.

Plakiás is a typical example of just what happens when a place turns to tourism as its main source of revenue. It used to be an insignificant little village and due, to its natural beauty and fine beach, it has experienced what could be referred to as an economic upsurge. In other words, it is bursting at the seams.

Further west, almost in the rural district of Sfakiá, renowned for its fighting men, are the villages of **Ano Rodákino** and **Káto Rodákino**. Long ago the feuding families Papadópouli and Páteri lived here. For years, violent acts of vengeance perpetrated by these families on each other in their long, drawn-out vendetta led to the deaths of so many of them that they finally buried the hatchet and made peace. As so much has been written about the islanders' violent characters and thirst for vengeance, here at least is one example of Cretan good sense.

East of Koxaré: Spíli is a lovely place in a bad position. People are always on the way through, usually on the way to Préveli, Agía Galíni, Mátala or Festós. Yet Spíli has far more to offer than just its refreshing spring water. The fountains are one of the main attractions of the town, but the old churches and comfortable *tavérnes* are not to be overlooked. Stop and sit a while.

Arriving in **Agía Galíni** in the evening, which is the loveliest time, is like wandering into a dreamland. A terrace of coloured lights seems to hang in the velvet sky. From the breakwater in the harbour one can see the lights of Mátala twinkling in the distance.

The car park on the harbour is usually packed and the narrow streets are crowded with people. One huge restaurant takes up a whole street. It doesn't sound very cosy, but don't be put off by first impressions – the centre of Agía Galíni is quite charming.

It is obvious what tourists come here

Spíli is one spot where you can drink spring water from the mouths of "lions".

for – a beautiful beach, scenery and a great social life. There are visitors of all age groups here. The inhabitants of Agía Galíni – the name means "Holy Peace of the Sea" – are said to have been successful smugglers before they turned their attention to tourism. That may well be true, for there is no denying a certain rather charming rakishness in their expressions. Agía Galíni, its pretty houses climbing up the steep hillside terraces around, is definitely a place to come back to.

The Valley of Amári: This incomparably lush valley is reached by turning south at Missíria. Even if you have passed by all the other cultural points of interest, you should not exclude this place. The main agricultural crops are olives and fruit, and trees alternate with a profusion of wild flowers, including wood and prickly bindweed and yellow ox-tongue.

Mount Samítos at 1,014 metres (3,327 ft), stands right in the middle of the valley and divides the way through – one on each side of the mountain. One route takes you through **Apóstoli**, where in 249, the men now known as the 10 holy ones or Agii Déka, were put to death for their Christian faith. It takes about five hours to climb **Kédros** – 1,777 metres (5,830 ft) from **Gerakári**.

The other road goes from Apóstoli to the 17th-century **Assomáton Monastery**, which these days houses a School of Agriculture. **Monastiráki** is reached by way of the village of **Thrónos** in the northeast, where the 14th-century Panagiá Church is worth a visit to see its well-preserved frescoes. Near Monastiráki a mid-Minoan settlement was discovered (approximately 2000–1800 BC). The storage jars from this settlement are exhibited in the Archaeological Museum of Haniá.

From here you go on to **Amári**, an exceptionally pretty village, at least

ía Galíni
rbour.

1,500 years old. It was the main village of the district of Amári even in Venetian times. Through the villages of **Fourfourás**, **Kouroútes** and **Níthavlis** one comes to **Apodoúlou**. There the 13th-century frescoes in the Agios Geórgios Church are worth seeing.

A late Minoan mansion and a dome grave have also been discovered and excavated at the southern side of the village. The four sarcophagi are housed in the Archaeological Museum of Réthimnon.

Moní Arkádi: There are many little villages on the way from Réthimnon via **Adele** (birthplace of Konstantin Gaboudákis), such as **Pigí**, **Loutró**, **Kiriánna** and **Amnátos**. The latter is almost 300 metres (984 ft) above sea level in a fertile region of great contrast, with its slopes and steep gorges. Here you will find colourful gorse bushes and olive trees, as well as Greek saffron, briers and the Greek strawberry tree.

The Monastery of **Arkádi** is a haven of peace, but that impression is at variance with its history. It has existed since the 14th century, but its appearance was completely altered in the 16th century. The fort-like arrangement extends for more than 5,200 sq metres (6,219 sq yd) and has entrances on all four sides.

Later additions make it difficult to visualise the original structure at the beginning of this century. The main entrance is in the west, rebuilt in 1872 after the damage of 1866. This leads to the Early Baroque facade of the church built in 1587. The belltower still shows traces of the fighting in 1866.

The interior of the church was renewed later. The altar wall was carved in 1927 out of cypress wood and includes parts of the original iconostasis which withstood the fire. The west wing has two storeys and the galleries have bow-shaped openings into the courtyard. The monks' cells are almost ex-

Below left, the peaceful Monastery of Arkádi viewed from the outside; right, interior vaulted roof Arkádi.

clusively on the second floor. In the northeast corner is the powder storeroom with a memorial tablet; in the north wing, the guesthouse and refectory surrounded by kitchen rooms.

The museum is in the south wing. Apart from ecclesiastical manuscripts and religious relics, you can see memorabilia of 1866 and personal effects of the Abbot Gabriel. You will also discover that the international arms trade began long ago – some of the Turks used Prussian arms.

The tragedy for which the monastery is famous took place on 8 and 9 November 1866. Earlier in May of that year, preparations for a rebellion were underway in Arkádi. Since as many as 15,000 Cretans had met here, it was not surprising that the scheme was discovered by the Turks. Abbot Gabriel was ordered to disband the revolutionary committee. When he refused, the Turks attacked Réthimnon, whereupon about 700

women and children fled to Arkádi and sought refuge there. When Abbot Gabriel refused a second ultimatum, the vastly superior troops of Mustapha Pasha attacked the monastery.

Despite the small cache of weapons at their disposal, the Cretans managed to hold off the first onslaught. But by the next morning the rounds of ammunition had been expended. The survivors, mainly women and children, gathered in the powder storeroom. No one was to be taken alive by the Turks. Just as the Turks forced their way into the storeroom, Konstantín Giaboudákis, with the agreement of Abbot Gabriel, ignited the powder kegs. The explosion killed many Turkish soldiers too.

Thirty-six men survived, either because they didn't make it to the storeroom, or because they disagreed with the suicide pact. They hid in the refectory, where they were later brutally murdered. Legend has it that an infant

reek
rthodox
·coration
the
onastery
Arkádi.

girl was blown into a tree, and survived; she later became a nun.

Bullet marks and sword cuts can still be seen on the door of the refectory and on some of the tables. The monastery was set on fire. In the ossuary just outside the monastery, the skulls of the victims are laid, and an inscription honours the heroes. The news of the tragedy of the Arkádi Monastery was received with horror throughout the rest of Europe. The shock of the mass suicide and destruction of a monastery altered Cretan politics. Now 8 November is the "National Day" of Crete in memory of the victims.

Via Margarítes to the Nída Heights: Go along the coast a little further eastwards until you turn inland near the little village of **Stavroménos**, which is in the rural district of **Milopótamo**. Just south of **Aléxandrou** is the pottery village of **Margarítes**. The workshops are just above the village. Here, all kinds of pots are made, in particular the large storage *pithoi* which were known in Minoan times. In some places one can still see ovens made from oil barrels, used for firing smaller objects. Next to these are the walled ovens, several metres high, for the *pithoi*.

As you wander through the lovely village, stop to have a look in the former monastery church of Agios Ioánnis Prodrómos (John the Baptist). The architecture of the church and the well preserved 12th-century frescoes are most interesting. In the nearby church of Agios Geórgios there is a most expressive painting of the Virgin Mary.

If you cross the road to the southwest, you reach **Prinés**. To the west are the ruins of the Dorian city of **Eléftherna**, important right up to the Byzantine era, then destroyed by the Saracens.

Then it's back to Aléxandrou via Margarítes, and from there a wide road leads to Anógia. At **Pérama** is the

Below and right, striking painting conjunction colours on the facades of houses in Margarítes.

Melidóni Cave where long ago Hermes was worshipped in hollows filled with stalactites. The altar there is now a reminder of more recent history. In 1824 several hundred Cretans used the cave as a hide-out. However, the Turks lit a fire at the cave entrance, and all the Cretans suffocated.

Axós, mythology has it, was founded by Oaxon, a grandson of Minos, and was inhabited from late Minoan times. Ruins of an acropolis indicate a period of glory in the past, and later historical indications are reflected in various Byzantine churches. In the 13th century the inhabitants were driven out for their resistance to the Venetians. They moved southeast and founded **Anógia**.

The village is 800 metres (2,625 ft) up in the Ida Mountains in terrace form, reflecting the Resistance mentality of its founders. The Turks destroyed it twice, once in 1821 and again in 1866, but it was rebuilt each time.

One of the worst periods in the history of the village was during World War II, when on 15 August 1944, following the abduction of the German General Kreipe, all the males in the village were shot, and the place was destroyed.

Nevertheless, despite or perhaps because of that, the character of Anógia has remained unique. The people here are very friendly and inquisitive. It is easy to meet them, but not so easy to understand what they are saying, as they speak an old dialect which has only survived here. But one doesn't need to speak their language to buy their beautiful crafts, and speech is quite unnecessary to appreciate their wonderful music and dance performed in their national costume.

Anógia is a good point from which to set off into the Ida Mountains. There is a 20-km (12-mile) path to the **Nída Plateau** at 1,370 metres (4,495 ft). In summer the shepherds of Anógia gather up here. At the edge of the plateau, in a rugged, wild landscape lies the **Ida Cave**, believed to be Zeus' childhood home. In this extraordinary vault, bronze shields, gold jewellery, hand drums and many other objects were found. An altar was discovered too, making this one of the oldest places of worship on Crete.

The landscape and climate – perhaps the people too – have hardly changed since mythical times. The shepherds still keep bees on the Nída Plateau and live in stone houses called *mitáta* built on the same principles as the Minoan dome graves. The plateau is a good place to start out on longer tours of the Ida Mountains.

Inexperienced climbers are strongly advised to use a guide. The **Tímios Stavrós** at 2,456 metres (8,058 ft) is the highest peak of the Psilorítis range, and the ascent takes about five hours. Once there, the view of the island from Crete's loftiest peak is magnificent.

HANIÁ AND SURROUNDINGS

The capital city of **Haniá**, in the administrative district of the same name, has about 62,000 inhabitants, making it the second largest city on Crete. Regular flights and shipping links to Athens, and the expansion of the charter business have given it a cosmopolitan air. Although the newer parts of the city are cold and functional, the old city, especially around the Venetian Harbour, has retained its unique charm, and is home to many foreign expatriates.

The history of Haniá is particularly interesting as the attention of Crete's conquerors has always been focussed here. There are, of course, traces of the Byzantines, Venetians, Turks and Germans. Linear-B Tablets found in ancient workshops indicate that Haniá was the site of the Minoan city of Kydonía. Homer describes West Crete as the home of the Kydonians. The name originated from their king, Kydon, who is sometimes said to be the son of Minos, and at other times his grandson. Kydon was renowned for his immense hospitality. Perhaps Kydon's prestige contributed to the fact that in late antiquity, Crete and Kydonía were one and the same.

It is not surprising that nearby states coveted this strategically important island, and there were many attempts to invade. In 429 BC, Athens failed in its attempt to overrun the island. The Romans, after a long siege, finally added Crete to their empire in 67 BC. In the ensuing period, many splendid edifices were built on the island, especially during the time of Caesar Hadrian, who visited Crete in AD 123.

Onorio Belli, a Venetian who lived in what later became Canea reported that even after 1583, remains of a Roman theatre could be seen. As the Venetians then began using the ancient site as a quarry, there is nothing to be seen there today. Some underground burial sites and fragments of beautiful floor mosaics can only give an indication of those glorious times.

During the first Byzantine Epoch from AD 352, Crete remained a military base in the Mediterranean. The Byzantines reinforced the city wall of Kydonía to ward off attacks by pirates. However, these fortifications were not enough to repel the stronger attacks of the Saracens, and Kydonía eventually fell in 826. Much of the city was destroyed, and it lost its former importance. For a long time it was even known as "City of Rubbish". Nikefóros Fokás, later Emperor, reconquered Crete and settled many noble and military families from Constantinople in Kydonía, but the city never regained its former greatness.

After the Crusaders had conquered

Constantinople, Crete was given to Bonifatius II, the Margrave of Monferrat, who in turn sold the island to the Venetians. In the expectation of lucrative trading connections, many merchants moved from Venice to the city which was then known as La Canea. The Venetians renewed the city wall and fortified the Byzantine castle, known as "Kastéli". As a result, La Canea prospered.

By 1537 the Venetians had to admit that their defences were inadequate, for Chaireddin Barbarossa easily took the city and plundered it. The specialist in fortifications, Michele Sanmicheli, was summoned all the way from Verona, and he was responsible for the forts built at La Canea and Cándia/Iráklion. These took almost 20 years to complete, and two bastions, the shipyards and part of the sea wall can still be seen. These works marked a peak in the history of La Canea, which was then referred to as

"The Venice of the East." The monasteries of San Francesco (St Francis), San Nicolo (St Nicholas) and San Salvatore had by then been founded outside the town.

The fortifications were adequate to repulse several attempted Ottoman invasions, but finally in 1645, after 55 days of siege, the Turkish army under Yussuf Pasha conquered the city. The Turks, as was their custom, quickly altered the appearance and character of the place. Churches and monasteries were turned into mosques.

Today the Archaeological Museum of Haniá is found in the San Francesco Basilica. In the inner courtyard the 12-sided Turkish fountain can still be seen. The dramatic changes of history are particularly evident in the San Nicolo Church which has a minaret as well as a campanile, and is now a Greek Orthodox Church called Agios Nikólaos.

In 1692 an attempt by the Venetians

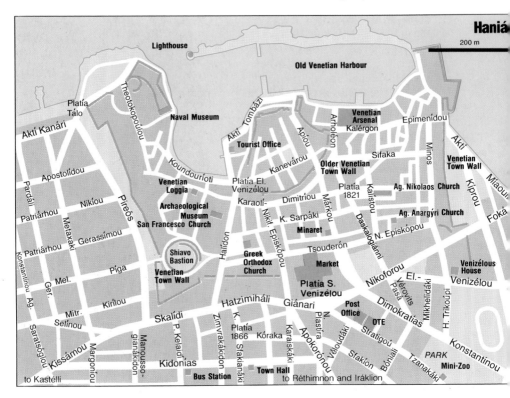

to retake La Canea failed. The Turks established themselves on the island, and in 1850 Haniá became their seat of government. But there were still many uprisings against the Turks. In 1866, after the fall of Arkádi, these revolts reached such proportions that the Great Powers finally turned their attention to Crete. But it was not until 1898 that allied troops occupied Haniá, and Prince George of Greece took up his official post as High Commissioner.

In the so-called "Battle for Crete" in 1941, the city was badly damaged by German bombs, although many ancient monuments did escape the bombing. The Djamissi Mosque, better known as the **Janissary Mosque** at the Venetian Harbour (EOT nowadays), and the minaret of the **Aga Mosque** in Daskalogiánni Street survived.

The Janissaries were often described as the "elite troops" of the Sultan. But it must not be forgotten that these were in fact abducted Christian children who, by brutal methods, were "re-educated" and made into the worst enemies of their own people.

Some great buildings of the Venetian period remain, such as the Loggia, the Arsenal, the Archives and some palaces near the harbour, which are now hotels and guesthouses. The Pacific Hotel was once the Renieri Palace.

The area around the Venetian Harbour, although on the edge of the city, is actually the natural centre of activity. There are cafés and restaurants, and the whole place is always full of life. But it is not merely a tourist area. No local resident would miss an evening stroll around the harbour. One can walk out as far as the breakwater and look back on the city and in the distance to Lefká Ori.

It is also a great place to get away from the loud disco music. Admire the harmony of the design of the lighthouse, and then decide whether it is of

oonlight
ecomes
aniá.

Venetian or Turkish origin. You are entitled to your own opinion on that, as even the experts can't seem to agree.

Another aspect of foreign domination now completely accepted by the Cretans is the city park in Tzanakáki Street, which was originally a private garden belonging to Reouf Pasha. There is a quaint small zoo with an enclosure containing the rare kri-kri mountain goat. This place too is a favourite attraction for the people who live in the city. In summer there is an open-air cinema. Musical performances are also held here during this season, making the park a good alternative to the harbour.

Of course, the loveliness of the garden cannot conceal evidence of the Turks' reign of terror. Their cruelty penetrated into all aspects of Cretan life. Traces of the persecution of the Christians at this time are particularly evident in what was then the capital city. Haniá retained its position of capital until

1972. In **Splántzia**, the once completely Turkish part of town, there is a memorial tablet to the murdered Bishop Melhisedék, one of the leaders of the Resistance to the oppressors, and his fellow fighters.

The **Market Hall** of Haniá is very famous. Its layout is in the form of a cross, and it is situated on the old Turkish marketplace. But much of its fame is misplaced, as in fact it is no more than a copy of the market hall in Marseilles. But there is no denying that it brings prosperity to the town. In its crowded area, fish, meat, fruit and vegetables are traded. But one can also buy medicines, shoe soles and books. For hardened city dwellers this early form of buying, selling and bartering in a crowded and friendly atmosphere is a welcome change from the modern supermarkets and department stores.

Traditionally, the marketplace has been a meeting place for people interested in airing their political views. If you don't mind the noise, you can sit and relax in one of the restaurants. However, the food here is not particularly good, and it's a little more expensive than elsewhere.

There are so many people buying and selling in Haniá that the market stalls are never sufficient. On certain days, those who do not manage to get a stall set out their wares around the hall.

Skrydlof Street is one of the tourists' favourite places, and because of the crowds it has been made into a pedestrian precinct. Here are plenty of leather articles, as well as hand embroidered items, ornamental jewellery and ceramics – all surrounded by heaps of kitsch.

If you manage to grab a seat in the little *tavérne* in the middle of the street, you can watch the action over a glass of beer or *oúzo* and *souvláki*. Of course you can also have your shoes and boots made to measure. You can even watch the cobbler at work. Otherwise, you can just place your order and pay in ad-

Left, Cretan boots are world-famous. Right, handmade lace for sale

vance. Service in terms of quality and quick delivery are guaranteed and the Cretans are internationally famous for their buff-coloured boots.

The museums of Haniá are most interesting. Details of the resistance of the Cretans to the various foreign occupations are documented in detail in the **Historical Museum**. In the **Nautical Museum** there are many models of ships, while the **Archaeological Museum** has a collection of artefacts from the whole region.

The administrative part of the city, **Halépa**, in the east, is worth seeing. These buildings were very cleverly put under a preservation order early on to protect the area from property speculators and attendant architectural alteration. The old government building today houses the administrative offices of the region (the Nomarchía).

The motorists of Haniá are probably the most impatient on the island. Their carelessness often becomes a hazard, and to recuperate from the traffic of Haniá, it is a good idea to take refuge in one of the many green parts of the town.

Even if the days of Kydon are over and in place of the legendary hospitality one finds the hotelier's routine, Haniá is still well worth a visit. There's merriment in the air, an international flair and a special warmth which will remain with the traveller long after leaving.

Hero's land: The Peninsula of **Akrotíri** lies northeast of Haniá. It is an easy place to get to, as buses leave every half hour to the different villages.

You should definitely not miss the memorial to **Venizélos**, on the western slope of Akrotíri. On this historical spot, Elefthérios Venizélos (1864–1936) and his son Sophoklís (1896–1964) are buried. It was here that in 1897 the revolutionary committee met in the **Elías Monastery** under the leadership of Venizélos. Finally, in 1913 the

Vegetable market, Haniá.

demand for union with Greece was granted. All that remains of the monastery today is the little St Elías Church. Nevertheless, the view overlooking Haniá and the Rodopós Peninsula is spectacular.

On the road to the airport there is a turning to the village of **Korakiés,** where the convent of the *Prodrómos* (literally the Forerunner, thus John the Baptist) is situated. This place played a particularly important role in the struggle against foreign oppression. In times of trouble it became an asylum for young women who wished to avoid being sent either to a Venetian brothel or to a Turkish harem.

Today, 20 nuns live here under the care of an astonishingly young mother superior, who sometimes serves coffee and biscuits to visitors. It is always interesting to see how nuns look after their convents, in contrast to how monasteries are kept (although it must be

admitted that often there are only a couple of old men living in them). The monasteries have a neglected air about them. In a small room, the nuns sell their embroidery and hand-painted icons.

After **Stavrós,** which you should see if you enjoyed the film *Zorba the Greek*, you come to the villages of **Profilías, Kounoupidianá** and **Horafákia.** All are equally well known for their excellent honey and mild Attic climate. But if the wind does blow, you'll certainly know about it. The bay and sandy beach of **Kalathá** are worth a detour, and from there you can make your way northwards to Stavrós.

Stavrós lies on the seaside, and is made up of small hotels, bungalows, a tiny harbour and a beautiful beach. Opposite is the slope on which the "Boss" cable car was erected for the film *Zorba the Greek*, and which was so photogenically caused to collapse. The place itself has nothing to offer today, apart from a

edding
kes, Haniá
arket

tavérna ("Mama's Restaurant") and a new restaurant, the dimensions of which, reminiscent of a gymnasium, give an indication of what it is like in the high season.

The highlight of Akrotíri is the 17th-century Monastery of **Agía Triáda**. Another name given to the monastery is Tzangaroli, which is the name of the Venetian merchant family who erected it. A handful of monks currently live here, keeping the surrounding olive groves and vineyards in excellent order. Agía Triáda was always a rich monastery, due to the support of its own workforce. In 1821 the Turks laid it to waste, but soon after it was rebuilt in 1830, it managed to regain its wealth.

The massive, somewhat severe building is impressive, and houses a library of more than 700 volumes, some extremely old. Here you will also find several icons by the Byzantine painter Skordíli. Fortunately, many of the treasures were saved from destruction. However the only icons on view in the church nowadays are those from the 18th and 19th centuries.

About 4 km (2½ miles) to the north of Agía Triáda is the 16th-century Monastery of **Gouvernéto**. The monks' cells, uninhabited now, are grouped around an inner courtyard. In 1821, a year of terror, most of the monks were murdered and the monastery was razed to the ground.

The library and icon collection have been completely destroyed by fire, so there are no art treasures to attract the visitor here today. Sculptures of mythical beasts, seemingly carved by a soul mate of Hieronymus Bosch, decorate the church portal. Unfortunately, the soft sandstone used by the sculptor is crumbling away.

Further to the north, slightly downhill, the road leads to the so-called **Bear's Cave**. The name comes from a

The deserte Monastery o Katholikó of Akrotíri.

huge stalagmite, larger than a man, in the shape of a bear. Findings confirm that this cave was a place of worship in Neolithic and late Minoan times. There is a tiny Lady Chapel here now, just near the entrance under the overhanging rocks. It was built during the 16th and 17th centuries. On 6 and 7 October each year processions and services are held here in memory of St John, who was killed by a huntsman's arrow on 6 October 1042.

Down a path which ends in a flight of steps in the rocks, you finally arrive at the **Cave of St John**. It apparently goes 135 metres (443 ft) back into the mountain and its rather complicated layout takes some time to figure out.

The legendary **Monastery of Katholikó,** which dates from the 10th and 11th centuries, is close by. The founder was none other than St John himself, and the monastery is possibly the oldest on Crete. The church, the belltower with its

facade, and other additions came into being much later in the 16th century. Pirate attacks forced the monks to move to Gouvernéto.

Even without the monastery and cave, Akrotíri would still be worth visiting because the scenery here is outstandingly beautiful. However, enjoyment of this peaceful landscape is somewhat disrupted by the piercing noise of Greek military jets screeching across the sky.

A Trip to the South: The area around Haniá can easily be explored by bus, taxi or even on foot. **Mourniés**, for example, is only 6 km (3½ miles) south of the city. Though a humble place today, Mourniés once played an important role – at great cost to itself – in the history of the island. When the Turkish commander Mustapha Pasha raised the level of taxation beyond the endurance of the people, he caused an armed demonstration in Mourniés. During the

ew monks
ll live in
e Agía
iáda
onastery.

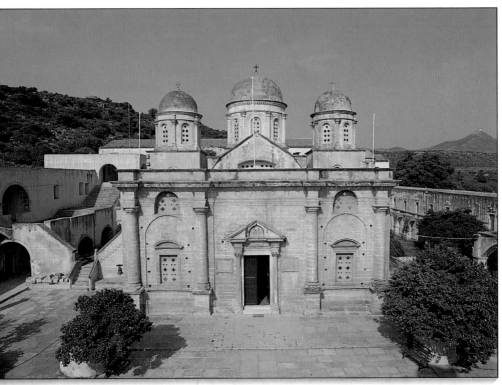

course of the action, most of the Cretan peasants were captured by Turkish soldiers, then hanged on mulberry trees.

The village also suffered during the German occupation. When, after an attack on German headquarters, the culprits could not be found, "punitive action" was immediately taken: all males between the ages of 15 and 50 were assembled under an old plane tree, which is still the centre of the village, and shot. These gruesome events are still talked about by the locals.

The birthplace of Elefthérios Venizélos is here, too. South of the village, built into a rock face, is the church of Agía Varvára. Nearby are the entrances to tunnels built by Cretan forced labour and used by the Germans as arms depots. The German mines were still being used during the 1950s by fishermen, with mixed results. The seas around Crete appear to be quite lifeless now; after the so-called "dynamite fishing"

the number of blind victims and amputees in the area is high.

Approximately 15 km (9 miles) from Haniá are the ruins of **Aptera**, the great ancient city in this part of the island, and undoubtedly one of the most prosperous of its day. It was inhabited from about 1000 BC, and its name was probably derived from Apteron, the Minoan king who ruled around 1800 BC. The city was situated on a plateau and surrounded by a wall almost 4 km (2½ miles) long, of which about 600 metres (¼ mile) survive. The city was destroyed by an earthquake in AD 700 and most of the survivors were forced to leave the area. As a result, it was not difficult for the Saracens to take the city in 823.

Sadly, Aptera was plundered by antique smugglers before being put under archaeological protection by the authorities. Statues, inscriptions, vessels and many coins minted in Aptera were simply sold. Since World War II, however, more statues, clay tablets and vessels have been found and these are now exhibited in the Archaeological Museum of Haniá. In the area of ancient Aptera, remains of a Doric and a Hellenic temple, Byzantine ruins, parts of a monastery, Roman cisterns, rock graves and a small theatre have been discovered. While in Aptera, don't miss the magnificent view of Soúda Bay.

There are other Minoan remains which can be seen in the nearby villages of **Stílos** and **Samonás**.

Térisso, 16 km (9¾ miles) from Haniá, is accessible through the gorge of the same name, also known as the Venizélos Gorge. Its strategic position – 580 metres (1,903 ft) above sea level – made it an ideal base in the struggle against the Turks. In 1905 Venizélos and his revolutionary committee lived here. Today it is an ideal place from which to set out on tours to **Mesklá** and **Soúrva**, or for climbing **Páchnes** the highest peak of the Lefká Ori at 2,452 metres (8,045 ft).

Left, down the steps of the Monastery of Katholikó. **Right,** detail of the wall at the Agía Triáda Monastery.

WESTERN CRETE

A bus leaves the long distance depot in Haniá every hour for **Omalós**. The picturesque journey takes you inland through lush gardens, eucalyptus woods and orange groves. And 9 km (5½ miles) out of the city is the village of **Agiá**, which was founded under Arab rule (AD 800–1100). In this village you will also find a three-naved basilica which is built on the ruins of an ancient temple. Unusual pillars of red marble and granite survive from the earlier structure.

There are two interesting churches in the village of **Alikianós**. The older, Ai Kyr Jánnis, dedicated to John the Hermit, dates from the 10th and 11th centuries and has interesting murals and mosaics. In the Church of Agios Georgios (St George) of 1243, there are also some well preserved frescoes.

The road continues through **Fournés**. Not far from there is the cave of **Hiróspilios**. A turning leads to the village of Meskla with the ruins of the Dorian city of **Rizinía**. Archaeological finds indicate that the city of Rizinía reached a period of greatness around 400 BC. There are remains of a wall and an acropolis.

The road then winds its way up to almost 1,100 metres (3,609 ft) to the 25 sq-km (10 sq-mile) Plateau of Omalós. Up here the soil is extremely fertile, and cereals, potatoes and tomatoes are grown. Sheep graze in between the crops. The tiny hamlet of Omalós is only inhabited in the summer, and if you intend to stay overnight here on the way to the **Samaria Gorge**, you must book your accommodation well in advance. There are a couple of guesthouses for travellers.

In winter, the plateau, almost circular in shape, is flooded by water coming down from the surrounding mountains. Fortunately, the water can flow down

the 2.5-km (1½-mile) long **Tzanís Cave**. Legend has it that on moonless nights, a shepherd, enchanted by a water sprite, plays his lyre and sings of his sorrow at the mouth of the cave. The geographical position of the plateau made it ideal as a base for resistance to the Ottoman Turks, and on one of the hills is the grave of Hatzí Micháli Giannári.

Just before the descent to the Samaria Gorge there is a path leading to the Greek Mountaineers' Association Hut. It lies at an altitude of 1,650 metres (5,413 ft) and can serve as a starting point for mountain treks. You climb down into the gorge on a path still known as "Xilóskalo", which means wooden ladder. The name is a reminder of the days when the only access to the gorge was by ladders.

Botanically speaking, this is a fascinating place. Apart from cypresses and kermes oaks, pines and plane trees, the Greek yellow ox-tongue, Cretan corymb and the Cretan campanula grow here. Eagles and falcons soar above the steep rock faces. In earlier times, when there were fewer people about, one could often see the extremely shy mountain goat or "kri-kri" (*Agrími* in local parlance) as it climbed about on the mountainside.

You reach the Church of Agios Nikólaos 4 km (2½ miles), and about 2 km (1 mile) further up is the deserted settlement of Samariá with its Byzantine church of Osía Maria the Egyptian. This is the place which gave the gorge its name. There is a spring here, a refreshing spot for tired travellers. An underground stream emerges just behind the village, and this will have to be crossed several times as you continue on through the gorge.

The last 4 km (2½ miles) are the most interesting as you go through high cliffs where all the sounds are magnified. When the wind howls through the narrow *Sideróportes* (Iron Gates) one can

e way West.

understand how tales of water sprites, demons and other strange creatures came about.

The last stretch is extremely narrow, only 3 metres (10 ft) wide with 500-metre (1,640 ft) high vertical cliffs towering above. You look through the gap to a wide valley which stretches right down to the sea.

The little village of **Agía Rouméli**, still unspoiled despite the number of visitors to the gorge, is at the far end. The few inhabitants only make their living from tourism during the hiking period from April to October; the rest of the year they keep themselves busy with their cattle and bee-keeping. They also sell *Díktamos*, a very rare plant which grows in particularly inaccessible parts of the gorge and is used in herbal teas, especially in what the Greeks call "mountain tea".

Recently, a Samariá Round Tour has been organised. You arrive by ship in

Agía Rouméli, take a few steps in the gorge, and then leave.

From Agía Rouméli to Frangokástello: Near what is now Agía Rouméli was once the Minoan city of **Tárra**. The few finds, which include a stone tablet inscribed with the double axe are displayed in the Archaeological Museum of Haniá. In mythology, Apollo is said to have come to Tárra. After conquering Crete, the Dorians erected a temple here to their revered Apollo. On this site, the Panagía Church was built in the 12th and 13th centuries.

The coins from Tárra show the head of a goat and a bee, very similar to coins from other towns in the Cretan League of Cities, to which Lissós, Elyros-Syia, Poikilássos and Irtakína also belonged, around 300 BC. The town also had a trading agreement with King Magas. In AD 66 an earthquake destroyed Tárra, and it was never rebuilt.

There are good connections from Agía Rouméli to **Loutró**, **Hóra Sfakíon**, **Soúgia** and **Paleóhara**. A walk to Loutró is recommended. It is not a difficult walk, although it does take about five hours and you are advised to arm yourself with hat and sun-block. From the turning to Agios Pávlos you can hitchhike to **Anópoli**. Then it is only 3 km (1¾ miles) south to Loutró.

There's nothing left in Loutró now of its former glory. Once known then as **Fínix**, the city was famous in ancient times as the rich port of Anópolis. Together the two towns probably had 60,000 inhabitants. West of the village are a few scattered ruins. The **Sotíros Christoú Chapel** with frescoes from the 14th and 15th centuries is lovely. In Byzantine times it was a bishopric.

There are hardly any fishermen left in Loutró. Up until the beginning of the 19th century there was a fleet of small trading ships, but that has now dwindled to a couple of boats. As in so many coastal villages, tourism is now the mainstay. Private houses and rooms are

Left, Gingilo Mountain. **Right**, the Samariá Gorge.

rented out to visitors, and there are quite a few *tavérnes* to choose between. In the old days, the village could only be reached by boat, but a new road now ensures its survival.

Anópoli lies north of Loutró, some 600 metres (1,968 ft) up, at the foot of Mount **Kástro** at 2,218 metres (7,277 ft). One of the most famous of all Crete's freedom fighters, Joánnis Vláhos was born here. His wide education earned him the nickname Dhaskalojánnis, or Teacher John. It was he who led the rebellion of 1770.

Anópoli was one of the most important of the ancient Cretan settlements. It was burned to the ground in 1365 for resisting the Venetians. In 1867 it suffered the same fate, but this time at the hands of the Turks.

To the west 12 km (7½ miles) away is **Hóra Sfakíon**, the capital of the Sfakiá region which is famous for its fierce fighters. The buildings are arranged around the harbour in an amphitheatre. There is plenty to do here. There are many hotels, pensions and cosy *tavérnes*. A bus leaves every two hours for Haniá, and in summer there is a ship to Agía Rouméli every three hours. Twice a week you can go to Gávdos island and once a week to Agía Galíni.

Climate, food and lifestyle seem to be particularly beneficial here, as when you look at the inhabitants of this western part of Crete you will notice plenty of healthy-looking old folks, despite the embroilment of so many in feuds and vendettas over the years.

There are, in fact, quite a few centenarians. The inhabitants of Sfakiá have the reputation of being strong, traditionalist and belligerent. During the long years of foreign rule, they never gave in to oppressors, whether Venetians, Turks, Saracens or Germans. The message is clear – resistance keeps you young, as long as you manage not to get

Below left, you need good shoes to cross the rugged Samaria Gorge. Right, so many villages to explore.

194

killed. Some say the people of Sfakiá are fanatics for justice; others feel that they simply like violence. Evidence of the latter was the "Omalós Vendetta" which claimed 63 victims between 1947 and 1960. Visitors to the area still take locally made knives away with them as souvenirs – mementoes of western Crete's mountain men and their ready daggers.

Frangokástello is reached via **Patsianós** (Agía Galíni bus). This Venetian castle, built in 1340, was originally named after the neighbouring church of Agios Nikíta. But to stress its foreign nature, the Cretans christened it Frangokástello – Castle of the Franks, modern Greece's generic term for "foreigners from Europe". On 18 May 1828 there was a battle here between 700 Cretans led by Hatzimicháli Daliánis, and 800 Turks under Mustafa Bey.

On a morning between 17 and 30 May each year a strange phenomenon is said to take place, an event immortalised in legend and guidebooks of the 19th century. Just before sunrise a shadowy procession leaves the ruins of the Church of Agios Harálambos, and for about 10 minutes columns of armed black figures march along the castle walls. The locals believe that these ghosts who return each year are the unredeemed souls of the dead. Due to their appearance in the damp early morning air, they are known as *Drosoulítes*, or "dew men". Scientists have looked into the matter and their conclusion is that the whole phenomenon is merely a mirage from Libya, perhaps brought about by an unusual refraction of light.

If you want to see the dew men, you will need quantities of luck and patience. Luck, because the sea must be calm and the humidity just right, and patience, because no one, apart from the scientists, knows exactly where the procession appears from and when, and there are only 10 minutes when conditions are right for the phenomenon.

Thus, it may take a few years to catch a glimpse of the dew men. Nevertheless, the sandy beach and cosy *tavérnes* are inviting anyway.

North of Hóra Sfakíon, high on a plateau is the village of **Imbros**. It is only inhabited in the summer, and apparently the first people to live there were outlaws. This is where one of Crete's wildest and most beautiful gorges begins, the **Imbrou**. It is just 7 km (4 miles) long, and its walls reaching a height of up to 300 metres (984 ft) close in to a gap of no more than 2 metres (7 ft) at the narrowest point. There are hardly any tourists here, but the Imbrou Gorge is an excellent alternative to the Samariá Gorge, if one doesn't have the time for both. From Imbros the road leads on towards Haniá through the fertile plain of **Askyfou**, where there are lush vineyards, and potatoes, fruits and nuts are cultivated.

After **Krapi** the so-called "Wild

e Venetian
stle of
ango-
stello.

West" of Crete is at an end. Overall, this region gives the impression of being one vast battlefield of history. Almost every village was involved in fighting the Venetians, Turks or the Germans in World War II.

In **Vrísses**, a friendly village, you can fortify yourself for the 33-km (20-mile) journey to Haniá with sheep's yogurt and honey.

Two-beach town: The little town of **Paleóhora**, with about 900 inhabitants, lies on a peninsula jutting out into the Sea of Libya. This geographic situation means that there are two beaches, a long sandy beach to the southwest, and a pebbly stretch in the east. Sometimes, this pebbly beach offers a very welcome alternative, as the sandy one is often too windy to enjoy. Both have showers and restaurants nearby, making them ideal for holiday-makers.

Paleóhora has two ports, of which only one has been used to date. It is only suitable for small boats and links the place daily to Agía Rouméli at the Samaria Gorge, and weekly to Elafoníssi. A projected new harbour will be able to accommodate large car ferries and facilitate motor access to some of the interesting villages in the area which are still difficult or even impossible to reach by bus.

The new houses which have replaced the old in recent years have fortunately not spoiled the centre of the village of Paleóhora. Behind the breakwater of the harbour the little streets are still much as they were before the advent of the tourists. Here, in the evening, only a few metres from the bustle in the centre, the old women still sit with their needlework and chat. They look as if progress has completely passed them by. But tourism has changed even these people. Much of the traditional Cretan hospitality has been lost as a result of the tourist invasion. Nowadays, bus loads of for-

Overlooking the Paleóhor peninsula.

196

eigners descend half naked (that's how conservative Cretans view visitors dressed in shorts) and mill about taking pictures of the old folk. Yet the people are friendly and you can win their affection – but to do that you must first learn to speak a little Greek.

Go through the old part of the town bordering on the Panagiá Church with its resonating bell tower, and you will come to the ruins of a Venetian castle, built in 1282, called **Sélinou**. Nowadays, this is the name given to the whole region. Don't miss the Festival of the Virgin Mary held in March, when three Orthodox priests and two local singers demonstrate their musical prowess at the *paneyíri*, or Name Day feast..

Paleóhora is definitely the most important town on the southwestern coast. There is a medical station, and several doctors and dentists practise here. Since 1988, a pharmacy has been added to this service. There is also a post office, tele-

phone exchange, a police station, a kindergarten, a junior and senior school and two travel agencies. Children are transported from the surrounding area by specially laid on buses. Most people here manage to make a living from fishing and raising cattle, and supplement their income in the summer with the profits of tourism. During winter they grow vegetables (tomatoes and cucumbers) in greenhouses. The vegetable season in **Kondoúra**, a village to the west of Paleóhora, starts in September and goes on until the May–June of the following year.

Paleóhora earned a reputation as a hippy hangout in the 1960s, but that's all over, and the tourists these days are quite tame, although they are still predominantly young. In the summer season the main street is closed to traffic after six in the evening, and it is then that the evening siesta begins. In the cafés, restaurants and *tavérnes*, tourists and

sty orning: unrise over fká Ori.

locals mingle until the early hours. This is a lively spot and if you don't enjoy the fun here, you have probably only yourself to blame.

Around Paleóhora: There are several interesting trips which you can make from Paleóhora. One is to the village of **Anídri**, which lies just 5 km (3 miles) to the northeast. Here stands the beautiful Agios Nikólaos Church, which was decorated with paintings by Joánnis Pagoménos in 1323.

Only 2.5 km (1½ miles) further is **Asogirés**. Here the population has shrunk from 400 (1971) to 40. Just outside the village, next to the oil press, there is an enormous plane tree, the leaves of which remain green even in winter. Legend has it that the tree was planted by the 99 Holy Fathers. Scientific examinations have so far failed to come up with any explanation of this wonder of nature. The church, dedicated to the Holy Fathers (Agii Páteres) of 1864, is built into a rock face, just outside the village. A tour of the church and the little folk museum is conducted by a friendly custodian. You have to ask for him in one of the *tavérnes* and he will then take you around. Weapons, pots, books, clothing and other objects provide visitors with a lively picture of life on Crete in the 19th century.

The road to the **Cave of Souré** in which the 99 Holy Fathers lived winds its way up into the open countryside. Through a small door in the wire fence (right fork at the top), you reach a path which leads downhill first, then up again. A black cross marked on a rock indicates the entrance to the cave. There are three iron ladders to enable you to get down about 15 metres (49 ft) to the floor of the sacred cave. It is quite cold down there and you get a strong feeling of the ascetic environment of the hermit's life. You have to feel your way forward with the help of a rope. The cave goes back about 70 metres (230 ft), slightly uphill into the mountain. Fur-

ther up, the path becomes oppressively narrow. If you want to go right to the far end, you need a reliable torch.

Then it's on to **Teménia** – 17 km (11 miles) from Paleóhora – a village which supplies the whole of western Crete with mineral water. Nearby are the ruins of the ancient city of **Irtakína**, which was an important autonomous city in the Hellenic period. Fountains and parts of buildings can still be found between plants growing wild. Irtakína, like the other towns in the League of Cities, minted its own coins. The dolphin and stars depicted on these coins indicated the seafaring tradition. For years, no one bothered about this place; people just took the debris from the ruins to finish building their own houses. However, no one ever found any use for a 3rd-4th century BC headless statue of Pan, so it is now displayed in the Archaeological Museum of Haniá.

According to the records made avail-

A familiar relic to remind visitors of the port of yesteryear.

able by the private archaeologist Dr. Paterakis, the city of Lissós, to the west of present day Soúgia, was founded by old men who had been driven out of Irtakína because of famine there. Irtakína did not benefit, but Lissós soon became so rich that it was able to send supplies to Irtakína as well.

If you stop a while in the village of **Rodováni** do try the delicious black bread which is still made from a traditional recipe. East of Rodováni are the ruins of the Dorian city of **Elyros** with a view of the harbour of Soúgia. Pictures of goats and bees on coins which have been found there indicate that the people of Elyros were hunters and beekeepers. Ruins of a Byzantine church show that the place was later a the site of an early bishopric. All appearances indicate that the place was eventually destroyed by the Saracens. Also east of Rodováni is the little **Cave of Skotiní** in which ceramic remains from the Classical epoch (550–67 BC) have been found.

The road then goes on towards Haniá through **Agía Iríni**, the last village before the Omalós Plateau. It would of course be possible to begin a walk through the Samaria Gorge from here. About 11 km (7 miles) south of Rodováni, you come to **Soúgia**, a village with a broad pebble beach, which is now definitely on the tourist map. Here lay ancient Elyros-Syia, and in the church built in 1875 there is a beautiful mosaic floor which originally belonged to a 6th-century basilica.

From an archaeological point of view the ruins of **Lissós** are more interesting. During its heyday in the Roman epoch, the town was so rich that it could afford to mint coins in gold. Only Irtakína was comparably wealthy. Lissós also became famous for its mineral springs. Remains of bath chambers show that this place was a spa in ancient times. Most impressive of all is the Asklepios Shrine. Everywhere you look are ruins of houses, theatres and public buildings, a fascinating sight. Various statues are exhibited in the Archaeological Museum of Haniá.

From Paleóhora to Hrissoskalítissa:

Most of the way the road is asphalted, and the few gravel stretches do not pose any problems. You drive in the direction of Haniá through **Plemenianá** to **Drís** and **Strovlés**, villages set among the chestnut groves. The next stop is **Elos**, which is a larger village where a chestnut festival is held every year in October. Cretan visitors rave about the excellent chestnut cake baked at this time and the traditional music.

The last stage of the journey is through **Váthi**. The Convent of Hrissoskalítissa, set high up on a cliff on the west coast unfortunately does not shimmer as brightly in the distance as it used to up until a few years ago. The sky-blue roof which was the building's hallmark had rotted and so had to be repainted

crificial mb.

with a darker but more durable paint. The name of the convent means "Virgin of the Golden Step," and thereby hangs a tale.

The 90 steps leading up to the convent are said to have been fashioned from gold which can only be seen by a pure, sinless person. So you can find out for yourself how virtuous you are. Perhaps you will see the "elusive" gold. The place is really well worth a visit. It is a very isolated place, but when asked recently if she finds the solitude extreme at times, the abbess merely replied that she could not even begin to imagine living anywhere else.

Elafoníssi and Gávdos: The island of **Elafoníssi** is about 6 km (3½ miles) to the south of the convent. But the road is so bad that it seems much further. In a certain light the sand has a pink glow. Here you will find everything you need for a good holiday: sea, sun, fresh air, pines and hardly any people.

Easter of the year 1824 was a day of sorrow and tragedy on this island. A terrible slaughter took place. Many Cretan women and children had fled from Ibrahim Pasha Messez and his followers. They hid themselves here. In those days, the Turks had a simple strategy: if they couldn't seize the men, they would simply make off with the women and children. The Turks found their hiding place and killed 850 people. After the massacre, the soldiers prepared to plunder the convent, but bee-keepers living there set upon the Ottomans and put them to flight. The convent was thus spared from destruction.

From 1 July to 15 September, a boat leaves twice a week for **Gávdos Island** – the southernmost point in Europe. The 37-km (23-mile) journey takes about three hours. When you arrive, you will find that you can camp overnight in the small harbour of **Karavé** with its sandy beach. It is an idyllic spot, but dramati-

Snow-cappe Lefká Ori.

cally cut off from the main island, along with everything else. The loveliest beach there is **Sarakíniko**, to the north of the harbour, and there is a pension there too, where visitors love to stay to get away from it all. In spring and autumn, however, the sudden and unpredictable storms can cause one to be stranded for several weeks on Gávdos.

Despite the advent of electricity, the island is really only for those who are prepared to rough it. Compared to Crete, Gávdos is tiny, but it still takes two days to walk round the 37-sq km (14-sq mile) island. The path is rough but not dangerous; so as long as you are careful, it should not present any problems. Settlements on Gávdos remain as yet unexcavated. Apparently it was densely populated in the Byzantine epoch, with some estimates putting the number as high as 8,000 inhabitants. In those days it even had its own bishop. There is a headless statue of a woman dating from this period, but to see it one needs to go to England. In Venetian times Gávdos was a Corsair hide-out. During the period of Turkish domination it became one of the most important refuges of the Resistance fighters.

Today there are about 100 people on Gávdos, mainly in the principal town of **Kastrí** and in the villages of **Ambelos**, **Vatsianá** and **Metóhia**. On the island is the cave where the nymph Calypso is supposed to have lived.

In another version the nymph lived on the Maltese island of Gozo. Whether on Gozo or Gávdos, it was she who was able to detain Odysseus for a period of seven years. The 99 Holy Fathers stopped here on their way from Egypt to Crete. There they intended to spread the Gospel among the Cretans. John the Hermit was among the group.

On the way to Kastrí from the harbour, you pass the Panagía Church, the bell of which once belonged to a ship.

hat all
eek men
rry.

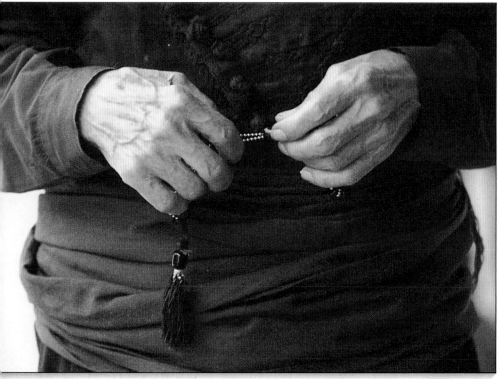

This ship was wrecked on the rocks near Gávdos during a storm. Later, one of the islanders saw the bell deep in the water, and with some help managed to dive down and salvage it. But diving to such depths caused him to lose his hearing so he became known as *Koufidákis*, the deaf one. There have been many attempts to remove the bell from the island but all were mysteriously thwarted, and somehow it never left.

When, during World War II, German soldiers were stationed on Gávdos, a great deal of fighting took place against the British. The Germans mined the island, which led to numerous casualties among the civilian population. Many fishermen and farmers left their homes and moved to safety in Paleóhora on Crete.

Kándanos and Rodopós: On the way back to Haniá from Paleóhora one should stop at **Kándanos**. As this place has the highest rainfall in Crete, the vegetation is lush, with olives, chestnuts, fruit trees and vineyards growing in profusion. The rich meadows are ideal for cattle. The river Kándanos is narrow but has the great advantage that it does not dry up in summer. With its post office, telephone exchange, doctors, dentists and ambulance as well as a police station and several cafés and restaurants, Kándanos has become a centre for the 15 surrounding villages.

Its history goes back a long way. A little to the south lay the ancient city of **Kantánou**, which was situated on a hill, and split in two by an earthquake. Later, rich Venetian families lived here, and when the Turks took over the city, the Venetians converted to Islam. Kándanos then became an administrative centre for the region, with a high concentration of military installations. There were many bloody confrontations leading to a great many casualties. The area is rich in old churches with

Seeking refuge in the olive grove.

good examples of Byzantine art, such as that in the **Panagía Tsivremiana Church**. There is nothing left of old Kándanos. After the Germans landed in **Máleme** on 20 May 1941, they got as far as Kándanos. The Cretans managed to kill 25, which led to heavy reprisals: the village was bombed on 25 May and almost destroyed. Very few inhabitants survived the attack. A bilingual (Greek and German) tablet refers to this terrible day. On it is written this stark message: "Here Kándanos once existed…"

The return journey takes you through the village of **Voukoliés**, where a market has been held on Saturdays for hundreds of years. Every year in August a week-long concert festival is organised, to which the best known Cretan musicians are invited. This is a great attraction for locals and tourists alike.

Another plus: if you get a stomach upset in Voukoliés, consider yourself relatively fortunate. The sparkling mineral water here is famous for curing disorders of this nature.

If you go on further to the northwest, through **Tavronítis**, you will reach the **Peninsula of Rodopós**. This is one of the most beautiful parts of Crete, although it isn't easy to get to. The asphalt road ends suddenly at **Afrátas** and **Rodopós** and proceeding north by car becomes very difficult. But it is definitely worth the effort, as you cannot possibly say you know Crete if you have not visited Rodopós.

Just by the river on this peninsula is **Kolimbári**, a peaceful, shady place with a hotel, restaurant and lovely long beach. North of the village, also on the waterside is the Monastery of **Goniá**. There is a pottery school here as well as a large library and a notable collection of icons. Goniá was always a well known centre of resistance. Behind the monastery is the Orthodox Academy of Crete. Seminars for priests are held here

ıng and
ıding
ad to
ıra Sfakíon.

but, otherwise, things are really quite unorthodox. The exchanges from West to East are by no means limited to theological ideas. New methods of agriculture are tried out here too, all thanks to the Bishop Irenéos Galanákos who, from 1972 to 1980, was Greek Orthodox Metropolitan in Germany.

Not far north of Afrátas is the fascinating cave of **Ellinóspilios**. It is not only large at 165 metres (541 ft) long and beautiful, but archaeologically important, too. Human and animal remains were found here, as well as ceramic fragments. Some dating from the early Neolithic period (about 10,000 BC) and one skull was dated at 20,000 to 25,000 BC, which makes the finds the oldest human artefacts in the Aegean.

In the north of the peninsula near Kap Skala is the **Diktínaion**. Originally there was a 7th-century Doric temple here, dedicated to the nymph Diktynna. The nymph, identified with the Cretan goddess Briómartis, is said to have leapt into the sea here to escape the attentions of King Minos. She was saved from drowning by fishermen with their nets. The Emperor Hadrian is reputed to have ordered a new temple to be built here after his visit to Crete. Ruins of the temple, which was built in the 2nd century AD, can still be seen today. At least, during the Roman era, the importance of this religious centre extended beyond the boundaries of Crete.

From Rodopós there is a road leading north to the church of **Agios Ioánnis**. There are many turnings and no signposts, so remember to turn right at the cistern. Soon you reach a point where you can see the church lying deep in the valley. On 29 August thousands of believers come here to commemorate the beheading of St John.

Binoculars are a great asset on Rodopós, as there are so many birds of prey to watch. It is so peaceful here that a day

Whitewashe simplicity: Greek architecture Georgioúpol

on Rodopós is definitely preferable to a visit to the Samaria Gorge if one really wants to get away from it all.

Kastélli and Gramvoússa: Kastélli, the main town of the region of **Kíssamos** lies between the two peninsulas of Rodopós and **Gramvoússa**. The little harbour, from which ferries leave regularly for the Pelopponese, has made the town a "trading centre" of western Crete. The inhabitants are fishermen and sailors and they also cultivate vineyards and olive groves. The favourable climate and abundant supply of water here give rise to a wonderfully green environment. As there are also lovely beaches, and hotels, pensions and *tavérnes*, Kastélli is gradually becoming a tourist resort.

This area has been inhabited since very early times. There was a late Minoan settlement here called **Kíssamos**, which was the independent port city of ancient **Polyrrhínia**. Above the present-day Polyrrhínia village, 6 km (3½ miles) from Kastélli, are the ruins of the city of that name, founded in 8 BC and destroyed by the Saracens in the 9th century. Once again it was the typical set up of a Dorian double settlement: a well-fortified city in the hills within sight of a port. Apart from the remains of a temple, cisterns and burial chambers, there are also ruins of a fort which was in fact rebuilt in Byzantine times.

The ancient city of **Agníon**, famous for its temple of Apollo, lay on the west side of the Gramvoússa Peninsula. Now the peninsula is uninhabited, and is a good place for walking and watching vultures and birds of prey. You can take a boat to the island of Imeri Gramvoússa, one of the oldest pirate islands in the Mediterranean. The Venetian castle (1579–1582) is well preserved in parts. Built 137 metres (450 ft) up, it proved invincible even to the Turks.

From Kastélli you can take a bus or

inging in e catch.

205

taxi to the peaceful village of **Plátanos**. In the church are some interesting icons, among them one depicting the 99 Holy Fathers. From here one can visit the ancient city of **Falássarna**, which was the port for Polyrrhínia. There is not much left of ancient Falássarna and it now lies far from the sea. For a long time it was assumed that the island rose in the west (Falássarna) as it dipped in the east (Eloúnda), but no longer.

One can ponder this question and other mysteries of Crete at leisure on the deserted beaches of Falássarna. There are a couple of *tavérnes* to take care of one's creature comforts, and it is possible to rent rooms.

Georgioúpolis and Kournás: The road follows the coast through countryside thick with reeds, through Tavronítis, numerous small villages and newly built modern hotels.

Then you go on past **Máleme** where a large beehive tomb was discovered. But the place became known for other reasons. In World War II, Haniá Airport was located here. In 1941, after heavy fighting, it was captured by German airborne troops. There are 4,465 graves in the German Cemetery of Máleme, mainly of very young men. Most of them lost their lives on 20 May 1941 on the night they landed. Their remains were kept in the Monastery of Goniá until the cemetery was founded in 1973.

The road carries on through Soúda Bay towards Réthimnon. There is no shortage of lovely places to stay on this stretch. In **Vámos**, for example, sporting events are held in winter and musical festivals in summer.

Even better is the pretty fishing village of **Georgioúpolis**, with a large village green. This was the site of the ancient city of **Amfímalla**, one of the ports of Láppa. But nothing remains of it now. The beach slopes gently to the sea and is ideal for young children and, although narrow, it stretches quite a way towards Réthimnon. It was named after the former high commissioner, Prince George. Although once infested with malaria, it is now a tourist resort.

It is then 7 km (4 miles) to the **Kournás Lake**. This freshwater lake is almost circular in shape and is set 200 metres (656 ft) up in a landscape reminiscent of the Alpine foothills. At one time the lake was going to be filled in, because of the mosquito infestation, but the fertility of the surrounding countryside depended on it, and it is cleaned twice a year instead. There is a legend which says that the lake was formed at the wish of a dishonoured maiden, and it is sometimes possible to see her out on the water at midday combing her hair.

Not far beyond the lake is the **Cave of Kournás** with its geological rarity: a stalagmite on which two stalactites form the shape of a cross. And at the village of **Keratidés**, you can treat yourself to a panoramic view over the lake to the sea.

Left, knotted only for a solemn purpose. Right, "You stay a monk as long as you toll the bell."

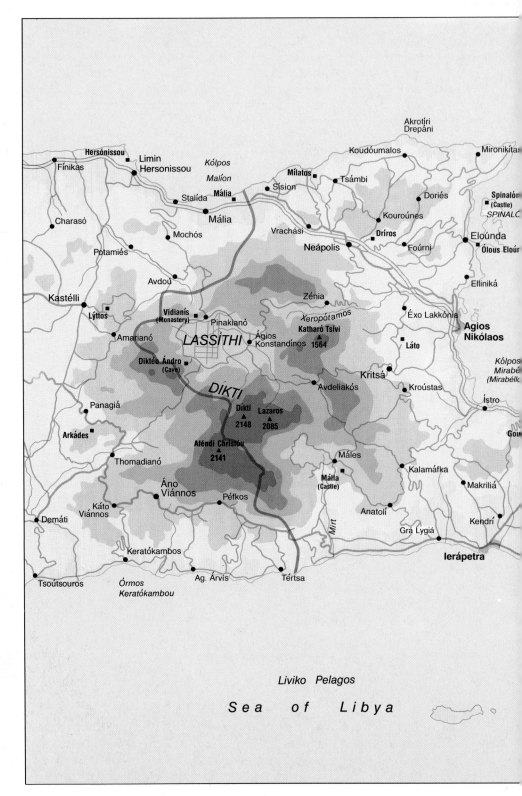

Akrotíri
Drepáni

Koudóumalos

Mironikíta

Fínikas   Hersónissou   Limin Hersonissou   Kólpos Malíon   Mílatos   Tsámbi   Doriés   Spinalór (Castle)   SPINALC

Stalída   Mália   Sísion   Kouroúnes   Eloúnda

Charasó   Mália   Vrachási   Dríros   Foúrni   Ólous Eloúr

Potamiés   Mochós   Neápolis

Avdoú   Zénia   Ellinká

Kastélli   Vidianís (Monastery)   Pinakianó   Xeropótamos   Éxo Lakkónia

Lýttos   Ágios Konstandínos   Katharó Tsívi 1564   Láto   Agios Nikólaos

Amarianó   LASSÍTHI   Kritsá   Kólpos Mirabé (Mirabéllo

Diktéo Ándro (Cave)   DÍKTI   Avdeliakós   Kroústas   Ístro

Panagiá   Díkti 2148   Lazaros 2085   Gou

Arkádes   Aféndi Christóu 2141   Máles

Thomadianó   Málla (Castle)   Kalamáfka   Makriliá

Áno Viánnos   Péfkos   Anatolí   Kendrí

Káto Viánnos   Grá Lygiá

Demáti   Mirt   Ierápetra

Keratókambos

Tsoútsouros   Órmos Keratókambou   Ag. Árvis   Tértsa

Liviko Pelagos

S e a   o f   L i b y a

212

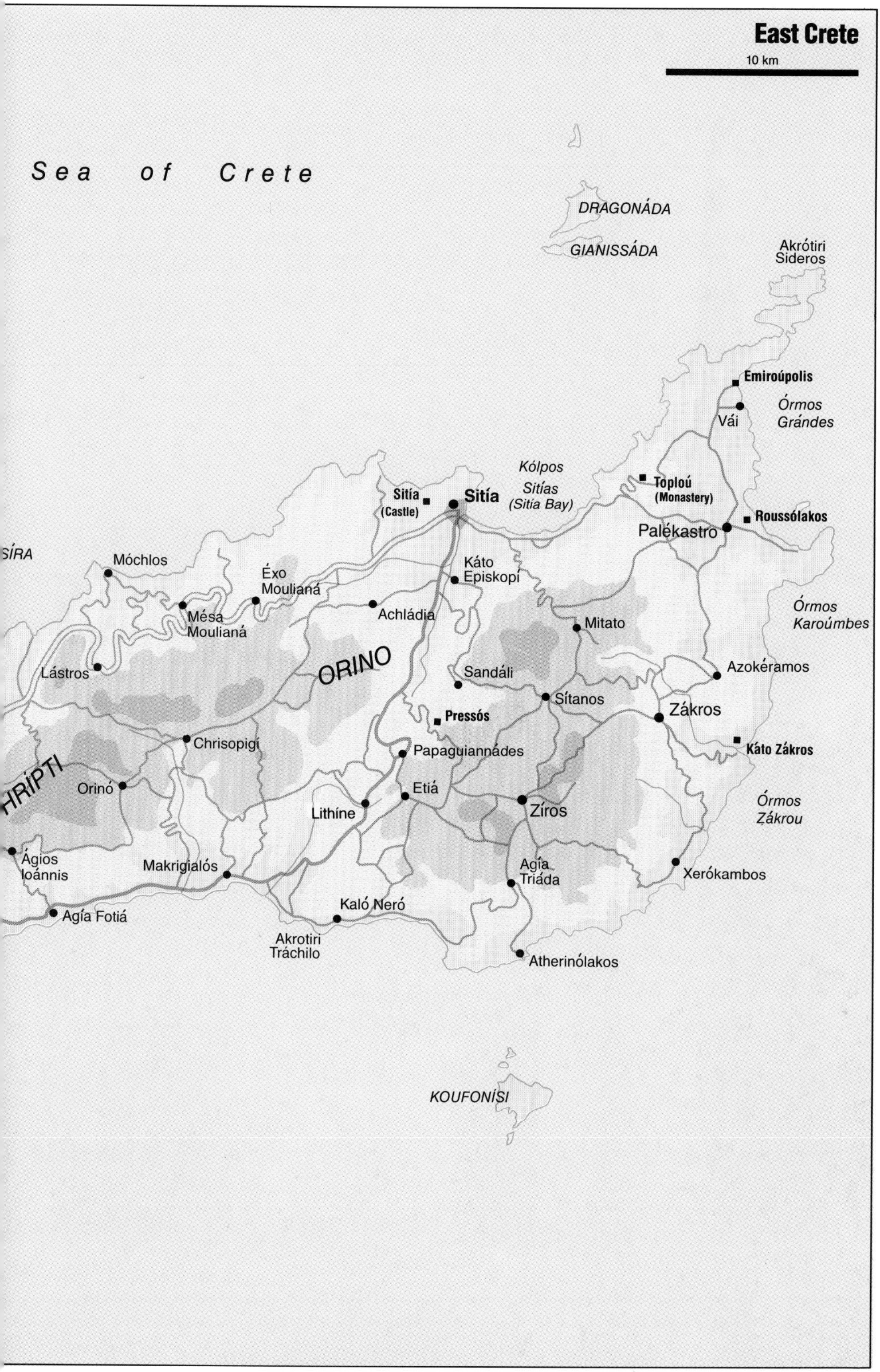

Sea   of   Crete

DRAGONÁDA

GIANISSÁDA

Akrótiri
Sideros

■ Emiroúpolis

Órmos
Grándes

● Vái

Kólpos
Sitías
(Sitía Bay)

Sitía
(Castle)

● **Sitía**

■ Toploú
(Monastery)

■ Roussólakos

Palékastro

SÍRA

● Móchlos

Éxo
Mouliná

● Káto
Episkopi

Órmos
Karoúmbes

● Mésa
Mouliná

● Achládia

● Mitato

● Azokéramos

● Lástros

ORINO

● Sandáli

● Sítanos

Zákros

● Pressós

■ Káto Zákros

HRIPTI

● Chrisopigí

● Papaguiannádes

Órmos
Zákrou

● Orinó

● Etiá

● Zíros

Lithíne

Ágios
Ioánnis

● Makrigialós

● Agía
Triáda

● Xerókambos

● Agía Fotiá

● Kaló Neró

Akrotiri
Tráchilo

● Atherinólakos

KOUFONÍSI

AROUND AGIOS NIKÓLAOS

Agios Nikólaos, with its 8,500 inhabitants, is a very pleasant little city. It lies on a promontory and is bordered by the sea along its eastern side. As its houses are also grouped around a hill, it is not always easy to get one's bearings here. Despite the natural beauty of the place, it is not immediately apparent why it has become such a popular tourist centre, as there is no particularly good beach here. Better bathing is to be found further along, but even those places are no match for the best beaches of the island. It soon becomes clear, however, that water is not the main attraction of this area. Agios Nikólaos is quite simply a magnet for the trendiest of Crete's tourists – the one resort on the island which is reminiscent of Mykonos.

Agios Nikólaos is the ideal spot for people who want more than just a tan. It's a place for those who like the bustle of a town and who like crowds and enjoy wandering through the streets and going shopping. Nowhere on the island is the mix of nationalities more colourful. Nowhere, apart from Haniá, is it easier to get to know people. A respite from the noise may be found in the peaceful countryside, or in any of the many beautiful spots on Mirabéllo Bay.

One of the sights here is **Voulisméni Lake**. The lake is almost round, and according to myth, the goddess Artemis bathed in it, which was said to be unfathomable. More recently it has been measured and found to be 64 metres (210 ft) deep. Whereas in earlier times it was famous for its "sweet" water – the water was supposed to come, or have come, from an underground spring – nowadays it is regarded as salty.

Culturally, Agios Nikólaos has not much to offer. The **Panagía Church** to the east of **Venizélos Square** is worth a visit to see its 14th-century frescoes.

More important is the **Agios Nikólaos Chapel** a little further out, behind the Minos Beach Hotel. This is one of the oldest churches on Crete but, if you compare the ages usually given for the church and its frescoes, you come to the illogical conclusion that the frescoes came first.

The oldest parts of the fresco are interesting, for following the iconoclasm of Leo III (726–843), no figures were to be represented, only ornamentation. This makes the Agios Nikólaos Chapel unique on Crete. The name of the town was taken from the chapel.

On no account should you miss the Archaeological Museum, if you are interested in the Minoan Epoch. Although the most spectacular items are housed in Iráklion, important exhibits can be found here too, such as the "Goddess of Mirtos", the skull of a Cretan contest victor, various vessels and containers

Agios Nikólaos
250m

Akti St.
Estiás
Konstantínou
Lefkón-Oreón
Erithroú Stavroú Stratigón
Koúndourou
Miltou
Lasithioú
Archaeological Museum
Paleológou
Antistáseos
Vitsénsou-Komárou
Apostólou-
Dimokratías
Epimenídi
Títou
Dimokratías
N. Plastíra
Filelínon
Tompázi
Giampoudáki
Kritsás
Geórg.
Kondogiánni
Anapáfseos
Akti Atlantídas
Platía Venizélou
Ag. Triáda Church
Modátsou
OTE
Kont.-Stakianáki
Stakianáki
Ariádnis
Akti Themisoktí
Voulisméni Lake
Lighthouse
Harbour
Folk Museum
Tourist Information
Kóraka
BUS STATION

such as a small cosmetic box, wine goblets, weapons, double axes, sarcophagi and idols.

It is true that there is nothing particularly sensational by way of rare artefacts, but that has its advantages. As only finds from the east of the island are displayed here, the collection is more comprehensible than the more extensive exhibition in Iráklion, and you also get a good idea of Minoan culture.

In the eight rooms, there are exhibits dating from the Neolithic period, the Minoan and Post Minoan era right up to Roman times.

Not much is known about the historical development of the town of Agios Nikólaos. In Dorian times the port **Lató y Kamára** of the mountain town of **Lató** was situated here. Remains of an acropolis were found up on a hill where the city centre now stands. On the same site, the Venetians erected a castle, Mirabello, of which hardly a trace remains. In the Turkish era, the place was almost uninhabited. It was not until 1870 that the present town of Agios Nikólaos was built.

Special mention should be made of Agios Nikólaos' unique climate. According to records, in summer the humidity level here is nil. For star-gazers and more serious astronomers, this is of great importance, as the stars can be seen exceptionally clearly.

Panagía i Kerá: The Church of **Panagía i Kerá** (Church of our Lady, Mother of God) is about 500 metres (¼´mile) outside of Kritsá on the right side of the road in a grove of oaks, olives and cypresses. Some say that this is the most beautiful church on the island. In fact it would be difficult to find one which can compete from a purely architectural point of view.

What is interesting is that the aesthetic charm of the building, rather than being a calculated effect, in fact stems

Still waters at the waterfront of Agios Nikólaos

from the necessity of holding the vault together. The impression of size is modified somewhat when one looks at the interior. It is over 100 sq metres (119 sq yd) in area. Its apparent unity would seem to indicate that it was built in a single phase. History, however, tells otherwise. The central nave is the oldest part, dating from the mid-13th century. The frescoes in the apse and on the walls of the tambour are from the same period. The south nave was built and painted between 1300 and 1340, the north nave 100 years later.

The central nave is dedicated to Mary, the Mother of God, and is decorated with pictures of the archangels, the prophets and evangelists. Many well-known biblical scenes, including Herod's massacre of the innocents and the raising of Lazarus are also depicted.

The south nave is dedicated to St Anna and the north to St Anthony. Photography inside the church is prohibited but slides and books may be purchased in the small café next door.

Doric city: The ruins of the Dorian city of **Lató** are easy to find, lying 3 km (1¾ miles) northwest of Kritsá. Just before the Kritsá signpost, a road suitable for vehicles leads off to the right, into the hills. For visitors wishing to walk from Kerá to Lató there is a path behind the café which is just along the road to Lató.

Lató was founded in the 7th and 8th centuries BC, and is a typical double settlement of a fortified town set between two hills within sight of the port. Its most important period was probably during the 4th and 3rd centuries BC, when it expanded in area as well as in population. A document from the year 193 BC gives the name of the hill city as **Lató y Etéra**.

One of the great advantages of Lató is that it still offers an accurate picture of a double settlement. The port of the former hill city **Lató y Kamára** lay on

eat wave at
e harbour?

the site of present-day Agios Nikólaos. Although originally the more important of the two, Lató y Etéra was eventually left deserted. One can only speculate as to why this happened. Most probably there was a long period of peace, when there was no need to take refuge in the hills. After that time the port took over all the necessary functions.

This Post Minoan place was also discovered by Arthur Evans towards the end of the 19th century, but was excavated by a French archaeologist.

The best way to approach Lató is from the city gates below. You can take the steps up to the centre which will give you a clear impression of just what an inhabitant of the city saw 2,500 years ago. This area, which one can still enjoy walking through today, is only a small part of what was once the large expanse of the original city. If you have time, just take a look into the bushes to the side, and you will be amazed at how far the

settlement extended, and just how much there is still to discover.

The village of **Kritsá** is 11 km (7 miles) from Agios Nikólaos, in the foothills of the Díkti Mountains. With 2,000 inhabitants, Kritsá is one of the largest villages on the island. As most visitors to Agios Nikólaos come here, it is usually crowded, so it's a good idea to leave your car in the car park at the entrance to the village. From there one can also go to the Katharó Plateau.

In the village, you are greeted by a bronze statue "The Maid of Kritsá," **Kritsotopoúla**. She is revered as a freedom fighter against Turkish oppressors. The Turkish Pasha Husein, who lived in **Houmeriáko**, a village northwest of **Neápolis**, had chosen this daughter of the priest of Kritsá as his mistress. On the very first night, she stabbed the pasha, dressed herself as a man and joined the freedom fighters on the Lassíthi Plateau. It was not until she was

Sponge seller, Agios Nikólaos.

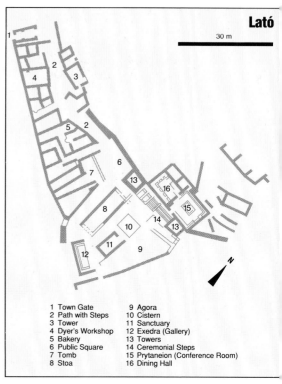

Lató

30 m

1 Town Gate
2 Path with Steps
3 Tower
4 Dyer's Workshop
5 Bakery
6 Public Square
7 Tomb
8 Stoa
9 Agora
10 Cistern
11 Sanctuary
12 Exedra (Gallery)
13 Towers
14 Ceremonial Steps
15 Prytaneion (Conference Room)
16 Dining Hall

wounded that her true identity became known to her comrades.

There are several churches worth seeing in Kritsá. Just at the entrance to the village, on the right, is the Cemetery Church of Agios Ioánnis with its late 14th-century frescoes. To the south is the **Agios Geórgios tou Kavousióti Church**, dating from the early 14th century with frescoes of the same date, and then the **Agios Konstantínos** Church with its frescoes of the mid-14th century, as well as the churches of Agíou Pnévma and Agía Paraskeví.

The main street is one huge, colourful bazaar, a mass of cloth, material and blankets. There is a wonderful selection of handicrafts here, although the label "Kritsá" doesn't indicate a low price. If you can manage it, do walk through the streets up to the lovely road lined with almond trees which runs along the hill above the village. From there you will have a glorious view over Kritsá and the valley, and Kerá shimmers white in the distance through the olives, oaks and groves of cypresses.

There's no doubt that Kritsá is a lovely place, especially its location. Then there are the weavers and potters, but these are not the real reasons for its fame. It is the **Panagía i Kerá Church** on the way from Agios Nikólaos which is the main attraction.

In Kritsá the road to the **Katharó Plateau** branches off left from the main road. The road is asphalt for a short stretch, then gravel, although still passable. But the 16-km (10 miles) drive is well worth the effort, for the plateau lying at 1,100 metres (3,609 ft) has the most wonderful scenery imaginable. It is only inhabited and cultivated during summer, as it is usually snowed in during the winter. Potatoes, various vegetables and vineyards are the main crops up here.

Further south from Kritsá on the road

Kritsá, the rgest llage in rete.

to **Kroústas** is the Church of **Agios Ioánnis o Theológos**, which once belonged to the Monastery of **Toploú**. The iconostases in the three naves are exceptionally beautiful. After about 4 km (2½ miles) you reach Kroústas. Then if you drive just as far again, you come to a left fork in the road which will take you to another Church of Agios Ioánnis where the frescoes dating from 1347 are worth seeing.

Gourniá: Approximately 18 km (11 miles) southeast of Agios Nikólaos a road leads into the hills, to the Monastery of **Faneroméni**. Although the monastery seems very near, don't be misled: the road actually winds around for almost 8 km (5 miles) to get there.

Further down the road you come to the Minoan city of **Gourniá**, which lies on a hill just outside **Pahía Ammos**. Gourniá is an archaeological godsend, as it is larger and better preserved than **Palékastro**, **Mírtos** or the surroundings of the Palace of **Káto Zákros**. These sites, although interesting, do not give as clear an indication of a Minoan city layout.

Findings in a necropolis on the edge of the city indicate that the period of habitation here was from about 3000 BC to 1100 BC. Most parts of the city which have been excavated are dated from about 1600 BC, the Late Minoan period. However, the great catastrophe of 1450 BC destroyed much of the settlement and it was uninhabited for a long time, before being finally resettled in about 1300 BC.

On almost the highest point of the hill is a building which is generally thought to have been a Minoan palace. It lies in a north–south axis and the layout of the rooms around a central courtyard is reminiscent of the island's other great palaces. A governor of some kind probably ruled here, under the authority of either Knossós or Káto Zákros.

Cool cover.

In the sanctum various cult objects were found, most of them ornamented with snakes, as well as a sacrificial table, bulls' horns, double axes and a clay goddess whose outstretched arms are wound around with snakes.

Much more important than any theory, is the opportunity for the visitor to wander the ancient streets at will. Fascinating comparisons can be made with other Dorian cities (Lató, for example), and also with the present-day mountain villages of Crete. Many finds from the graves in Gourniá are displayed in the Archaeological Museum of Iráklion.

The little village of **Paheía Ammos** used to have an attractive harbour. The completion of the coastal road led to the stagnation of its growth, and it now relies on tourism for prosperity. This is the narrowest point of the island, and this fact played an important part in the founding of Gourniá.

Opposite the lilac-coloured hills is the wedge-shaped **Monastiráki Gorge**. If you make your way through the gorge you can reach the peak of the 1,476-metre (4,842-ft) high **Aféndis Stavroménos Mountain**, from which there's a wonderful view of the island. The recommended route to take is along the 27-km (17-mile) coastal road from Agios Nikólaos through **Kavoússi Xerámpela** and the 850-metre (2,789-ft) high **Thrípti Alm**.

Heading further south for 3 km (1¾ miles) is the village of **Vassilikí** with its famous early Minoan excavation site. The black and red ceramic work has become known as the Vassilikí style. To locate the site, you should turn left at the signpost and then continue on for about 150 metres (165 yd).

Another 3 km (1¾ miles) to the south is the friendly village of **Episkopí**, with its lovely little Agios Nikólaos Church in the shape of a cross.

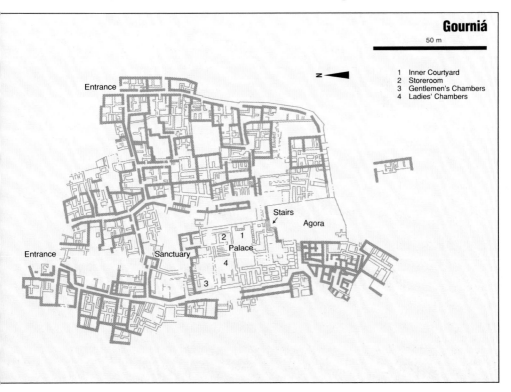

Gourniá

50 m

N

1 Inner Courtyard
2 Storeroom
3 Gentlemen's Chambers
4 Ladies' Chambers

Entrance

Stairs

Agora

Entrance

Sanctuary

Palace

The most eastern town on Crete is Sitía, 73 km (45 miles) from Agios Nikólaos. It is set in gentle mountain scenery and lush vineyards. The fertile soil makes the gardens of the 7,000 inhabitants gloriously colourful. A picturesque harbour links Sitía to the mainland and other islands. There are connections to Piraeus, Rhodes, Kárpathos, the Cyclades and the Aegean Islands.

Tourism is definitely booming. Whether it will grow too quickly and overwhelm the town as some observers fear is left to be seen within the next few years. The place has already made concessions to the industry – box-like hotels, promenade restaurants and beach discos abound these days – but, to date, it has still managed to keep its own laid-back character despite all that.

Burial findings indicate that the Bay of Sitía was inhabited in Minoan times. The ancient town of Itia or Etia or even Itis, with **Pressos** as its port, was probably not located on the site of present-day Sitía, but 1 kilometre inland on a hill.

According to Diogenes Laertius in his *Philosophical History of Greece*, Myson, one of the seven wise men of Greece, was born here. For Cretans today, Vinzentos Kornáros (1600–77) seems a more important figure. His *Erotókritos* is one of the most significant national poems of Greece.

In Byzantine times Crete was a bishopric. As this bay always attracted pirates and invaders, the Byzantines built a fort at the turn of the millennium, which soon encompassed almost the whole settlement. The Genoese, and later the Venetians fortified the walls, but very little of these works can be seen today. As the Turkish attacks increased after about 1648, the Venetians moved the people to places easier to defend. In earlier times the inhabitants had already

__Left__, the waterfront in Sitía.

had to cope with the loss of their homes. In 1303 and 1508, they were destroyed by earthquakes, and in 1538 by the ruthless Ottoman admiral Chaireddin Barbarossa. The fears of the Venetians proved well founded when, in 1651, a single attack by the Ottomans was enough to take their fort. The evacuated town fell into decay and was eventually brought back to life only on the initiative of the Turks in 1879.

If you are interested in the history of names, Sitía is a treasure trove, with a great variety of optional meanings to choose from. The name can be traced from a Linear-B inscription tablet, and was possibly included in Egyptian lists of place names. It may also be connected to "Lassíthi" (from or to La Sitía). A connection with the above-mentioned Itia or Etiá is also possible as, until recent times, there was a place called Etiá (or Ethiá, "Willow Tree") just 25 km south of Sitía. A hilltop sanctuary was discovered here during the 1950s.

A Franciscan monastery and a Venetian palace which once stood here were both destroyed. The fort is now the only building worth seeing in the town. The name **Kasárma** comes from *casa di arma* (House of Arms). Below the fort, about 50 metres (55 yd) to the east, are the remains of a horseshoe-shaped Roman pond with a diameter of about 6 or 7 metres (20 or 23 ft). It is now located underwater and seems to indicate that East Crete has sunk. Strong doubts have been expressed by some geologists about the theory that there was a simultaneous rising of the western part of the island (Falássarna) as the east sank, a view once held by some scholars.

One of the sights of the town is the recently opened **Archaeological Museum**. There all the important finds from the area are beautifully displayed. In a small **Folklore Museum**, you can see, among other things, the simple equipment used to make the elaborate

Cretan national costume in earlier times. The kitchen utensils and living rooms of 100 years ago are interesting too, and give a fascinating insight into the Cretan lifestyle of the 19th century.

To the east of Sitía is a long beach, which is quite steep in places. As the currents are strong, particularly when it's windy, children must be supervised if they swim at all. It is not really a place recommended for family outings.

There are differing opinions about Sitía. While some see it as the typical although rather rough but vital Levantine trading city, others grumble that it is a provincial one-horse town. One thing is certain, though. There are few lovelier sights in the world than the lights of Sitía glimmering in the darkness as you drive towards the city along the coast from Toploú or Palékastro.

The village of **Agía Fotía** is 5 km east of Sitía. In 1971 an early Minoan necropolis was discovered here which,

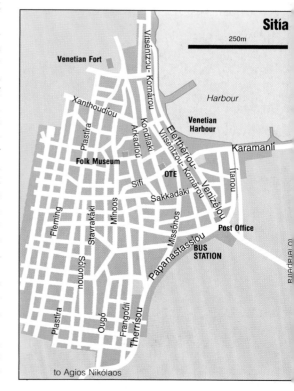

with its 250 graves, is one of the largest on the island.

Toploú and Vái: The landscape between Sitía and **Toploú** becomes more bizarre and surrealistic as you approach the Toploú Monastery. The steep road is asphalted these days. The clearly recognisable rock strata all around will bring joy to the heart of any geologist. After a while the monastery comes into sight between the mountain crests, its tall Italianate belltower beckoning like the minaret of an isolated mosque.

Toploú is actually only the nickname of the monastery. It probably comes from the Turkish word *top,* meaning cannon ball. In Venetian times the monastery did possess a renowned cannon and used it successfully against the numerous pirates in the area.

The monastery's real name is **Moní Panagía Akrotirianí,** Monastery of the Mother of God of the Foothills, also of the Cape. It was built in the 15th and 16th centuries on the ruins of the monastery of Agios Isodóros and then destroyed by a strong earthquake. It was during the subsequent rebuilding under the supervision of Abbot Gavríl Pantógalos that the monastery took on the appearance it has today. It was often attacked during Turkish rule as a suspected meeting place for secret revolutionary committees.

During World War II, it was a contact point for the Cretan partisans and the British. The Germans found out about this, and in retaliation shot the abbot and several monks. There is a memorial near the entrance to commemorate these events.

It may be better if you have not visited the monastery before and therefore do not remember the way it used to be. Then you will not be disappointed. The inner courtyard was once glorious, with white stone walkways, arcades and balustrades, but it is now unrecognisable.

alm beach
Vái.

The whole place has been filled with dark wooden scaffolding, which has been erected in order to make getting around easier: as a result the aesthetics have suffered.

In better days, 150 monks lived here, but now there are only two. The older monk, who only a few years ago posed proudly beside the wonderful icon – "Great are you, my God" – of Ioánnis Kornáros, now makes a sullen impression. And no wonder. He has seen his monastery taken apart and downgraded into a tourist attraction. But despite this, the Monastery of Toploú is still an impressive sight in the barren landscape of East Crete.

Northeast of Toploú, on the east coast of the island, is the palm-fringed, "tropical" beach of **Vái**. From Toploú, the quickest way to get there is via the direct road to the northeast; from Sitía it is easier to go via **Palékastro**.

The sandy beach of Vái lies in a small bay, like a lagoon, and is famous for its palm trees. The locals will tell you this date palm "forest" sprouted when Roman soldiers seeded the area – in passing – with date stones. It is a wonderful beach for children, as it slopes gently and the waves are not strong. The water is supposed to be slightly warmer here than elsewhere too. There is a restaurant, as well as showers, changing huts and lovely shady spots under the palm trees. You will find all you need for a delightful beach holiday. Campers overnighting in the past made such a mess of the little beach and the woods nearby that now camping and overnighting are forbidden. That is also the reason why the palm wood is fenced in nowadays and is a protected area.

The place is not, however, anything like the usual cliché of a tropical beach but is more reminiscent of the North African coast. But Vái would probably be just as famous if it had hazelnut

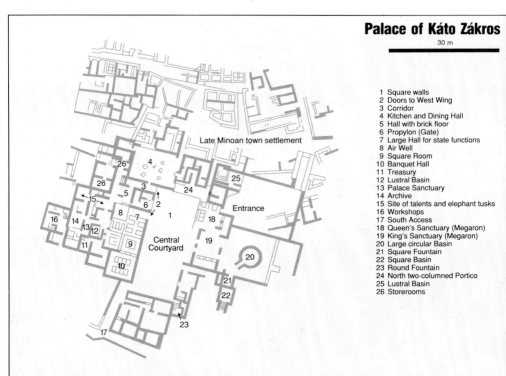

Palace of Káto Zákros

30 m

1 Square walls
2 Doors to West Wing
3 Corridor
4 Kitchen and Dining Hall
5 Hall with brick floor
6 Propylon (Gate)
7 Large Hall for state functions
8 Air Well
9 Square Room
10 Banquet Hall
11 Treasury
12 Lustral Basin
13 Palace Sanctuary
14 Archive
15 Site of talents and elephant tusks
16 Workshops
17 South Access
18 Queen's Sanctuary (Megaron)
19 King's Sanctuary (Megaron)
20 Large circular Basin
21 Square Fountain
22 Square Basin
23 Round Fountain
24 North two-columned Portico
25 Lustral Basin
26 Storerooms

Late Minoan town settlement

Entrance

Central Courtyard

bushes or oaks instead of palms, as its charm is really due to the contrast to the surrounding landscape.

Not far north of Vái is the little village of **Erimoúpolis**. This site on the cape was settled even during Minoan times. It was once the site of the powerful city of Itanos, from which regular trade was conducted with the Orient during Greek and Roman times. Below the acropolis, very little of which remains today, sections of streets as well as the ruins of an early Christian basilica have been discovered. More impressive than the excavations, however, is the view to the northeast of the rugged **Kap Síderos** with its lighthouse.

Káto Zákros and the Valley of the Dead: The most interesting way to reach the Palace of **Káto Zákros** is via Palékastro, for the roads are better and they take you through a fascinating mixture of lush countryside and totally barren landscapes. Beaches about a mile away,

especially at the southern end of the bay, are worth visiting.

Palékastro is a delightful place, and also has an excavation site 2½ km (1½ miles) away to the east at **Roussolákos**. Here are the remains of a Minoan port, second in importance only to Gourniá in terms of archaeological significance. As there is relatively little left to see here, the site receives far fewer visitors than the great palaces. In fact, Palékastro depends on the popularity of the monastery of Toploú and the beach at Vái for visitors.

Further south, visitors to Káto Zákros and Zákros, also known as Ano Zákros or Epáno Eákros, can find shops, *tavérnes*, hotels and rooms to let. The scenery around Zákros is surprisingly green. This is because near the village there is a spring which provides water for the whole area.

Luckily the old days of dust and frazzled nerves on this stretch are over, and you can drive the 8 km (5 miles) to the excavation site of Káto Zákros on an excellent road. The last curvy and rather steep stretch is interesting as it leads through the most extraordinary scenery, rather like a moonscape. Yet the valley where the Palace of Káto Zákros is found has lush vegetation. Spring water flows from Zákros, sometimes so strongly that parts of the palace area are flooded.

At the end of the motorway, the first place you come to is the lovely beach of Káto Zákros. In high season there is a lot going on here during the day, but the evenings are so quiet that you feel as if time has stood still and the Minoans could reappear at any moment. Also, this is one of the few places on the island where you can camp anywhere you wish. You can also spend the night in either of the two *tavérnes* which, with a couple of other houses, make up the village of Káto Zákros.

The Palace of Káto Zákros is one of the most significant excavations on

Broken bones in the Valley of the Dead.

Crete and certainly the most important to be discovered since World War II. It is comparable to the palaces of Knossós, Festós and Mália in type and layout, although smaller in size. The reason for the importance of this palace, which dates from about 1600 BC, is not so much that it is the only one of its kind in East Crete. What is really fascinating is the fact that after the great catastrophe of 1450 BC, it was neither plundered nor altered in any way. Thus an extraordinary number of artefacts, over 10,000 individual articles, were found here. This "posthumous preservation" is also important in solving the mystery of the nature of the catastrophe which destroyed civilisation on Crete in 1450 BC. Evidence from Káto Zákros indicates that life was not wiped out by ashfall, but by tidal waves following the volcanic eruption on Santorini.

The entrance is from the northeast through the city settlement to the palace itself. The four chutes to the left of the path were once ventilating shafts in a metal melting works. In the northeast corner of the courtyard, which is on a north-south axis, is a stone square, possibly once the wall around a holy tree, but more likely an altar. Due to the absence of evidence, the specific functions of some of the palace rooms cannot be clearly defined. But one was probably a workshop as various kinds of stone, presumably for artistic work, were stored there. It can be assumed that the large hall with six pillars at the northern side of the courtyard was a dining room, as kitchen utensils were found in the small room next to it.

The archives were so named because of the clay tablets found there inscribed with Linear-A figures. But much remains unclear, such as use of the two basins, one round and the other square, found behind the so-called "Megaron of the King." In Room 8 of the Archaeo-

Cutting bamboo cane, Ierápetra

logical Museum of Iráklion the considerable finds from Káto Zákros are displayed, including elephant teeth, bronze talents, stone rhyta, ceramics, weapons and tools.

Past the palace site and the recently planted banana plantation, you come to the **Valley of the Dead**, named thus because it was here that the Minoans buried their dead. They placed them in caves or niches in the rocks of the gorge. Now and then a stray goat bleats here today, but apart from that the valley is completely silent, just as it must have been in ancient times.

Ierápetra and Mírtos: The best way back to Agios Nikólaos from Sitía is to take the inland road through **Piskokéfalo**, **Lithíne** and then drive along the south coast to **Ierápetra**. There is much of interest to see on the way: goats clambering up in the trees, and strange buildings which seem to merge the old with the new – they are concrete structures which encase the old houses which, apparently, no one wanted to knock down.

The road runs on past **Férma** and **Agía Fotía**. Both places have lovely beaches and beautiful bays, which are mainly shadeless.

Iérapetra is probably the largest city in the Lassíthi district, and the southernmost in Europe. Estimates of the population vary astonishingly between 7,000 and 11,000 inhabitants. Ierápetra is like Sitía in that although one may like the place, it is difficult to recommend it to others, as there's not much to go on and the beach is not a great one.

It is a prosperous town, due to the cultivation of tomatoes, cucumbers and beans, grown mainly in greenhouses. This part of the island is known as the vegetable garden not only of Crete but of the whole of Greece, for it grows produce for the whole country. The olive harvest is considerable, as is that of

irls sewing,
erápetra.

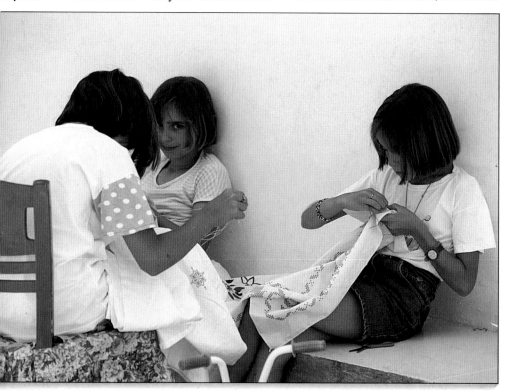

oranges and mandarins. The reason for much of this prosperity is the artificial lake north of the city, which has solved the water problems of the past.

The history of Iérapetra goes back to Minoan times. Its location on the narrowest part of the island made it an ideal place from which to trade with Libya and the islands of the Aegean. It is possible that there was an overland route from sea to sea. It is quite likely that the town of Gourniá was built on this route. Like the town itself, its name went through a series of metamorphoses: first it was called Kyrva, then in succession Pytna, Kamiros, Ierapytna and, finally, Iérapetra.

There are not many attractions in the town, and those that are can be found in the old part of the city. The Venetians built a castle at the end of the 13th century to protect the harbour. Even then, Iérapetra was not the important trading port for Africa that it had been in Roman times. The famous house in which Napoleon spent the night on his way to the Egyptian campaign lies east of the Agio Nikólaos Church.

There are various Roman artefacts on display in the little Archaeological Museum, including a selection of (mostly headless) statuary. On the western edge of the old city is a dilapidated Turkish mosque. The minaret is damaged and this unfortunately means that one cannot go in. An octagonal fountain stands in front, and there is an inviting *tavérna* nearby. In the shadows of the tamarisks on the square, the men spend their time playing cards and *távli*.

Ierápetra lies on a latitude of 35 degrees, further south than much of the Mediterranean coast of Algeria and Tunisia. The sun shines almost all year round, making it an ideal place for an autumn holiday.

The little village of **Mírtos** is 14 km (8½ miles) west of Ierápetra. On the way there you can visit two excavation sites. The first is **Foúrni Korífi**. Just by the

sign "Nea Mírtos" is a hill on the right. Here traces were found of a huge family made up of more than 100 members who lived and worked in a multi-roomed communal building. There, they manufactured various products in an almost industrial way as far back as 2400 BC. Then there is **Pírgos**, a hill just outside Mírtos, with a Minoan mansion dating from the 16th century BC.

The little fishing village of Mírtos has adapted well to foreigners. But despite the concrete promenade along the sea front, the place has not lost its charm.

Then you drive back towards Ierápetra, and turn off at **Grá Lygiá** to **Kalamáfka**. Just behind Kalamáfka is the one spot on the island where you can see the Sea of Crete and the Sea of Libya. The place is not marked, but it is easy to find. Just climb a small hill on the right, and the wonderful panorama opens out. Even the artificial lake of Ierápetra can clearly be seen.

A modest harvest.

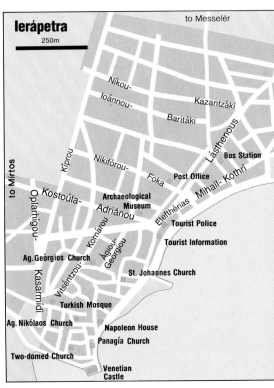

230

OLIVES

And he stayed yet another seven days; and again he sent forth the dove out of the ark;

And the dove came to him in the evening; and lo in her mouth was an olive leaf plucked off; so Noah knew that the waters were abated from off the earth. – Genesis, 8 : 10–11.

Even in the Old Testament, the olive tree was a symbol of life, so it is clear that it has long been known and treasured. On Crete, evidence shows that olive trees have been there since Mycenaean times. Locals call it the blessed tree because everything from it is precious: the fruit, the leaves and the wood.

As one can make use of its components for food, soap and medicaments, and the tree seems so tailor made for man, it is small wonder that it has taken on such a religious significance. According to Homer, the gods rubbed themselves with perfumed olive oil.

The olive tree propagates easily. A new tree will grow from an olive stone or a piece of root. To "domesticate" the tree is more difficult. The wild tree must be three years old before it is transplanted to a convenient place for cultivation. The first few years then mean nothing but hard work for the farmer: grafting, transplanting, digging, fertilising, watering and protecting the tree from parasites. The trees spaced 10–12 metres (33–40 ft) apart react quickly to these measures, but it is still 15 to 18 years before the olive tree is profitable.

Different Mediterranean countries utilise varying methods of cultivation. In Spain three trunks are grown, whereas in Greece a single tall trunk is preferred. The tree flowers in April, and by May the first fruit is visible. It is a local belief that 20 May – Prophet **Respite from work in the olive grove.**

Elias's Day – is when the oil is formed.

Olive trees do need water, and in winter ditches are dug around the trees to catch every drop. In the hot Cretan summer, wells, ditches, pumps and hoses, all expensive ways of watering, have to be used. Olive groves have to be watered at least once a week. On watering days, the trees have absolute priority. Houses set in the groves have no running water – however hot it is. Man and beast must give way. The harvest varies from year to year. A good harvest exhausts the tree, so that in the following year it will not yield much. In October, nets are spread out under the trees; from the beginning of November onwards, the ripe olives fall. Every three weeks the fruit is collected and sold in the market, or taken to the oil mill. Some types are harvested directly from the trees, using monstrous comb-like implements or compressed-air machines.

As in all Mediterranean countries, people in Crete cook with plenty of olive oil. The top-grade oil is from the first pressing; middle-grade oil from the second hot pressing is used for soap, creams and fuel. Oil presses used to be enormous vats in which a round stone was turned by hand. Nowadays, the olives are pulverised by machine, and the oil extracted from hydraulic presses.

There are no black and green olives; green olives are simply unripe black ones. However, there are different kinds of olives, and they are quite easy to tell apart. The large, almost round *Koroliá-Aetoniholiá* yield about 125 per kilo. The longer sort, *Ladoliá*, which are rich in oil, take about 1,000 to make up a kilo. There are some 500 other species of this dicotyledonous *Oleanceae* family, among them ash, jasmine, privet and, in a few corners of southern Europe and East Asia, forsythia and elder. Of all the souvenirs available on Crete, pure olive oil in tins is one of the finest.

**he harvest
fter the
bour.**

SPINALÓNGA AND LASSÍTHI

The village of **Eloúnda** lies about 12 km (7½ miles) north of Agios Nikólaos in a long bay formed by the off-shore **Peninsula of Spinalónga**. This bay would be a perfect harbour had the depth in certain places not been a mere 3 metres (10 ft). This of course makes it quite impossible for large ships to berth. On the seaward side is the famous fortified island also known as **Spinalónga**.

Eloúnda spreads out over the hillside and the town is divided into various areas. **Shísma**, with its harbour installation, is actually the centre. The large square near the harbour is particularly popular, and there you can sit in one of the lovely cafés or restaurants and simply watch the world go by. In contrast to Agios Nikólaos, which always seems overcrowded, Eloúnda is much more pleasant and relaxing, as the tourists who come here tend to spread out more.

In ancient times this was the site of **Oloús**, one of the most important and richest of all the cities on Crete. It is highly probable that Oloús was the port city of the Dorian city of **Dreros**. This was founded in the 6th and 7th centuries BC and lay in the hills west of Oloús. The strong tectonic activity in the 4th century AD led to most of Oloús sinking into the water.

A road leads to the Peninsula of Spinalónga, passing across a narrow piece of land that is split by a canal. On the way you will pass salt production basins, set up by the Venetians and used until recently. After a bridge, you can see three windmills and an excavation site. The foundations of an early Christian basilica can be examined on foot, the main attraction being an exceptionally beautiful mosaic floor decorated with fish motifs.

If you drive on a little further, you will come to a spot where, on a calm day, you can see the remains of Oloús beneath the water. Not much is known about this ancient city. It was mentioned in 2nd-century BC documents and in travel records by the Roman "travel writer" Pausanius in the 2nd century AD. According to him, Briómartis, a Cretan Artemis, was worshipped here.

In the city there were once apparently all kinds of treasures, including a statue of the goddess Briómartis fashioned by the artful Daedalus. Of course many present-day divers would love to explore the sunken city but, for obvious reasons, diving with compressed-air cylinders is forbidden on Crete. The island has simply lost too many artefacts in the past and now intends to preserve its ancient heritage. Bathing, on the other hand, is excellent in any of the little bays around the peninsula.

Eloúnda is the most fashionable corner of Crete, with the highest concentra-

ft and low, ling in e sun is way of life these etans.

tion of luxury hotels as well as scores of new apartment developments.

The Island of Spinalónga: This rocky island is about 400 metres (¼ mile) long and no more than ´half its length in width. There are various points from which one can take a boat to reach it. The distance from Agios Nikólaos is greatest, making this the most expensive way. The usual way is from Eloúnda, but the shortest is from **Pláka**, a little fishing village north of Eloúnda.

The days when taking people across to the island afforded a good second income for the people of Pláka are over. Things are more organised these days but Pláka is still the best place to embark. If the captain is happy with the price, he will take a turn around the whole island, which gives the visitor another insight into the fascinating history of the place.

Just what the island looked like in antiquity is not clear. There was proba-

bly a fort named **Kalydon** which protected the harbour town of Oloú. The island served the Christians as a refuge from the Saracens. However, there must have been fortifications, since flight to a barren island would have served very little purpose.

Its greatest importance was under the Venetians, who in 1579 transformed the place into one great fort. This strategic measure was intended to provide security for the military port near present-day Eloúnda. It seems that the Venetians, whose decline was beginning to become apparent to them, decided to change tactics. As they realised the approaching Turks would probably prove stronger in the long run, they concentrated on fortifying selected bases. By doing this they hoped to maintain some degree of superiority at sea. In fact Spinalónga did in the end prove invincible. In 1669, when they conquered Iráklion, the Turks nominally

"What's in store for me"

took Crete, but they were forced to hoist the white flag before this little island and its 35 Venetian cannons. The same thing happened at Soúda and Imere Gramvoússa, which were equally well fortified. Forty-six years later, the problem resolved itself. Venice had become so weak that all three of its forts had to capitulate.

For a long time the Turks left Spinalónga unchanged. It was not until the 19th century when tension with the Christian population of Crete increased, that Turkish families began to settle on the island. By 1881 there were over 1,000 Turks living here. When Crete became "autonomous under the rule of the Sultan" in 1898, most of the Turks left. Those living on Spinalónga, who had become successful traders, were among the few who chose to stay. They were tolerated by the rest of the population until 1903. Then parliament under Prince George decided to turn

Spinalónga into a leper colony. This was the final move, and it was not long before the Turks were gone for good.

Whether this was a political manoeuvre or whether there had indeed been previous plans for establishing a leper colony, is not clear. The fact that the sick were left isolated for four years would seem to argue for the first supposition. A strange thing did happen on the "Island of Dreams", however. In time a real feeling of community was born of the enforced communal living there. But the leper colony was finally closed in 1957 and little remains to be seen.

The Lassíthi Plateau: On the way to the **Lassíthi Plateau** you pass through **Neápolis**. The place was founded in the 16th century under the name of **Neohorió** (New Village). In 1870 the Turkish prefect Kostis Pasha moved the district administration and bishopric here. Then the name was no longer adequate and it was changed from New Village to

*iling past
ínalónga.*

New Town: Neápolis. But today, apart from the district court and the bishopric, all the important offices are situated on the coast in Agios Nikólaos.

The road winds its way up through the villages of **Vrísses**, **Amigali**, **Zénia** and **Exo Potámi**, beyond which there is a wood. At one point where the road widens, perched on the side of the cliff is a tiny *tavérna* and souvenir shop.

Behind **Mésa Potámi** there is a pass at about 1,000 metres (3,281 ft) above sea level. After scaling the heights, the road gently leads down to the plain of Lassíthi, which lies at about 850 metres (2,789 ft).

This basin, which has an area of about 40 sq km (15 sq miles), is enclosed by the Díkti Mountains, and is one of the most fertile areas of Crete. Potatoes, fruits and cereals are the main crops grown here. There is no trace now of the windmills which pumped the underground water up here.

The Lassíthi Plateau was inhabited as early as Neolithic times. Remains of fortifications at entrance points to the plain indicate that it was a place of refuge for the Minoans. The tradition was retained by the Cretans as they fled here from the Venetians.

This led to all the inhabitants of the plateau being banished in 1263. All forms of land cultivation were forbidden then. As nothing changed for almost 200 years, the plain fell into obscurity. It was not until there was a long period of food shortages that the Venetians remembered the place at all. Then the land was recultivated and rented to the people.

After the victory of the Turks on Crete the place once again became a centre of resistance. The result was that in 1866 revenge was taken, and during the great uprising, the plain was completely laid to waste by 30,000 Turkish soldiers. Of the 21 villages encircling

A shepherd of Oros Díkti ponders.

the plain, **Tzermiádo** and **Psichró** are particularly noteworthy. North of Tzermiádo, the capital of the plateau, is the **Cave of Trapéza**. Arthur Evans discovered it and Pendlebury explored it. The latter was able to ascertain that it was used as a burial place in Neolithic times. Over 100 burial niches and similar finds dating from all epochs were discovered in the cave.

Of greater importance, however, is the **Díkti Cave** near Psichró. The popularity of this cave is reflected in the crowds that make their way here every day. A large car park has been constructed behind the village to cope with the traffic.

There are more mountain and tourist guides here than anywhere else on the island, so it's best to decide before you arrive, whether you would like a guide or not. The descent into the cave and some spots inside are a bit slippery, and engaging a knowledgeable guide might

be a good idea. Their charges are quite reasonable, too.

The cave can be reached in about 15 minutes if you enter from the southwest. Its importance stems from the fact that it is generally regarded as the birthplace of Zeus. Those interested in mythology will note that Zeus is the late Greek form of a Minoan boy god. He was the son of the fertility goddess who was worshipped in the cave. There is a small rock chamber called "The Cradle of Zeus" and a large stalactite named "The Coat of Zeus."

The many idols and votive offerings found in the cave are now displayed in the Archaeological Museum of Iráklion in Rooms 7 and 13.

Where else on the island of Crete could you find a more appropriate place to complete your trip? Here, at the end of your own 20th-century journey, you find yourself back at the beginning of Greek mythology.

ow over
ıs Díkti.

INSIGHT GUIDES
Travel Tips

FOR THOSE
WITH MORE THAN
A PASSING INTEREST
IN TIME...

Before you put your name down for a Patek Philippe watch *fig. 1*, there are a few basic things you might like to know, without knowing exactly whom to ask. In addressing such issues as accuracy, reliability and value for money, we would like to demonstrate why the watch we will make for you will be quite unlike any other watch currently produced.

"Punctuality", Louis XVIII was fond of saying, "is the politeness of kings."

We believe that in the matter of punctuality, we can rise to the occasion by making you a mechanical timepiece that will keep its rendezvous with the Gregorian calendar at the end of every century, omitting the leap-years in 2100, 2200 and 2300 and recording them in 2000 and 2400 *fig. 2*. Nevertheless, such a watch does need the occasional adjustment. Every 3333 years and 122 days you should remember to set it forward one day to the true time of the celestial clock. We suspect, however, that you are simply content to observe the politeness of kings. Be assured, therefore, that when you order your watch, we will be exploring for you the physical—if not the metaphysical—limits of precision.

Does everything have to depend on how much?

Consider, if you will, the motives of collectors who set record prices at auction to acquire a Patek Philippe. They may be paying for rarity, for looks or for micromechanical ingenuity. But we believe that behind each $500,000-plus

bid is the conviction that a Patek Philippe, even if 50 years old or older, can be expected to work perfectly for future generations.

In case your ambitions to own a Patek Philippe are somewhat discouraged by the scale of the sacrifice involved, may we hasten to point out that the watch we will make for you today will certainly be a technical improvement on the Pateks bought at auction? In keeping with our tradition of inventing new mechanical solutions for greater reliability and better time-keeping, we will bring to your watch innovations *fig. 3* inconceivable to our watchmakers who created the supreme wristwatches of 50 years ago *fig. 4*. At the same time, we will of course do our utmost to avoid placing undue strain on your financial resources.

Can it really be mine?

May we turn your thoughts to the day you take delivery of your watch? Sealed within its case is your watchmaker's tribute to the mysterious process of time. He has decorated each wheel with a chamfer carved into its hub and polished into a shining circle. Delicate ribbing flows over the plates and bridges of gold and rare alloys. Millimetric surfaces are bevelled and burnished to exactitudes measured in microns. Rubies are transformed into jewels that triumph over friction. And after many months—or even years—of work, your watchmaker stamps a small badge into the mainbridge of your watch. The Geneva Seal—the highest possible attestation of fine watchmaking *fig. 5*.

Looks that speak of inner grace *fig. 6.*

When you order your watch, you will no doubt like its outward appearance to reflect the harmony and elegance of the movement within. You may therefore find it helpful to know that we are uniquely able to cater for any special decorative needs you might like to express. For example, our engravers will delight in conjuring a subtle play of light and shadow on the gold case-back of one of our rare pocket-watches *fig. 7*. If you bring us your favourite picture, our enamellers will reproduce it in a brilliant miniature of hair-breadth detail *fig. 8*. The perfect execution of a double hobnail pattern on the bezel of a wristwatch is the pride of our casemakers and the satisfaction of our designers, while our chainsmiths will weave for you a rich brocade in gold *figs. 9 & 10*. May we also recommend the artistry of our goldsmiths and the experience of our lapidaries in the selection and setting of the finest gemstones? *figs. 11 & 12.*

How to enjoy your watch before you own it.

As you will appreciate, the very nature of our watches imposes a limit on the number we can make available. (The four Calibre 89 time-pieces we are now making will take up to nine years to complete). We cannot therefore promise instant gratification, but while you look forward to the day on which you take delivery of your Patek Philippe *fig. 13*, you will have the pleasure of reflecting that time is a universal and everlasting commodity freely available to be enjoyed by all.

Should you require information on any particular Patek Philippe watch, or even on watchmaking in general, we would be delighted to reply to your letter of enquiry. And if you send

fig. 1: The classic face of Patek Philippe.

fig. 4: Complicated wristwatches circa 1930 (left) and 1990. The golden age of watchmaking will always be with us.

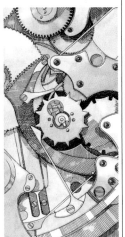

fig. 2: One of the 33 complications of the Calibre 89 astronomical clock-watch is a satellite wheel that completes one revolution every 400 years.

fig. 5: The Geneva Seal is awarded only to watches which achieve the standards of horological purity laid down in the laws of Geneva. These rules define the supreme quality of watchmaking.

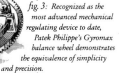

fig. 3: Recognized as the most advanced mechanical regulating device to date, Patek Philippe's Gyromax balance wheel demonstrates the equivalence of simplicity and precision.

fig. 6: Your pleasure in owning a Patek Philippe is the purpose of those who made it for you.

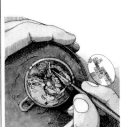

fig. 7: Arabesques come to life on a gold case-back.

fig. 8: An artist working six hours a day takes about four months to complete a miniature in enamel on the case of a pocket-watch.

fig. 9: Harmony of design is executed in a work of simplicity and perfection in a lady's Calatrava wristwatch.

fig. 10: The chainsmith's hands impart strength and delicacy to a tracery of gold.

fig. 11: Circles in gold: symbols of perfection in the making.

fig. 12: The test of a master lapidary is his ability to express the splendour of precious gemstones.

PATEK PHILIPPE
GENÈVE

fig. 13: The discreet sign of those who value their time.

your card marked "book catalogue" we shall post you a catalogue of our publications. Patek Philippe, 41 rue du Rhône, 1204 Geneva, Switzerland, Tel. +41 22/310 03 66.

So, you're getting away from it all.

Just make sure you can get back.

AT&T Access Numbers
Dial the number of the country you're in to reach AT&T.

*AUSTRIA†††	022-903-011	*GREECE	00-800-1311	NORWAY	800-190-11
*BELGIUM	0800-100-10	*HUNGARY	00◇-800-01111	POLAND¹◆³	0◇010-480-0111
BULGARIA	00-1800-0010	*ICELAND	999-001	PORTUGAL¹	05017-1-288
CANADA	1-800-575-2222	IRELAND	1-800-550-000	ROMANIA	01-800-4288
CROATIA¹◆	99-38-0011	ISRAEL	177-100-2727	*RUSSIA¹ (MOSCOW)	155-5042
*CYPRUS	080-90010	*ITALY	172-1011	SLOVAKIA	00-420-00101
CZECH REPUBLIC	00-420-00101	KENYA¹	0800-10	SOUTH AFRICA	0-800-99-0123
*DENMARK	8001-0010	*LIECHTENSTEIN	155-00-11	SPAIN•	900-99-00-11
*EGYPT¹ (CAIRO)	510-0200	LITHUANIA◆	8◇196	*SWEDEN	020-795-611
*FINLAND	9800-100-10	LUXEMBOURG	0-800-0111	*SWITZERLAND	155-00-11
FRANCE	19◇-0011	F.Y.R. MACEDONIA	99-800-4288	*TURKEY	00-800-12277
*GAMBIA	00111	*MALTA	0800-890-110	UK	0500-89-0011
GERMANY	0130-0010	*NETHERLANDS	06-022-9111	UKRAINE†	8◇100-11

Countries in bold face permit country-to-country calling in addition to calls to the U.S. **World Connect™** prices consist of **USADirect**¹ rates plus an additional charge based on the country you are calling. Collect calling available to the U.S. only. *Public phones require deposit of coin or phone card. ◇ Await second dial tone. ¹May not be available from every phone. †††Public phones require local coin payment through the call duration. ◆ Not available from public phones. • Calling available to most European countries. ¹Dial ''02'' first, outside Cairo. ³Dial 010-480-0111 from major Warsaw hotels. ©1994 AT&T.

Here's a travel tip that will make it easy to call back to the States. Dial the access number for the country you're in to get English-speaking AT&T operators or voice prompts. Minimize hotel telephone surcharges too.

If all the countries you're visiting aren't listed above, call **1 800 241-5555** for a free wallet card with all AT&T access numbers. Easy international calling from AT&T. **TrueWorld Connections.**

AT&T

TRAVEL TIPS

Getting Acquainted

THE PLACE

Crete is 260 km (160 miles) long, between 12 and 60 km (37 miles) wide, and the coastline is 1,046 km (650 miles) in length. It is the largest of the Greek islands and the fifth largest in the Mediterranean. The most characteristic feature of the landscape is the silvery olive trees, whose cultivation was intensified during Turkish rule.

The geography of Crete is largely determined by three massifs running the length of the island: in the far west the Lefká Ori (White Mountains) whose highest peak is Páchne at 2,452 m (8,045 ft); in the centre the Ida or Psilorítis range, with Crete's loftiest peak, Mount Ida, at 2,456 m (8,057 ft); and in the east the Díkti range, which reaches a height of 2,148 m (7,047). The mountains at the far eastern end of the island are gentler, with the highest peak, Aféndis Stavroménos, reaching 1,476 m (4,843 ft). Within Crete's mountain ranges are two large and several smaller fertile plateaux. Crete also has over 3,000 caves – approximately half of all the caves in Greece – owing to the crystalline consistency of the island's limestone crust. The majority of these underground cavities have yet to be explored. The island's gorges are predominantly located in the south, the longest and most famous being the Samariá Gorge.

FLORA AND FAUNA

The island of Crete is renowned for its abundance and variety of flowers and herbs. One tenth of more than 2,000 botanical species are indiginous. Two percent of the land is forest, mainly cypresses, pines, oaks, chestnuts, planes, tamarisk, juniper and eucalyptus. The native goat, the *krí-krí*, is protected. There are hares, rabbits and martens, and a number of birds of prey.

CLIMATE

The southernmost of the Greek islands, Crete enjoys an average of 320 sunny days per year; an average temperature of 30–35°C (86–95°F)in the summer (rarely rising as high as 40°C, 104°F) and 10–18°C (50–65°F) in the winter. In **spring** (April and May) the weather is clear but not yet debilitatingly hot – this is a lovely time to visit, when the island is relatively empty of tourists and the countryside is at its greenest. The hottest **summer** months are July and August. Then, in addition to the hot sun, there is a fierce northwesterly wind called the *meltémi* which can blow across the Aegean for days at a time; the other (less common) wind is the *lívas*, which comes up from the Sahara desert laden with dust and sand. During the **autumn** months (September and October) it is still hot enough to suntan and swim in the sea. **Winters** in Crete are mild, though it can suddenly become cold for short spells between November and February; the rainiest months.

In general, the south coast of Crete is both hotter and drier than the north coast. The mountains of the interior act as a block to the rain, so bad weather in the north is often not experienced in the south (and vice-versa). From autumn to late spring the mountains are covered in snow, and it is even possible to ski (see Sports on page 257).

POPULATION

There are 11 cities and 1,447 villages on Crete. The last census counted a population of 520,000, more than half of whom live in the Nomós Iráklion. Crete is divided into four governmental regions called *nomí*: Haniá, Réthimnon and Iráklion, with their respective capitals of the same names; and Lassíthi, with Agios Nikólaos as its capital. The individual *nomí* are subdivided into districts, known as *eparchíes*. In 1972, Iráklion replaced Haniá as the capital of the island. The prevailing religion is Greek Orthodox.

TIME DIFFERENCE

Greece is normally 2 hours ahead of Britain, 1 hour ahead of western European countries and 7 hours ahead of the US (Eastern Standard Time). Greek summertime – from the last Sunday in March to the last Sunday in September – does not coincide exactly with British summertime, so during certain periods the time difference is 3 hours (the cause of many a missed flight!).

ECONOMY

Although only about 30 percent of the land can be cultivated, Crete has an agricultural economy. The most important crops are olives, sultanas, grapes for table and wine, tomatoes, cucumbers, citrus fruits, bananas and carob. Sheep and goats are kept for wool, meat and cheese.

GOVERNMENT

Greece is a republic with a president, eleceted by parliament, who holds ceremonial executive power. The parliament is a single chamber of 300 deputies, led by the prime minister. There are three main parties: New Democracy (ND), PASOK (socialist) and KKE (communist)

PLANNING THE TRIP

WHAT TO BRING

The following items might come in handy on Crete: a decent map of the island (see Maps & Guidebooks on page 231); an alarm clock for early-morning buses or ferries; a torch for exploring caves; an AC adaptor for electrical appliances; mosquito repellent and pyrethrum incense coils (both also widely available on Crete); film (which is expensive on the island); suntan lotion (more expensive on Crete, though widely available); medical supplies (easily obtainable on the island but generally more expensive).

In the summer, bring light clothing made of natural fabrics and a sweater or windbreaker for the evening, when it can get quite cool. Sunglasses and a hat are also recommended, as well as comfortable walking shoes for visits to archaeological sites such as Knossós or trips up into the mountains. Rainwear should be taken for visits in the spring or autumn. During the winter months, warm clothing and rain gear are both needed, since it can get quite damp and buildings are often poorly heated. For visits to churches and monasteries, trousers should be worn by men (shorts are unacceptable) and skirts or dresses by women (no bare shoulders). Women especially should dress modestly when visiting rural villages away from the main tourist areas. As for formal attire, it is rarely needed in Crete.

Electricity

Greece runs on 220 volts/50 Hz AC. Plugs are two-pinned, so adaptors (available at any supermarket in Crete) are required for British electrical appliances and transformers for US ones.

Maps and Guides

Island maps are notoriously inaccurate, particularly those distributed by car rental agencies. You are better off buying a decent map before you leave home – Nelles, Freytag & Berndt, Bartholomew, Hildebrand, HarperCollins and GeoCenter are all perfectly adequate 1:200,000 maps. The best maps for walking in Crete are produced by Harms Verlag – there are five in their 1:80,000 series, covering the island from west to east.

On Crete itself, there are a number of local guidebooks published in English with information on the island's flora and fauna, museums and archaeological sites – these can be found at just about any *períptero* (kiosk) or foreign-language bookshop.

Youth and Student Cards

Students or anyone under 26 years of age are entitled to concessions on museum and archaeological site admissions. Students will need to produce a valid international student card, and under-26s will need an FIYTO youth card (available from STA Travel in Britain or Council Travel in the US).

ENTRY REGULATIONS

Visitors from EU countries (including Britain and Eire), Canada, the US, Australia and New Zealand need only a valid passport and can stay for a period of up to three months. For longer stays a resident's permit must be obtained from the local police in Crete.

Customs regulations

Into Greece: Visitors from EU countries may bring the following goods duty-free into Greece (note that the same quantities apply to duty-paid goods from outside the EC): 200 cigarettes or 100 cigarillos or 50 cigars or 250 g tobacco (18 years or over); 2 litres wine or 1 litre spirits or 2 litres liqueurs (18 years or over); 60 ml perfume; 250 ml eau de toilette. Allowances for duty-paid goods from within the EC are significantly more generous. (For currency restrictions see page 232.)

Visitors using a prescription drug should bring a copy of the prescription to avoid any possible problems at customs. Note that the drug codeine (fairly common in headache pills) has been officially banned in Greece.

Out of Greece: Visitors from EU countries can bring home the same quantities of duty-free goods as are listed above. Note that the export of antiquities and archaeological artifacts from Greece is strictly prohibited.

HEALTH

There are no inoculations required for visitors to Greece, though tetanus and typhoid boosters are recommended. Under EU regulations, British and other EU nationals are entitled to free medical care in Greece (for UK residents to qualify an E111 form must be presented – these are available at any British post office). It should be noted, however, that public health facilities are limited in Greece and private doctors are sometimes the only satisfactory option. Comprehensive travel insurance is a sensible precaution – available from travel agents, banks and insurance brokers, this covers both private medical treatment and loss or theft of personal property.

Personal safety

The main health hazard in Crete is overexposure to

the sun – wear a hat and sunglasses during the summer months and use a high-factor suntan lotion, especially for the first week or so. Also, be sure to drink plenty of fluids to avoid any danger of dehydration.

The three underwater hazards to be aware of are sea urchins, jellyfish and weevers. Sea urchins are the most common – if you step on one of these use a sterilised needle and olive oil to extract the spine. Jellyfish stings can be relieved by ammonia or urine. Weevers are an extremely rare fish that bury themselves under the sand with only their venomous spines protruding; if you do tread on one, immerse your foot in very hot water and call for medical help immediately.

CURRENCY

The Greek unit of currency is the drachma (*drahmí* in Greek; plural *drahmés*). The most common denominations are notes worth 50, 100, 500, 1,000 and 5,000 drachmas and coins of 5, 10, 20 and 50 drachmas. You are officially allowed to bring into Greece no more than 100,000 drachmas, though any amount of foreign currency and travellers' cheques may be imported. Anything over US$1,000 (or equivalent) should be declared on entry, in case this money needs to be exported again.

There are banks in all major towns and resorts, but be prepared for long queues (see Buisness Hours on page 247). Exchange facilities are also available at post offices (which often offer a better rate than the banks), travel agents, hotels and tourist offices. Always take your passport with you when exchanging money or cashing travellers' cheques, and check the rates and commission charges beforehand, as they vary considerably. In the main towns, local currency can also be withdrawn on a credit card at most cashpoint machines.

Eurocheques are accepted by banks and post offices but not shops, while major credit cards are accepted by the more expensive shops, hotels and restaurants, as well as all car rental agencies.

PUBLIC HOLIDAYS

Listed below are the most important public holidays in Greece, when all banks, post offices, shops and offices are closed. If a holiday falls on a Sunday, the Monday is also a holiday.
New Year's Day (*Protochroniá*): 1 January. St Basil's Day, when you may be offered a sprig of basil as a symbol of hospitality.
Epiphany (*Agia Theofánia*): 6 January. Water is blessed in commemoration of the Baptism of Christ; this involves a crucifix being cast into the local harbour, which is then recovered by as many young men as are prepared to brave the icy waters.
Pre-Lenten carnivals: three weeks of festivities ending on Clean Monday.
Clean Monday (*Kathará Deftéra*): movable date,

occurring seven weeks before Easter Monday; marks the beginning of Orthodox Lent.
Independence Day and the **Feast of the Annunciation** (*Evangelismós*): 25 March. Both a national and religious holiday; parades in all the major towns to celebrate the beginning of the revolt against Turkish rule in 1821, and church services to honour the announcement of the Incarnation to the Virgin Mary.
Greek Orthodox Easter (*Páscha*): Good Friday to Easter Monday. The Orthodox Easter occurs up to a month after the Catholic/Protestant Easter. This is the holiest time of year, the culmination of the 40-day fasting period (Lent) and the entire Orthodox year. On Holy Saturday Midnight Mass is celebrated by the Orthodox faithful in churches throughout the country, and on Sunday thousands of lambs are sacrificed for roasting.
Labour Day (*Protomayá*): 1 May. A popular day for picnics in the country; people pick flowers and bind them into wreaths to decorate their cars and home.
Pentecost (*Agíou Pnévmatos*): movable date, occurring seven weeks after Easter Monday.
Assumption of the Virgin (*Kímisis tis Panagías*): 15 August.
Ohi Day: 28 October. Celebrates the Greeks' answer ("*óhi*" meaning no) to Mussolini's 1940 ultimatum; parades and folk dancing.
Christmas Day (*Christoúgenna*): 25 December.
Boxing Day (*Sínaksis tis Theotókou*): 26 December.

Local festivals
Businesses normally remain open during the following local festivals, religious ceremonies and commemoration days, which can provide entertainment and good opportunities for photographs.
1st Sunday after Easter: *Agios Thomás*; celebrated at Vrondissí Monastery near Iráklion.
23 April: *Agios Geórgios* (St George, patron saint of shepherds); celebrated in many rural villages around the island (postponed until the Monday after Easter if the date falls during Lent). Sheep shearing festival in Asigonía.
8 May: *Ioánnis o Theológos* (John the Evangelist); celebrated at Préveli Monastery near Réthimnon.
20–27 May: *Máchi tis Krítis* (Battle of Crete); celebrations in Haniá and a different village each year to commemorate the German air attack in 1941.
24 June: Summer solstice/*Ioánnis o Pródromos* (John the Baptist); bonfires and festivities.
Late June: Naval Week; fireworks and celebrations in Soúda and elsewhere.
20 July: *Profítis Ilías* (Prophet Elijah); celebrated on mountain-top shrines and villages named after him.
26 July: *Agía Paraskeví*; celebrated at the Skotinó Cave east of Iráklion.
Late July: Wine festival in Réthimnon; a week of music, dancing and wine sampling.
July and August: Iráklion Festival; cultural events from folk dancing to modern drama.

American Express offers Travelers Cheques built for two.

Cheques *for Two*℠ from American Express are the Travelers Cheques that allow either of you to use them because both of you have signed them. And only one of you needs to be present to purchase them.

Cheques *for Two* are accepted anywhere regular American Express Travelers Cheques are, which is just about everywhere. So stop by your bank, AAA* or any American Express Travel Service Office and ask for Cheques *for Two*.

A Wise Man Never Thinks How Far He's Come. He Thinks How Far He Can Still Travel.

REMY XO BECAUSE LIFE IS WHAT YOU MAKE IT

6 August: *Metamórfosis* (Transfiguration of Christ); celebrated on Mount Joúchtas near Arhánes.

Mid-August: Sitía Sultana Festival; a week-long celebration of the harvest.

15 August: *Kímissis tis Panagías* (Assumption of the Virgin Mary); celebrated at many villages as well as the monasteries of Faneroméni, Hrissoskalítissa, etc.

25 August: *Agios Títos* (patron saint of the island); big procession in Iráklion.

27 August: *Agios Fanoúrios*; celebrated at Valsamónero Monastery, outside the village of Vorízia.

29 August: *Agios Ioánnis* (John the Baptist); commemoration of the beheading of Saint John the Baptist. Major pilgrimage to the church of Agios Ioánnis on the Rodopós peninsula west of Haniá and mass baptism of boys named John.

14 September: *Tímios Stavrós* (Raising of the Cross); celebrated in Axós, Anógia and Réthimnon; procession to Aféndis Stavroménos.

Mid-October: Elos Chestnut Festival; celebration of the chestnut harvest in Elos and other villages.

3 November: *Agios Geórgios o Methistís* (Saint George who "makes the others drunk"); a day for tasting the new wine and the fresh *tsikouthiá* (Crete's version of *rakí*).

7–9 November: Big celebrations to commemorate the anniversary of the holocaust at Arkádi Monastery on 8 November 1866.

11 November: *Agios Minás*, patron saint of Iráklion.

21 November: *Panagías Isódia* (Mary's introduction to the Temple); celebrated in Haniá and Réthimnon, of which Mary is the patron saint.

3 December: *Agios Nikólaos*; festivities in Agios Nikólaos, of which Saint Nicholas is patron saint.

GETTING THERE

By Air

There are three ways to get to Crete by air:

1. Direct charter flight to Crete, arriving in Iráklion or Haniá
2. Scheduled flight to Athens, then connecting flight to Crete
3. Scheduled or charter flight to Athens, then ferry to Crete

There are no international scheduled flights direct to Crete so most visitors arrive on charter flights either as part of a package holiday or on a flight-only deal. Direct charters are to Iráklion and less frequently to Haniá; they depart from regional airports in the UK (flight time: 4 hours), as well as from Ireland and other European cities (no direct flights from the US).

Greek airline regulations require that visitors arriving on charters must stay for a minimum of three days and a maximum of four weeks and must have accommodation on Crete – in practice this means being issued an accommodation voucher which is not intended to be used.

All scheduled flights involve changing planes in Athens. For airlines apart from Olympic Airways, this means changing terminals, too (to be on the safe side allow about 30 minutes for this, as the two terminals are a bus ride apart). Olympic Airways, the main carrier, operates direct flights from Britain (London, Heathrow) and from the US (New York) to Athens. The airline also runs up to eight scheduled flights daily from Athens to Iráklion (flight time: 50 minutes) and from six flights daily to Haniá (flight time: 45 minutes).

Most airlines require passengers to confirm their return passage a few days before departure – it is advisable to do this to avoid overbooking problems.

Olympic Airways in Britain:
11 Conduit Street, London W1R OLP
Tel: (0171)409 2400.
In the US:
645 Fifth Avenue, New York 10022
Tel: (212) 838 3600.

By Sea

Bear in mind that ferry schedules change frequently, especially between the summer and winter seasons. The best place to gain up-to-date information is from the Greek tourist office, or from any travel agent in Greece (the latter also sell ferry tickets).

From the Greek mainland: ANEK and Minoan shipping lines operate daily car and passenger ferry services from Piraeus (the port of Athens) to Iráklion and Haniá (Soúda Bay). Both trips take approximately 12 hours and run through the night, leaving Piraeus in the early evening (berths and cabins available). Another company, Rethimniakí, offers a service from Piraeus to Réthimnon several times weekly. Ferries also run between the Peloponnese and the island of Kíthira, from where there are connecting services to Kastélli in western Crete.

From other Greek islands: There are frequent ferries from many of the Cycladic islands (daily from Santoríni/Thíra). A regular ferry service also operates from Rhodes to Agios Nikólaos, Sitía and Iráklion.

From Italy: Ferries run regularly from Brindisi, Ancona, Bari and Otranto in Italy via the Greek island of Corfu to Pátra and Igoumenítsa on the Greek mainland (connecting ferries to Crete are described above). Two shipping lines, Adriatica and Marlines, offer a direct service from Italy to Crete in July and August – the former runs from Venice to Iráklion and the latter from Ancona to Pátra and Iráklion. It is essential to book all ferries in advance if travelling by car during peak season.

From Cyprus and Israel: Ferries run weekly to Iráklion from Limassol, Cyprus and Haifa, Israel.

By Train

The main rail route from London to Athens takes around three and a half days, travelling down through France and Italy, and crossing over to Greece by ferry from the Adriatic port of Brindisi. (The train across the continent to Athens via

Belgrade is no longer possible through the former Yugoslavia.)

Regular train tickets are valid for two months and allow as many stops as you like on a pre-selected route; all ferry crossings are included.

Rail passes: An Inter-Rail pass represents the best value for money for anyone under 26 years of age. It allows one month of unlimited 2nd-class travel on all European railways (34 percent reduction within Britain and reduced rates on some ferries). Anyone living outside Europe and North Africa can buy a Eurailpass before leaving home or within six months of arriving in Britain. This permits unlimited 2nd-class travel on European railways for anyone under 26, and unlimited 1st-class travel for anyone 26 and over. Senior citizens can obtain a Rail Europ Senior card which gives a 30 percent reduction on the regular fare.

By Coach

The cheapest – and most strenuous – way of travelling to Greece from Britain is by coach , which takes three and a half days via France and Italy. Eurolines provides the most reliable service; tickets are available from any National Express office. For further information from the UK:

Eurolines (UK) Ltd, 52 Grosvenor Gardens, London SW1W OAU. Tel: (0171) 730 8235.

By Car

Taking a car on to the island of Crete can be an expensive business, and car hire should be considered as an alternative.

The main route from London to Athens is through France and Italy, a distance of approximately 2,400 km/1,500 miles (not including the ferry crossing from Italy to Greece). The route via the former Yugoslavia is possible but it is no longer recommended: ask your local motoring organisation before setting out. Otherwise, for those determined to travel overland all the way to Greece, the best alternative route is via France, Belgium, Germany, Austria, Hungary, Romania and Bulgaria, arriving over the border in northeast Greece.

Before setting out consult the Greek tourist office or a motoring organisation such as the AA for advice on insurance requirements and any special regulations for countries en route. A national driving licence, vehicle registration documents and third-party insurance are all compulsory – though comprehensive cover is strongly recommended. If you are passing through any non-EU countries, an international driving permit and green insurance card will also be required (otherwise your cover will be third party only).

Many countries – including Greece – insist that you carry a first-aid kit, warning triangle and fire extinguisher. For a small fee the AA will provide up-to-date itineraries, including details on major road-works and other possible delays.

Petrol stations: *see Getting Around on page 250.*

Disabled Travellers

There are precious few facilities for assisting the disabled on Crete. Wheelchair users are advised to plan their trip carefully before they leave – the mountainous terrain of the island's interior and the poor state of the roads and sidewalks are a major obstacle to getting around. Organisations such as Holiday Care Service (Tel: (01293) 774535), in the UK, are worth contacting for advice.

Travelling with Children

The Greeks love children and they are welcomed pretty well everywhere. For younger children, baby-sitting services are offered by many hotels as well as "rooms" establishments (enquire before you check in). Buses are free for anyone under eight years of age. The sea is generally safe for kids, but do keep a keen eye on them as lifeguards are virtually non-existent in Crete; also be aware of the hazards of overexposure to the sun.

Embassies

Greece has diplomatic representation in all the major captails of the world.

Australia: 9 Turrana Street, Yarralumla, Canberra, ACT 26000. Tel: 73 3158.
Canada: 76280 MacLaren Street, Ottowa, Ontario K2POK6. Tel: 238 6271.
UK: 1a Holland Park, London W11 3TG. Tel: 0171 221.
USA: 2221 Massachusetts Avenue NW, Washington DC 20008. Tel: 667 3169.

Tourist Offices

The National Tourist Organisation of Greece (*Ellinikós Organismós Tourismoú* or EOT) maintains offices in most European capitals, North America and Australia. They will provide free of charge maps and brochures on Crete (in English), bus and ferry schedules, opening times of museums and archaeological sites, as well as hotel listings.

Australia: 51 Pitt Street, Sydney, NSW 2000; Tel: 241 1663, fax: 235 2174
Canada: 1300 Bay Sreet, Toronto, Ontario M5R 3K8; Tel: 968 2220, fax: 968 6533;
233 rue de la Montagne, Suite 101 Montreal, Quebec H3G 1Z2; Tel: 871 1535, fax: 871 1498
UK: 4 Conduit Street London W1R 0DJ; Tel: (0171)734 5997, fax: (0171 287 1369
USA: Olympic Tower, 645 Fifth Avenue, New York, NY 10022; Tel: 421 5777, fax: 826 6940;
611 West Sixth Street, Suite 2198, Los Angeles, California 90017; Tel: 626 6696, fax: 489 9744;
168 North Michigan Avenue, Chicago, Illinois 60601; Tel: 782 1084, fax 782 1091

Swatch. The others just watch.

seahorse/fall winter 94-95

shockproof
splashproof
priceproof
boreproof
swiss made

swatch+
SCUBA 200

INSIGHT GUIDES

COLORSET NUMBERS

PRACTICAL TIPS

EMERGENCIES

Crime
The crime rate in Crete is extremely low. Nevertheless, it is wise to keep cars and hotel rooms locked, and to watch your handbag in public. If you do have anything stolen, contact the police or tourist police (see Emergency Numbers below).

Foreign visitors are strongly advised against importing or using drugs in Greece. Possession of even small amounts can result in jail sentences of up to a year; anyone caught dealing can expect a much longer sentence.

Lost Property
Honesty is a matter of pride among the Cretans, so if you leave something behind in a shop or restaurant, chances are the proprietor will have scrupulously kept it to one side for you. If you do have any problems, however, then contact the tourist police (see Emergency Numbers below).

Pharmacies
Pharmacies (*farmakía*) are recognised by a red or green cross on a white background. Greek pharmacists are highly trained and can usually advise on treatments for minor complaints. They are also able to dispense a number of medicines which in other countries are available only on prescription. In the larger towns pharmacists operate a rota to provide 24-hour cover – details are posted in pharmacy windows.

Drinking Water
Tap water is safe to drink anywhere on the island, although it's usually bottled water that's offered to you at restaurants and tavernas. In people's homes, there is often a hot and cold tap for general purposes, and a separate tap for drinking water.

EMERGENCY NUMBERS

Police: 100
Ambulance/first aid: 166
Fire: 199
Road assistance: 174

Tourist police:
Iráklion: (081) 283190

Haniá: (0821) 51111 or (0821) 71111
Réthimnon: (0831) 28156
Agios Nikólaos: (0841) 26900

Hospitals:
Iráklion: (081) 237502 or (081) 239502 or (081) 269111
Haniá: (0821) 43811 or (0821) 44421
Réthimnon: (0831) 27491 or (0831) 27814
Agios Nikólaos: (0841) 25227

WEIGHTS & MEASURES
Greece uses the metric system. For quick and easy conversion, remember that 1 inch is roughly 2.5 cm, a metre is roughly one yard, 4 oz is just over 100 grammes and a kilogramme is just over 2 lb. As one kilometre is about five-eighths of a mile, so 40 km is 25 miles.

BUSINESS HOURS
Crete is a law unto itself when it comes to opening hours, which change with exasperating frequency. The best advice is to check everything with the EOT tourist office, and hope for the best that what they tell you is true.

Archaeological sites and museums. Opening hours vary considerably from site to site and from season to season. Summer hours – from about the beginning of April to the end of September – are longer than winter hours, though closing days usually remain the same. On public holidays and festivals most museums and sites either close entirely or open for Sunday hours only. The archaeological museums at Iráklion, Haniá and Réthimnon are normally open every day; the Agios Nikólaos, Sitía and Ierápetra archaeological museums are closed on Monday. Knossós, Agía Triáda and Festós archaeological sites are open daily; Górtis, Gourniá, Mália, Tílissos and Zákros are closed on Monday. Most sites remain open over the lunch hour, though the smaller ones often do not (never mind what the official schedules might say!). Closing times vary from as early as 3pm to as late as 7pm. However, except at the major archaeological sites, it is often possible to wander round outside the opening hours, as in many cases there is no enclosing perimeter fence.

Monasteries and convents. As a rule, they are open from 9am (or earlier) to 1 or 2pm, when they close their doors for an afternoon siesta, usually reopening from 5 to 7pm.

Banks: In general, opening hours are from 8am to 2pm Monday–Friday (Friday 1.30pm). In the larger towns, one bank will re-open its change desk from 5 or 5.30 to 7pm and for a few hours on Saturday. Bureaux de change may have more flexible hours.

Post offices. Local post offices are open from about 7.30am to 2.30 or 3.30pm Monday–Friday. Main post offices in large towns and post office caravans in tourist areas are generally open from 8am–8pm

Monday–Friday; the latter also open from 8am–8pm Saturday and 9am–6pm Sunday.

TIPPING

Service is included on most bills, but tips are still appreciated – the percentage given is usually quite small compared to other European countries. In smaller restaurants or tavernas, a tip of 5 to 10 percent is appropriate; in bars and cafés about 5 percent, or whatever loose change you might have. In the case of hotel dining rooms and smarter restaurants, a 10 or 15 percent service charge is usually already included, so either leave nothing or whatever change is left over after the bill has been paid.

Taxi-drivers do not expect tips, but they are not averse to them either – 10 percent is about right. Lavatory (toilet) attendants also expect a small contribution, as do cinema usherettes, hotel porters and chambermaids.

RELIGION

The island's population is virtually entirely Greek Orthodox. There are no Anglican or other Protestant churches on the island, nor is there a synagogue or mosque. Catholic churches are to found in Iráklion, Haniá, Réthimnon and Agios Nikólaos.

NUDE BATHING

Nude bathing is officially forbidden in Crete except on a few designated beaches. In practice it is more widespread, but be aware that Crete is still a very conservative society and it is extremely offensive to some Cretans, especially the older generation. Choose a beach that is either well secluded or well established as a nudist beach. Topless bathing is tolerated on most beaches in Crete.

THE MEDIA

Newspapers

Foreign newspapers are available at *períptera* (kiosks) and bookshops in all the major towns and resorts – they are usually a day old and the mark-up is substantial. Considerably cheaper and also widely available is the English-language daily *Athens News*. The larger hotels are often the best place to find magazines and weekly papers.

Radio and TV

Local Greek radio stations broadcast regular news bulletins in English, French and German. With a shortwave transistor radio you'll also be able to pick up the BBC World Service and Voice of America in the early morning and evening.

Most hotels have TV rooms and you'll find virtually all English-language programmes are subtitled rather than dubbed.

POSTAL SERVICES

Postboxes are bright yellow and, if there are two slots to choose from, *esterikó* means inland and *exoterikó* means overseas. Post offices (*tachydromeía*) and are also recognisable by their bright yellow signs – main branches will usually change money in addition to handling mail, but long-distance phone calls must be made from an OTE office (see Telephones below). Stamps (*grammatósima*) can be purchased at any post office or *períptero* (kiosk); the latter usually charge a small commission. Air-mail letters take anywhere from four days to a week to get to most European countries and just over a week to reach North America; for postcards allow anywhere from two weeks to a month.

The Poste Restante system is widely used in Crete – mail should be clearly marked Poste Restante, with the addressee's surname underlined and the name of the town to which it is being sent. Be sure to bring a passport or some other proof of identity when collecting mail.

TELEPHONES

Local calls can be made from hotel lobbies, *períptera* (kiosks), *kafeneía* (cafés) or telephone booths with a blue band. For international long-distance calls there are several options available: any telephone box with an orange band (assuming it actually works); any *períptero* with a metered phone; or any OTE (*Organismós Tilepikinonión Elládos*) office. The latter is the cheapest option, and indeed the only one if you plan to reverse the charges. A word of warning, however: the patience of Job is required at just about any OTE office – be prepared for long queues, and, when you finally succeed in getting a booth, be prepared to have to dial your number a dozen or more times before getting through. Operator-assisted calls can also take anything up to an hour to connect.

For international calls, dial 00, then the country code (44 for the UK; 1 for the US and Canada) followed by the number itself (leaving off the initial zero). Useful telephone numbers are listed below.
Operator: 151
International operator: 161
Local directory enquiries: 131
International directory enquiries: 01 169

TOURIST OFFICES

The National Tourist Organisation of Greece (*Ellinikós Organismós Tourismoú* or EOT) maintains offices throughout Greece. They will provide free of charge maps and brochures on Crete (in English), bus and ferry schedules, opening times of museums and archaeological sites, as well as hotel listings. EOT offices on Crete are located in:
Iráklion: Xanthoulidou 1 (opposite the Archaeological Museum); Tel: (081) 228225 or (081)

226081 or (081) 228203, fax: (081) 226020
Réthimnon: El. Venizélou Avenue (on the beach); Tel: (0831) 29148
Haniá: Kriári 40; Tel: (0821) 92624

EMBASSIES

All the main embassies in Greece are based in Athens. Addresses include:
British: Ploutárchou 1, 106–175 Athens; Tel: (01) 723 6211–9
American: Vassilíssis Sofías 91, 115–121 Athens; Tel: (01) 721 2951–9 or (01) 721 8400
Australian: D. Soútsou 37, 115–121 Athens; Tel: (01) 644 7303
Canadian: Gennadíou 4, Ypsilántou, 115–121 Athens; Tel: (01) 723 9511–9

Consulates in Crete
British: Papalexándrou 16, Iráklion; Tel: (081) 224012
Dutch: 25 Avgoústou 23, Iráklion; Tel: (081) 246202
German: Zográfou 7, Iráklion; Tel: (081) 226288

GETTING AROUND

DISTANCES

Iráklion, the main town on Crete, is 320 km (200 miles) from Athens.

From Iráklion to:
Knossós	5 km (3 miles)
Arhánes	14 km (9 miles)
Hersónissos	26 km (16 miles)
Kastélli/Pediáda	36 km (22 miles)
Festós	62 km (39 miles)
Agios Viánnos	65 km (40 miles)
Agios Nikólaos	70 km (44 miles)
Matala	75 km (47 miles)
Réthimnon	78 km (49 miles)
Agía Galíni	84 km (53 miles)
Haniá	137 km (85 miles)

Réthimnon to:
Moní Préveli	37 km (23 miles)
Amári	39 km (24 miles)
Agía Galíni	62 km (39 miles)
Hóra Sfakíon	70 km (44 miles)
Haniá	58 km (36 miles)

Haniá to:
Kastélli	42 km (26 miles)
Omalós	42 km (26 miles)
Hóra Sfakíon	72 km (45 miles)
Paleóhora	75 km (47 miles)
Soúgia	70 km (44 miles)

Agios Nikólaos to:
Kritsá	11 km (7 miles)
Eloúnda	12 km (8 miles)
Ierápetra	36 km (22 miles)
Sitía	73 km (45 miles)
Moní Toploú	91 km (57 miles)
Palékastro	94 km (58 miles)
Zákros	110 km (68 miles)

PUBLIC TRANSPORT

Taxis
Taxis are plentiful in the main towns and very cheap – especially if shared. They can be flagged down on the street or found in ranks by the harbour, bus and train stations. Within the towns they generally run on meters, which are set at "1" during the day and "2" (double fare) at night. For trips further afield a fare should be agreed in advance – if there are several of you a trip of some length can prove quite economical, and may be not add up to much more than the cost of going by bus. By taking taxis you are also likely to benefit from the driver's knowledge of the area.

Rural villages generally have at least one taxi (*agoréon*). It is usually possible to arrange for the driver to drop you off somewhere and pick you up a few hours later, or alternatively, you can negotiate a private sightseeing tour (again, it is worth checking the fare before setting off).

Note that a tip of about 10 percent is customary, but not obligatory, for taxi-drivers.

Buses
Buses are the only form of public transport on the island. Run by a group of companies known as KTEL, they are modern, reliable and inexpensive. There are frequent services connecting Iráklion, Agios Nikólaos, Haniá and Réthimnon, as well services to the main archaeological sites, the Samarian Gorge and many of the island's villages. Each city has its own bus terminal (or terminals) – just ask for the "KTEL". Timetables (also in English) can be obtained there, as well as at travel agencies, tourist information offices and the airport.

Coach tours
Coach tours are offered by most travel agents on the island. These include trips to the major archaeological sites, the Samarian Gorge, various beaches, as well as excursions into the mountains. If you don't have your own transportation, this is certainly an option worth considering, though obviously don't expect to go anywhere off the beaten track this way.

Driving in Crete

(See also Getting There: By Car on page 234.)
Driving is on the right in Greece and road signs follow standard European conventions, though on country byways you may come across some signs in Greek only. There is a good network of roads on the island, and what your road map may still show as a gravel road may turn out to be paved. A word of caution, nonetheless: the Cretan style of driving takes some getting used to – on highways motorists pass on the right or left without warning and frequently use the hard shoulder as an extra lane; in villages red lights are commonly viewed as a suggestion rather than a rule.

High speeds (usually not possible anyway) are not recommended – there are too many unexpected hazards, whether it be a paved road that suddenly becomes a dirt track without warning, a huge pothole or rock in the middle of the road, or an entire herd of sheep appearing out of nowhere. The speed limit on national highways is 100 kph (62 mph) for cars and 70 kph (44 mph) for motorbikes; on country roads it is 70 kph and in towns 50 kph (31 mph).

Although usually ignored, the use of seatbelts in cars is required by law, as are helmets for motorcyclists. Every so often the police clamp down and on-the-spot fines are dished out. Parking and speeding tickets must be paid at the local police station or car rental agency – be sure to ask for a receipt.

Should you break down or require emergency road assistance while driving on the island, the number to ring is 174. The **Automobile and Touring Club of Greece** (ELPA) will also help members of affiliated motoring organisations such as the AA or RAC. Their numbers are as follows – Iráklion: (081) 289440; Réthimnon: (0831) 20554; Haniá: (0821) 26059; Agios Nikólaos: (0841) 22620.

Car Hire

There are scores of car rental agencies on the island offering the normal range of hire cars as well as four-wheel-drive vehicles. International companies such as Avis and Hertz are considerably more expensive than their local counterparts, who are generally just as reliable. Whoever you rent from, be sure to check carefully the insurance being offered – full coverage is strongly recommended – and whether it is included in the price quoted. Payment by credit card is usually preferred; if not a large cash deposit will be requested. You will need to produce an international driving permit or a valid national licence that has been held for at least one year (a passport is also sometimes requested). The minimum age for renting a car in Crete varies from 18 to 21, depending on the agency.

Bicycle and Motorbike Hire

Motorbikes, mopeds and bicycles are widely avail-able in all the resort towns. Mopeds are ideal for short distances on reasonably flat terrain, but the interior is too mountainous for anything but a motorbike. Make sure, whatever you hire, that the vehicle is in good condition and that the price includes proper insurance. Be sure too to wear a helmet – all rental outfits have them, though often they won't actually give you one unless you ask.

Petrol Stations

Petrol stations are plentiful in towns, but harder to find in rural areas – always set out with a full tank if you're planning to travel any distance. The price of fuel is comparable to other European countries and unleaded petrol is available in all the main tourist resorts. Filling stations are generally open on weekdays from 7am–7pm and Saturday till 3pm; a few also stay open all night and on Sunday.

Public transport is exceptionally cheap on Crete, so hitching is really only worthwhile if you are trying to get somewhere out of the way (or if you've missed the last bus back!). Allow plenty of time in rural areas as there's usually not much in the way of traffic and rides are often short. Although Crete is a relatively safe place to hitch, women travellers are advised not to travel alone and to dress modestly.

WHERE TO STAY

Most visitors come to Crete on a package tour which includes pre-booked accommodation – this means that during the high season many of the larger, more luxurious resort hotels are fully booked in advance by foreign tour operators. There are, however, decent hotels to be had in all the towns, ranging from A-class downwards. Official tourist offices – called the EOT (National Tourist Organisation of Greece) – can also provide a comprehensive list of hotels and pensions, giving all facilities and prices. Alternatively, when you arrive in a new town, park your car and explore the old quarter on foot – you'll usually find a convivial hotel or pension fairly quickly (see also Places to Rent and Youth Hostels page 241). Another solution – which on a warm, starry night can be very pleasant indeed – is "roof-space" – i.e. a mattress on the roof of a cheap hotel or taverna.

The list below covers hotels and pensions in and around the main tourist resorts of Haniá, Réthimnon, Iráklion, Eloúnda, Agios Nikólaos, Sitía and Ierápetra. Hotels are graded by the tourist police as Luxury, A, B, C, D or E, and pensions as Luxury, A, B, C, D or E – note that all except the top category (Luxury) have to keep within set price limits.

HANIÁ

Amfora. Theotokopoúlou 20. Tel: (0821) 93224, fax: (0821) 93226. Beautifully restored 13th-century mansion with lovely views of the Venetian harbour from some of the 14 rooms. A-class. Open year-round.

Casa Delfino. Theofánous 9. Tel: (0821) 93098, fax: (0821) 96500. 17th-century Venetian mansion in the heart of the old town. Most of the 12 air-conditioned rooms are on two levels and overlook the medieval harbour. B-class. Open year-round.

Contessa. Theofánous 15. Tel: (0821) 98565, fax: (0821) 98566. Refurbished Venetian house with six rooms furnished in traditional Cretan style. Needs to be booked well in advance. A-class. Open March–November.

Dóma. Eleftheríou Venizélou 124. Tel: (0821) 21772 or (0821) 21773, fax: (0821) 21775. A converted 19th-century mansion in the suburb of Halepa decorated in tradtional Cretan style; formerly the Austrian consulate and British vice-consulate. B-class. Open March–October.

Eva. Theofánous and Zambelíou. Tel: (0821) 55319. Small 6-bedroom pension in a renovated Venetian house with wooden ceilings and brass beds. Open April–November.

Piraeús. Zambelíou 10, 73100 Haniá. Tel: (0821) 54154, fax: (0821) 94665. Fairly basic E-class hotel, but clean, friendly and full of character with a wonderful location overlooking the harbour. Open year-round.

Porto Veneziano. Aktí Enósseos. Tel: (0821) 59311 or (0821) 29312 or (0821) 59313, fax: (0821) 44053. Modern but comfortable B-class hotel on the waterfront. 63 air-conditioned rooms with balconies overlooking the Venetian harbour. Open year-round.

Thereza. Angélou 8. Tel: (0821) 40118. Beautifully restored Venetian house with magnificent views from its rooftop terrace and rooms. Needs to be booked well in advance during high season.

Villa Andromeda. Eleftheríou Venizélou 150. Tel: (0821) 45263 or (0821) 45264, fax: (0821) 45265. Formerly the German consulate, a beautifully restored neoclassical mansion with views over the sea and mountains. B-class. Open year-round.

RÉTHIMNON

Achíllion. Arkadíou 151. Tel: (0831) 22581. Run-down but atmospheric E-class hotel in a good, central location; can be noisy at night. Open year-round.

Brascos. Daskaláki 1, corner of Moátsou. Tel: (0831) 23721. Clean though somewhat bland B-class hotel with views of the harbour from its balconies. Open year-round.

Fortezza. Melissinoú 16. Tel: (0831) 21551, fax: (0831) 20073. Modern B-class hotel on the edge of the old town below the Venetian fortress, three minutes from the beach. Excellent value for money. Tennis courts and swimming pool. Open year-round.

Garden House. N. Foká 82. Tel: (0831) 28586. Small historical building near the fortress with lovely rooms.

Ideon. Platía Plastíra 10. Tel: (0831) 28667. B-class hotel with a small swimming pool and a good location by the ferry dock. Open year-round.

Kyma Beach. Platía Iróon. Tel: (0831) 21503 or (0831) 21504, fax: (0831) 22353. Comfortable C-class hotel overlooking the town beach. 40 rooms with shower. Open April–October.

Liberty. Moátsou 8, corner of Prevalaki. Tel and fax: (0831) 21851. Friendly, family-run B-class hotel opposite a park. Attractive rooftop terrace with a view of the harbour and 24 rooms with shower.

Porto Réthymno. Paralía. Tel: (0831) 20821, fax: (0831) 27825. Opened in 1992 and five minutes from the town centre, this modern hotel has more the feel of a resort with its own beachfront, watersports, swimming pool, fitness club, Jacuzzi and Turkish bath. 200 air-conditioned rooms with bath.

Rithymna Beach. Adelianós Kámbos, 7 km (4½ miles) east of Réthimnon. Tel: (0831) 29491, fax: (0831) 71441. Mammoth A-class resort complex with 556 rooms and bungalows on its own private beach. Almost always full in season – needs to be booked well in advance. Open March–November.

IRÁKLION

Agapi Beach. Amoudára, 4 km (2½ miles) west of Iráklion. Tel: (081) 250502 or (081) 250524, fax: (081) 258731. Sumptuous A-class resort hotel with 203 rooms and bungalows, private beach, swimming pool and tennis courts. Open March–October.

Astoria. Platía Eleftherías 11. Tel: (081) 229002, fax: (081) 229078. Old-fashioned A-class hotel opposite the Archaeological Museum and overlooking the traffic-filled Eleftherías Square. 120 air-conditioned, moderately priced rooms with bath. Rooftop swimming pool. Open year-round.

Atrion. K Paleológou 9 (behind the Historical Museum). Tel: (081) 229225 or (081) 242830, fax: (081) 223292. Congenial, well-run B-class hotel offering 50 air-conditioned rooms with bath or shower. Generous breakfast served buffet-style and evening drinks in the terraced garden. Open year-round.

Cretan Sun. Meintani 10. Tel: (081) 24394. Atmospheric but noisy E-class hotel overlooking the market.

Daédalos. Daedálou 15 (near the Archaeological Museum). Tel: (081) 224391. Slightly shabby but very friendly C-class hotel centrally located on a pedestrianised street. 60 rooms with shower and balcony decorated with paintings by local artists (the owner, Takis Stoumbidis, used to run an art gallery). Open year-round.

Galaxy. Leofóros Dimokratías 67. Tel: (081) 238812 or (081) 232157, fax: (081) 211211. Modern A-class hotel conveniently located on main road to Knossós. 144 air-conditioned rooms overlooking a central court with swimming pool. Open year-round.

Hellás. Kandanoleontos 11. Tel: (081) 225121 or (081) 243842. Just behind Venizélou Square, a clean but noisy D-class hotel with a pleasant courtyard and friendly atmosphere.

Idi. Zarós, 45 km (28 miles) southwest of Iráklion. Tel: (0894) 31302. C-class hotel with a swimming pool in the foothills of Mount Ida; ideal base for excursions in the mountains.

Olympic. Platía Kornárou (top of Odhós 1866). Tel: (081) 288861 or (081) 288864. Reasonably priced C-class hotel situated in one of the town's more modern sections.

Rea. Kalimeráki 4, corner of Handakos. Tel: (081) 223638. Quiet, cheap D-class hotel near the sea. Open year-round.

ELOÚNDA

Aktí Oloús. Tel: (0841) 41270, fax: (0841) 41425. Friendly, family-run hotel overlooking the Gulf of Mirabéllo and a short swim away from the sunken city of Oloús (bring your goggles and snorkel!). 65 small rooms with balconies decorated in traditional Cretan style. Open April–October. No credit cards.

Astir Palace. Tel: (0841) 41580–4, fax: (0841) 41783. Luxury-class resort hotel offering 200 plush rooms and 97 bungalows overlooking the Gulf of Mirabéllo. Tennis courts, two swimming pools and a private sandy beach. Open April–October.

Eloúnda Beach. Tel: (0841) 41812 or (0841) 41412, fax: (0841) 41373. Built in 1973 and regarded as Crete's leading Luxury-class resort hotel, the Eloúnda Beach offers a total of 300 rooms (half of them bungalows overlooking the sea); a miniature Cretan village comprising a *kafeneíon* (coffeehouse), Orthodox chapel and open-air amphitheatre; two sandy beaches and all manner of watersports. Open April–October.

Eloúnda Island Villas. Tel: (0841) 41274. 15 apartments on Spinalónga Island (a leper colony from 1904 to 1957), across the bay from Eloúnda. Tennis courts and a small private beach.

Eloúnda Mare. Tel: (0841) 41102/3 or (0841) 41512 (reservations), fax: (0841) 41307. 49-room Luxury-class hotel with 48 traditional whitewashed bungalows, each with its own sea-water swimming pool and private garden of jasmine, bougainvillea, oleander and hibiscus. Private sandy beach. Three restaurants including the hotel's Yacht Club. Open April–October.

Porto Eloúnda Mare. Tel: (0841) 41903, fax (0841) 41887. Owned by architect Spyros Kókotos and his wife (proprietors of the more expensive Eloúnda

Mare Hotel next door), this establishment comprises over 100 rooms/suites plus ten seafront bungalows with private pools. Facilities include a nine-hole golf course.

AGIOS NIKÓLAOS

Green House Pension. Modátsou 15. Tel: (0841) 22025. Charming, family-run pension with small wooden rooms leading onto a central courtyard. Shared facilities.

Mínos Beach. Amoundi Beach, Agios Nikólaos. Tel: (0841) 22345–9, fax: (0841) 22548. Crete's oldest Luxury-class resort hotel with 132 modern bungalows set in handsomely landscaped gardens on the lovely Gulf of Mirabéllo. Tennis courts, swimming pool, private beach and three good restaurants. Open April–October.

New York. Kondogiánni 21A. Tel: (0841) 28577. A large, relatively cheap place to flop near the bus station – often has rooms when other establishments are booked up with package tours. C-class. Open year-round.

Panorama. Aktí Koúndourou. Tel. (0841) 28890. Moderately priced accommodation overlooking the outer harbour. All rooms with bath.

Pension Marilena. Erithroú Stavroú 14. Tel: (0841) 22681. Cheap and exceptionally good pension – the best of the bunch in this older part of town northwest of the tourist office.

SITÍA

Alice. Papanastasíou 34. Tel: (0843) 28450 (0843) 28441. C-class hotel in a good position opposite a park; puts on a Cretan evening once a week. Open year-round.

El Greco. Gabriél Arkadíou 13. Tel: (0843) 23133. C-class hotel in a quiet, central location. Open year-round.

Elysée. Karamanlí 14. Tel: (0843) 22312. Friendly, family-run hotel on the seafront. 24 rooms.

Itanós. Karamanlí 4. Tel: (0843) 22146, fax: (0843) 22915. Friendly but characterless C-class hotel near the park. 72 rooms with shower. Open year-round.

Kappa Crete. Karamanlí. Tel: (0843) 28821–4. Modern A-class beach hotel with 162 rooms, tennis courts, swimming pool and other sports facilities.

Seaside Pension. Odhós Karamanlí (200 metres/656 ft past the bridge going away from the town centre). Tel: (0843) 22815. Simple but extremely friendly establishment with a homely atmosphere.

IERÁPETRA

Astron. Mihaíl Kothri 5. Tel: (0842) 25114–7, fax: (0842) 25917. Opened in 1992, a comfortable, moderately priced C-class hotel on the edge of town offering 70 air-conditioned rooms with balconies overlooking the sea. Open April–October.

Ferma Beach. Ferma, 9 km (5½ miles) east of Ierápetra. Tel: (0842) 61352, fax: (0842) 61416. Resort hotel with 156 rooms and bungalows, swimming pool, tennis courts and private beach.

Ierápytna. Platía Agíou Ioánnou Kale, 72200 Ierápetra. Tel: (0842) 28530. One of the nicest cheap hotels in town.

Iris. Mihaíl Kothri 36. Tel: (0842) 23136. Pleasant D-class hotel situated right on the waterfront. Open year-round.

Koutsounári Traditional Cottages. Koutsounári, 7 km east of Ierápetra. Tel. (0842) 61291. A group of restored houses decorated in traditional Cretan style and rented out as holiday villas with full cooking facilities. Beach just less than 1 km (½ mile) away. A-class. Open April–October.

Lyktos Beach. Koutsounári, 7 km (4½ miles) east of Ierápetra. Tel: (0842) 61280, fax: (0842) 61318. A-class resort hotel with superb sports facilities and lavish entertainment from discos and piano bars to video libraries and satellite TV. Other facilities include floodlit tennis courts, basketball and volley-ball courts, gymnasium, sauna, Jacuzzi. 250 air-conditioned rooms with bath. Open April–October.

Petra Mare. On eastern edge of Ierápetra, on the beach. Tel: (0842) 23341, fax: (0842) 23350. Large A-class resort complex with 219 rooms, swimming pool, private beach and live music entertainment. Open April–October.

Sunwing. Makrigialós, 20 km (12 miles) east of Ierápetra. Tel: (0843) 51621, fax: (0843) 51626. Mammoth A-class resort hotel with 371 rooms and apartments, tennis courts, swimming pool and private beach.

PLACES TO RENT

Villas

These are almost always rented out through foreign tour operators, and must be arranged from home. It is much safer to book before travelling if you are going in high sumer when accommodation in whole islands may be booked up. Reliable British companies include Simply Crete (Tel: (0181) 994 4462 or (0181) 994 5226) and Sunvil Holidays (0181) 568 4499), both based in London. National newspapers and specialist magazines also often carry private advertisements for villas and apartments to rent.

Rooms

Rooms to rent – *dhomátia* in Greek, but usually signposted in English "Rent Rooms" – are generally cheaper and more congenial than hotel rooms. The tourist office does not provide rooms listings, so it is usually a question of finding them for yourself on the spot.

In smaller villages away from the coast rooms for rent tend to be in people's own homes (ask at the local taverna for help finding somewhere to stay). In the larger resorts they are more often than not in characterless concrete blocks, and their owners will usually seek you out at the ferry or bus terminal.

Note that it is standard practice for rooms proprietors to keep your passport, which is then returned to you on departure.

YOUTH HOSTELS

There are half a dozen official youth hostels in Crete located in or near most of the major tourist resorts. They offer simple but clean accommodation and cheap meals or cooking facilities. Youth Hostel Association (YHA) membership cards are rarely (if ever) asked for in Crete – though to be on the safe side it is probably still worth obtaining one before leaving home. YHA addresses in Crete are as follows:

Iráklion: Víronos 5. Tel: (081) 222947. Cheap dormitory beds in a central location just off 25 Avgoústou.

Haniá: Drakoniánou 33. Tel: (0821) 53565. Friendly and quiet establishment on the edge of town.

Réthimnon: Tombázi 45. Tel: (0831) 22848. Cheap, clean and exceptionally friendly place a few blocks from the tourist office. Showers, cooking and clothes-washing facilities available.

Mália: A new youth hostel with an attractive setting just east of town.

Sitía: Therísou 4. Tel: (0843) 22693. One of the better youth hostels in Crete.

Plakiás: A small youth hostel just outside town; often noisy.

CAMPING

There are more than a dozen official campsites in Crete, and they are generally open from April to September (three campsites are open year-round: Arcadía, Agía Galíni and Síssi). Camping on beaches or unrecognised sites is officially forbidden, though it is still fairly common (and generally tolerated) in remoter areas.

Listed below are just some of the campsites on Crete – a complete list can be obtained from the Greek tourist office.

Karavan. Tel: (0897) 22025. Upmarket campsite on the coast just outside the tourist resort of Límin Hersoníssou (about 26 km/16 miles east of Iráklion).

Haniá. Tel: (0821) 31138 or (0821) 64203. Small, pleasant campsite 4 km (2 miles) west of Haniá and a short walk from the beach; limited facilities.

Agía Marína. Tel: (0821) 68555 or (0821) 68596. Fairly large site on a good beach outside Agía Marína village, 8 km (5 miles) west of Haniá.

Elizabeth. Tel: (0831) 28694. Large campsite with all modern facilities on a beach 4 km (2 miles) east of Réthimnon.

Arcadía. Tel: (0831) 28825 or (0831) 28746. Large year-round campsite a bit further east along the beach from the Elizabeth campsite.

Koutsounári. Tel: (0842) 61213. Small campsite about 7 km (5 miles) east of Ierápetra on the Sitía road; grey-sand beach 100 (330 feet) metres away.

Ierápetra. Tel: (0842) 61351. Another fairly small campsite 2 km (1 mile) further east along the beach from Koutsounári. Sandy beach 100 metres (330 feet) away, but otherwise flat, uninspiring country.

FOOD DIGEST

Food is an essential element in Greek culture, and plays a central role in the celebration of life in both the religious and social customs of the people. It is at the heart of every family gathering, feeding both body and soul. Hospitality and the generosity of spirit so characteristic of Crete are also expressed through food. No visitor is allowed to leave the house without being offered something to eat!

Greek cuisine is generally wholesome and robust rather than refined and sophisticated. The common assumption that Greek cookery represents a deviant form of Turkish cuisine is not in fact correct. Ottoman culinary arts were themselves enriched through contact with the ancient and independent Greek tradition.

The main ingredients bubbling away in Cretan kitchens today are vegetables, mostly locally grown and wonderfully fresh. Peas and beans, artichokes, wild greens picked from the hills, dandelions, leeks, spinach, cabbage, wild asparagus, stalk celery, onions, potatoes, tomatoes, aubergines and corn all have their place in Cretan cookery. Leafy parsley, dill, mint, garlic, spring onions and especially lemons are also used in abundance.

As in other countries, the "home-cooking" of Crete is very different from the charcoal-grilled or ready-baked fare typically served in most commercial restaurants and tavernas. The main meal of the day is usually eaten around two o'clock, when the whole family will sit down to such dishes as *avgolémono* (chicken broth cooked with rice, egg and lemon); *fasoláda* (bean soup) or *revíthia* (chickpea soup); *loukánika* (delicious spicy sausages); *dolmádes* (stuffed vine and cabbage leaves) or *yemistá* (stuffed vegetables); *keftédes* (meatballs made of minced lamb), *kléftiko* (large pieces of lamb, potatoes and vegetables cooked in foil or a terracotta pot) or *stifádo* (meat stew with tomato and onion). Delicious crusty bread fresh from the local bakery accompanies every meal.

Traditional home-cooking can also be found at the classic Greek *estiatórion*, the upmarket cousin of the taverna. Here there is a varied menu to choose from, starting with *mezéthes* (appetisers), and including the same sorts of dishes as those mentioned above. The simpler version of the estiatórion is the *mayériko*, a cooking stall where you select your food

directly from the hot stove. *Miá merítha* is "one portion" – that is, a plateful. It is not customary in Crete to take a bit of this and a bit of that from the various pots.

In traditional Greek tavernas, the food is all freshly prepared. Often the waiter will tell you verbally what your choices are, since many establishments have no set menu as such. The staple tourist dish is *souvlákia* (grilled *shish kebabs*), which is rarely eaten in Cretan homes. Tavernas serve food that is quick to prepare – grilled meat or fish served with chips; steamed or deep-fried vegetables; salads, among them *horiátiki*, a refreshing mixture of cucumber and tomato with *feta* (goat's) cheese, olives and onions, *taramosaláta* (smoked cod's roe purée) and *melitzanosaláta* (aubergine puréed with garlic and onion); baked savoury dishes such as *pastítsio* (baked minced meat and macaroni) and *moussaká* (mince, aubergines and potatoes topped with béchamel sauce) – most of which involve less work than the tastier vegetable-intensive dishes.

For a fish meal, the *psarotavérna* is the place to go. Here you will usually have a choice of seafood, with the "dish of the day" often being particularly good value. *Kalamári* (squid), *barboúnia* (red mullet), *xifías* (swordfish), *lithríni* (bream), *sardéles* (baked sardines) and *marídes* (fried whitebait) are all well worth ordering.

The Greek snack bars can be very tempting and hard to resist. A visit to the local *zacharoplastío* (patisserie) is a must for anyone with a sweet tooth – among the most popular pastries are *bugátsa* (a custard-filled pastry), *loukoumáthes* (doughnut-shaped honey fritters), *kataífi* (shredded wheat dripping with honey) and *baklavá* (thin layers of pastry filled with nuts and honey). The *galaktopolío* (dairy shop) sells *rizógalo* (rice pudding), local cheeses, eggs, yoghurt and other dairy products. A *psistariá* is the place to go for grilled kebabs, while a *souvlatzíthiko* (found on many street corners) serves delicious chunks of grilled meat with bits of tomato, chopped onions and *tzatzíki* (yoghurt, cucumber and garlic dip) all wrapped up in hot *pitta* bread, to be consumed either on the spot or as a take-away.

DRINKING NOTES

Wine has been produced in Greece since ancient times. *Retsina*, the resinated white wine originally produced in Attica on the mainland, was as popular then as it is today. (Don't be too surprised, though, if you don't take to it at first – the writer Kingsley Amis, for one, thought it tasted of "stewed cricket bats".) Although there are no outstandingly fine wines produced on Crete today, there are a few local brands that are certainly worth trying – Mínos, Olympía, Górtis, Logado and Lató, for example, are all perfectly palatable white wines.

Cretan red wine called *mávro*, meaning black, is full-bodied and notoriously alcoholic. Rosé, called *kókkino*, meaning red, is lighter and, like other wines, is often served by the kilo or half-kilo in restaurants, sometimes served in measured copper pots. The most popular mainland imports are produced by Boutári – Náoussa red and Rotónda white being about the best. Local brands of beer are also widely available in Crete, as well as European lager brewed under licence.

Tsikoutháthika and *rakáthika* are the places to go to enjoy the traditional tipple of the island, the homemade spirit *tsikouthiá*, which is the Cretan version of *rakí*. In a drinking house called an *ouzerí*, on the other hand, the aniseed-flavoured *oúzo* is the main drink, imbibed neat or mixed with water. For those with a sweet tooth, *mandaríni* is a delicious tangerine liqueur.

The classic among Cretan watering holes is the *kafeneíon* (coffeehouse) – still very much a bastion of the Greek male. Here customers pass their time discussing politics, playing cards and *távli* (Greek backgammon), reading newspapers or watching the passing parade. *Ellinikó* (Greek coffee – *never* to be referred to as Turkish in this part of the world) is served in tiny cups with an accompanying glass of iced water – either *skéto*, without sugar; *métrio*, medium sweet; or *varí glikó*, strong and sickeningly sweet. Instant coffee also enjoys considerable popularity among the Greeks – with Nescafé (abbreviated to "Nes") standing in for all brands. Served chilled and shaken with milk this becomes a *frappé* – a very refreshing drink on a hot summer's day.

WHERE TO EAT AND DRINK

The restaurants, cafés and bars listed below are predominantly patronised by locals and are not always easy to find, so you might need to take a taxi. These places will give you a good idea of everyday cooking and dining out on Crete. So, *kalí órexi* – enjoy your meal!

HANIÁ

Restaurants proliferate around Haniá's Venetian harbour and city walls. Though large sections of their menus are fairly touristy, you will also find plenty of authentic Cretan cuisine. A handful of tavernas in the villages around Haniá are included for anyone prepared to drive or take a taxi.

Aerikó. Aktí Miaoúli. Taverna/*ouzerí* in the Kum Kapí quarter of Haniá.

Bárbas Leftéris. Taverna in Kamissianá, on the westbound coast road just before you reach Kolimbári.

Bingasa. Galatás, just west of Haniá. *Estiatórion* serving Turkish and Greek food.

Fagotto. Angélon 16. Bar in an old vaulted building near the Firkás Fortress.

Fáka ("The Mousetrap"). Alfresco dining in the shadow of the Venetian town wall. Avoid tourist dishes such as moussaka and go for a *meze* of assorted starters.

Goniá. Polichronídi 33, corner of Geróla. A tiny restaurant in the Páno Kum Kapí quarter serving western Cretan specialities such as *sfakianés pítes* and *kaltsoúnia*, cheese puffs from Sfakiá and Haniá. Opens at 6pm.

Kiani Akti. On the eastbound coast road, just before you reach Kalíves. Classical fish taverna shaded by tamarisks and overlooking the sea. Closed in winter.

Kulurídis. Vamvakópoulo, just south of Haniá (follow signs to Alikianós). Taverna with excellent cuisine, but not cheap.

Les Vagabonds. Pórtou 44. French cuisine.

Maláxa. Maláxa, 8 km (5 miles) southeast of Haniá. Small taverna whose speciality is *stáka* (flour cooked in cream and eaten with bread).

Marco Polo. Aktí Tombázi. Fresh fish near the harbour behind the Turkish mosque.

Meltémi. *Kafeneíon* (coffeehouse) next to the Marine Museum.

Papagállos. Bar on Kondiláki near the harbour.

Tamám. Zambelíou 49. *Estiatórion* housed in the old Turkish baths on the harbour.

Tsikudakik. Soúda, just east of Haniá. Taverna serving delicious *mezéthes* (appetisers) on the main road opposite the mill.

RÉTHIMNON

Visitors are spoilt for choice in Réthimnon. As a rule, restaurants on the harbour are considerably more expensive than those in the surrounding backstreets.

Angela's. Dikastírion. The best place in town for squid.

Avlí. Xanthoudídou, corner of Radamánthios. Very refined restaurant with candlelight and soothing piano music.

Baluardi. *Mezethopolíon* (equivalent to a *tsikoutháthiko*) on the seaside drive below the Fortezza and near the harbour.

Galéro. Popular café/bar by the Rimondi Fountain.

Jeórjios. *Rakáthiko* (i.e. place to drink *rakí*) below the Archaeological Museum. Closed in winter.

Kiriá María. Moschovíti. *Mayériko* close to the Rimondi Fountain.

Kómbos. Taverna in Violí Haráki on the old road to Haniá.

Míltos. Maroulás, west of Réthimnon. Taverna serving two hot dishes a day such as lentils or aubergines.

Móna. Agías Varváras 13. *Rakáthiko* whose menu comprises *oftés patátes* (potatoes roasted in their skins), green olives and, of course, *rakí*.

O Psarás. Arambatsóglu 69 (formerly Thessaloníkis). Serves such culinary delights as *stifádo* with *ochtapódi* (octopus in red sauce).

Sérifos. Fish taverna on the Venetian harbour.

Sesília. Bar on Prokiméa E. Venizélou.

Sokáki. Pórtou 6. Taverna/*estiatórion*. Closed in winter.

Sokrátis. *Estiatórion* next to the Rimondi Fountain. Closed in winter.

To Methisméno Feggári ("The Drunken Moon"). Melissínou 34. *Ouzerí/kafeneíon*.

IRÁKLION

3/4. Theotokopoúlou 1. Very refined restaurant/bar in a neoclassical building on the old harbour.

Avantage. Chándakos 12. Cafeteria-style eating place.

Bugatsa. Opposite the Morosini Fountain. Tiny *zacharoplastío* (patisserie) selling puff-pastry sweetmeats with a cream cheese or sweet cream filling.

Doré. Platía Eleftherías. Sophisticated café/restaurant with roof garden on the fifth floor.

Giovanni. Straightforward taverna on Odhós Koraí.

Ippókambos ("Sea Horse"). Mitsotáki 3. *Ouzerí* on the old harbour. Closed from 3.30–7pm.

Irida. Odhós Koraí. Café occupying a marvellous neoclassical building.

Knossós. Opposite the Morosini Fountain. *Estiatórion* serving good plain food at reasonable prices.

Konstandin Lidakis. Arhánes, 14 km (8½ miles) south of Iráklion. Opposite the Panagía Church on the main road.

La Castella. Good-value fish taverna among the bars on the coastal strip. Popular with locals and tourists alike.

Onar. Chándakos 36B. Café/tearoom.

Várdi ("Shift"). *Ouzerí* on the old harbour. Opens at 4pm.

AGIOS NIKÓLAOS

Bland English/international fare is ubiquitous thanks to the large number of English tourists who come to Agios Nikólaos. The following places offer a more genuinely Cretan atmosphere. For those prepared to drive or take a taxi, the village of Pláka, 15 km (9 miles) north of Agios Nikólaos, is an ideal place to go for lunch or dinner.

Aktéon. A simple taverna on the harbour.

Café Plaza. Next to the Folklore Museum. Rather chic and expensive for some tastes, but right in the heart of things.

Itanos. Old-style *estiatórion* on Odhós Dyprou.

La Casa. Oktombríou 28. Taverna with a view over Voulisméni Lake.

O Sigos. *Estiatórion* in Kaló Horió, 11 km (6½ miles) south of Agios Nikólaos on the road to Sitía.

O Víos eínai Oneiron ("Life is a Dream"). Pasifáis 1. Cretan specialities and jazz music in a charming old taverna.

Tavern Aquas. Odhós Paleológou, near the Folklore Museum. Taverna with a large selection of hot dishes.

Tavern the Pine. Traditional *estiatórion* by the lake.

The Café. N. Plastíra 26. Café/bar perched above Voulisméni Lake; great views but rather small portions.

THINGS TO DO

ENTERTAINMENT

Bars, discos and **clubs** abound in the holiday resorts, but there is nothing distinctively Greek about them, in fact in most cases you feel you could be just about anywhere. Resort hotels often lay on evenings of "authentic traditional entertainment" which includes music, dancing and even costumes – the only thing missing are the Cretans themselves. The *kritiká kéntra*, traditional nightclubs located on the outskirts of town or even further out in the country, are used for weddings as well as evenings of live Cretan music. People also come here to eat and drink, but mainly to dance Cretan dances. The *skiláthika* are similar but sleazier clubs imported from the mainland, their dance music furnished by second- or third-rate *bouzoúki* ensembles. A *skiláthiko* is the final stop of many a late-evening tour of the nightspots, and is one of the few places where you're at all likely to see Greeks drinking heavily (whisky is sold by the bottle at grossly inflated prices).

Other alternatives include the **cinema** which is open-air in most towns (films are generally subtitled rather than dubbed). **Festivals** (*paniyíria*) are also held throughout the summer in Iráklion, Agios Nikólaos, Réthimnon and other towns (see Local Festivals on page 244). And last, but certainly not least, there is the *vólta*, or evening stroll, in which the entire populace partakes – this is a time to catch up with local gossip, to see and be seen.

PHOTOGRAPHY

Film and film processing are not cheap on the island, though they are both widely available. It is better to bring a supply of film with you and have it processed back home. Take care not to leave film or cameras in the heat for long periods, and be especially careful on the beach not to get sand in the lens mechanism – this can ruin a camera.

There are some restrictions on photography in Crete. It is illegal to photograph military installations, including the entire Soúda Bay region near Haniá and the area around Iráklion airport. Photography is permitted in museums and archaeological sites – a small fee is charged for hand-held photographic equipment and a more substantial fee for cameras on tripods. Taking pictures inside churches is usually not forbidden.

Cretan tourist resorts are choc-a-bloc full of souvenir shops selling over-priced kitsch and junk – however if you can manage to steer clear of these places, there are some genuine treasures to be had. These include hand-woven blankets, embroidery work, metal and wood crafts, ceramics and earthenware, as well as spices and herbal teas – all of which have been important export commodities as far back as Minoan times.

Crete, and above all Haniá, is famous for its **leather goods**: bags in all sizes, rucksacks, sandals and especially boots of cowhide imported from Africa. Unglazed **ceramic** storage jars of the kind produced on Crete 4,000 years ago (used mainly as flower pots today), plus other pots and jugs of all sizes are sold along the roads just outside towns. There is generally a big selection of everyday earthenware to choose from, some of it very attractive. Hand-woven, hand-embroidered or crocheted **blankets** and **fabrics** are still important products of the native crafts industry, although industrial copies are stepping up the competition. Inexpensive items include sheep's wool knits and countless cotton products from T-shirts to towels, as well as conventional linens with colourful stripes on a white background. These get much softer once they've been washed a few times.

Market vendors and small household goods shops sell woven **wicker baskets**, as well as **wooden spoons** and the traditional *bríkia* – the small copper **coffeepots** with long handles used to make Greek coffee. With a bit of luck, you should be able to find the matching long-handled copper spoon and whisk as well. A chinaware store is the best place to get the tiny cups to go with the set – the classical *kafeneíon* variety are white and unbreakable. And finally, to complete your Greek coffee-making ensemble, you'll need a brass **coffee grinder**. The smaller versions of these mills make excellent pepper grinders.

Cretan knives, originally part of the traditional costume, are long and curved with thick white handles and silver scabbards. The old ones are rare and expensive, but they also come in various shapes and sizes as souvenirs. A whole range of other knives are also available, from chopping knives to the curved knives used to prune grapevines.

Gold and **silver** are relatively inexpensive in Crete and Greece generally – which explains the abundance of jewellery shops, often selling machine-made merchandise. You'll also find a number of skilled gold- and silversmiths on the island.

For the gourmands among you, there are a number of **culinary delights** worth bringing home, including the sharp, firm cheese called *graviéra*; honey (*méli*), especially the kind derived from thyme blossoms; black and green olives in brine; wine (see Drinking Notes on page 242); and *tsikouthiá*, Crete's version of *raki*. The local marketplace is the place to go for most of these – here you'll also find

a whole array of herbs and spices, from *rígani* (marjoram) to Cretan saffron and spicy cinnamon bark. You can also stock up on *passatémpo* from any street cart – paper bags full of peanuts, pistachios, roasted chickpeas, pumpkin seeds, etc.

Greek music lovers might like to try a sampling of cassettes by the best-known and loved Cretan musicians. Psarantónis and his band from Anógia, for example, do interpretations – often quite unconventional – of traditional folk music. His *Erotókritos*, Crete's national 17th-century epic, is wonderful. The recordings of Ross Daly, an Irishman turned Cretan, are wonderfully creative – his *Lavírinthos*, for instance. This is also true of the albums by the famous and beloved singer who died at an early age, Níkos Xilúris, Psarantónis's brother. The music by a *lyra* player who "emigrated" to Piraeus, Kóstas Mountákis, is also highly recommended.

Cretans are great sports enthusiasts, though for the most part as spectators only. Whenever a major football match is televised, the *kafeneía* (coffeehouses) in the big cities are crammed with enthusiastic supporters. This enthusiasm rarely manifests itself, however, when it comes to engaging in any form of sport themselves. Don't let this discourage you: Crete offers all kinds of sporting possibilities from swimming, snorkelling, windsurfing and sailing to hiking, climbing and even skiing.

Watersports are the main attraction for the majority of tourists. The seas around Crete are warm enough to swim in from April till early November. They are generally safe as well, though they can get rough when the *meltémi* wind blows – take care, as life guards are almost non-existent in Crete. Most of the big coastal resort hotels hire out watersports equipment (usually to both guests and non-guests). Waterskiing is popular at all the major resorts and some of them also have facilities for paragliding and jet-skiing. Boats are also widely available and you'll find even the tiniest fishing harbours will often have a kayak to rent. **Fishing** enthusiasts require no special licence, but underwater spear fishing is restricted. Seabass, swordfish and dentex are the most common catch.

On account of the many underwater archaeological sites around the island, **scuba diving** is restricted to government-designated areas. **Snorkelling** is permitted everywhere, however, and it can actually be quite a rewarding pursuit, especially around Mirabéllo Bay, where from Eloúnda Beach you can swim out to see the sunken Greco-Roman city of Oloús.

Most of the big resort hotels have **tennis** courts, some of them floodlit. There are also tennis clubs in Haniá (Dimokratías Avenue; Tel: (0821) 21293) and Iráklion (Beaufort Avenue; Tel: (081) 226152), as well as a few public courts behind the Archaeological

Museum in Iráklion. Other outdoor activities include **horseriding**, which is possible just outside Iráklion at Amnissós (Tel: (081) 282005).

There are numerous possibilities for **hiking** and **climbing** in Crete. Excursions into the mountains are organised by the Greek Alpine Club (*EOS*), which have branches in Iráklion (Dikeosínis 53; Tel: (081) 227609), Réthimnon (Arkadíou 143; Tel: (0831) 22710) and Haniá (Stratigoú Tzanakáki 90; Tel: (0821) 24647). Guides and equipment are also available for climbers wishing to scale the heights of Mount Ida (Psilorítis) or peaks in the White Mountains (Lefká Ori). If you go on your own, wear sturdy, comfortable shoes and be sure to take food and plenty of water, as well as a jacket or sweater (even in the summer). An early start is also advisable, especially in the summer when it can get oppressively hot in the middle of the day. Bear in mind that everything grinds to a halt for the afternoon siesta (from around 2 to 6pm), including any monasteries you may wish to visit. In mountain villages the *kafeneíon* (coffeehouse) is the local "information office" for overnight accommodation; it is also the place to go for such things as the key to the local church.

Skiing is also possible in Crete during the winter months – though don't expect any resorts resembling Val d'Isère or Chamonix, or you're bound to be disappointed. For more information contact the Haniá branch of the Greek Alpine Club (address above).

LANGUAGE

It is possible to survive in most parts of Crete just knowing English. Cretans have seen so many English-speaking tourists and have such strong connections with the English-speaking world (through emigration, the media, education) that you are bound to find yourself understood.

This section is about being perceived as a *ksnos*, a foreigner or guest, instead of a *tourísta*. Greeks put great stock in their language and are highly responsive to the efforts of foreigners who try to learn it. Precisely because Greeks so effusively appreciate your efforts, Greek can be one of the most gratifying European languages to learn. With a little study and practise on your part, you too may soon be met with the stock praise: *Pos mathes tso kal ta elinik?* That is, How did you learn Greek so well?

The following crash course in Greek and listing of words and phrases will be useful to you. You'll also want to carry a pocket-sized English-Greek/Greek-English dictionary. Greek is a phonetic language. There are some combinations of vowels and consonants which customarily stand for certain sounds, and some slight pronunciation changes determined by what letter follows but, generally, sounds are pronounced as they are written, without additions or omissions. Thus, learning the phonetic values of the Greek alphabet, and then reading, say, street sounds out loud, is a good beginning to getting the feel of the language.

In addition to pronouncing each letter, you should remember that stress plays an important role in Modern Greek. When you learn a Greek word, learn where the stress falls at the same time. Each Greek word has a single stress (marked in the following list with an accent). Greek is an inflected language as well, and noun and adjective endings change according to gender, number and case. Case endings, the rules governing them, and the conjugation of Greek verbs, are beyond the scope of a guide. For visitors staying on for a long period, there are language classes at the Hellenic American Union and other teaching centres in metropolitan Athens.

Cap.	l.c.	Value	Name
Α	α	a in father	alfa
Β	β	v in visa	vita
Γ	γ	gh before consonants and a, o and oo; y before e, as in year	gama
Δ	δ	th in then	thelta
Ε	ε	e in let	epsilon
Ζ	ζ	z in zebra	zita
Η	η	e in keep	ita
Θ	θ	th in theory	thita
Ι	ι	e in keep	yota
Κ	κ	k in king	kapa
Λ	l	l in million	lamda
Μ	μ	m in mouse	mi
Ν	ν	n in no	ni
Ξ	ξ	ks in jacks	ksi
Ο	ο	o in oh	omikron
Π	π	p in pebble	pi
Ρ	ρ	r in raisin	ro
Σ	σ	s in sun	sigma
Τ	τ	t in trireme	taf
Ε	ε	e in keep	ipsilon
Φ	φ	f in favor	fi
Χ	χ	h in help	hi
Ψ	ψ	ps in copse	psi
Ω	ω	o in oh	omega

Dipthongs

Type	Value
αι	e in let
αυ	av or af in avert or after

258

Type	Value
ει	e in keep
ευ	ev or ef
οι	e in keep
ου	oo in poor

Double consonants

Type	Value
μ π	b at beginnings of words; mb in the middle of words
ντ	d at beginnings of words; nd in the middle of words
τζ	dz as in adze
γγ, γκ	gh at the beginnings of words; ng in the middle of words

·Note: This list is broken into syllables, the stressed syllable marked with an accent. Pronounce e as in pet; a as in father; i as in keep; o as in oh.

Numbers

one	é-na (neuter)/ é-nas (masc.)/mí-a(fem.)
two	thí-o
three	trí-a (neuter)/tris (masc, fem.)
four	té-se-ra
five	pén-de
six	ék-si
seven	ep-tá
eight	ok-tó
nine	e-né-a
ten	thé-ka
eleven	én-the-ka
twelve	thó-the-ka
thirteen	the-ka-trí-a/the-ka-trís
fourteen	the-ka-té-se-ra
etc. until twenty...	
twenty	í-ko-si
twenty-one	í-ko-si é-na (neuter and masc.)/ í-ko-si mí-a (fem.)
thirty	tri-án-da
forty	sa-rán-da
fifty	pe-nín-da
sixty	ek-sín-da
seventy	ev-tho-mín-da
eighty	og-thón-da
ninety	e-ne-nín-da
one hundred	e-ka-tó
one hundred and fifty	e-ka-to-pe-nín-da
two hundred	thi-a-kó-si-a (neuter)
three hundred	tri-a-kó-si-a (neuter)
four hundred	te-tra-kó-si-a (neuter)
one thousand	hí-lia (neuter)

Note: Since the word for drachma, *(thrak-mí,)* is feminine, a number preceding this noun will also be feminine. Thus, *hí-lies thrak-més,* for 1,000drs.

Days of the Week

Monday	Thef-té-ra
Tuesday	Trí-ti
Wednesday	Te-tár-ti
Thursday	Pém-pti
Friday	Pa-ras-ke-ví
Saturday	Sá-va-to
Sunday	Ki-ri-a-kí
yesterday	kthes
today	sí-me-ra
tomorrow	á-vri-o
day after tomorrow	meth-á-vri-o
next week	tin á-li ev-tho-má-tha

Greetings

Hello	yá sas (plural/polite) yá sou (sing./familiar) ya (abbreviated)
Good day	ká-li mé-ra
Good evening	ka-li spe-ra
Good night	káli ník-ta
Bon voyage	ka-ló tak-si-thi
Welcome	ká-los il-tha-te
Good luck	ka-lí tí-hi
How are you?	Ti ká-ne-te? (plural/polite) Ti ká-nis? (singular/familiar)
fine (in response)	ka-lá
so-so (in response)	ét-si két-si
me, too	kai egó
Pleased to meet you	há-ri-ka

Getting Around

yes	ne
yes (emphatic)	malista
no	ó-hi
okay	en dák-si
thank you	ef-ha-ris-tó
very much	pá-ra po-lí
excuse me	sig-nó-mi
it doesn't matter	then bi-rá-zi
it's nothing	tí-po-ta
certainly/polite yes	má-li-sta
Can I..?	Bó-ro na..?
When?	Pó-te?
Where is..?	Pou í-n-e..?
Do you speak English?	mi-lá-te ta an-gli-ka?
Do you understand?	Ka-ta-la-vé-ne-te?
What time is it?	Ti ó-ra i-ne?
What time will it leave?	Ti ó-ra tha fi-gi
I don't	then (plus verb)
I want	thé-lo
I have	é-ho
here/there	e-thó/e-kí
near/far	kon-dá/ma-kri-á
small/large	mi-kró/me-gá-lo
less/more	ligótero/perisótero
quickly	grí-go-ra
slowly	ar-gá
good/bad	ka-ló/ka-kó
warm/cold	zes-tó/krí-o

bus	le-o-for-í-on
tram	tró-li
boat	ka-rá-vi, va-pó-ri
bike/moped	po-thí-la-to/
	mo-to-po-thí-la-to
ticket	i-si-tí-ri-o
road/street	thró-mos/o-thós
beach	pa-ra-lí-a
sea	thá-la-sa
church	e-kli-sí-a
ancient ruin	ar-hé-a
centre	kén-tro
square	pla-tí-a

Athens airpoort:
East Air Terminal A-no-to-li-kó Er-o-thró-mi-o
(international flights)
West Air Terminal Thi-ti-kó Er-o-thró-mi-o
(domestic and Olympic Airways flights)

Hotels
hotel	kse-no-tho-hí-o

Do you have a room?
É-hie-te é-na tho-má-ti-o?
bed	kre-vá-ti

shower with hot water
douz me zes-tó ne-ró
key	kli-thí
entrance	i-so-thos
exit	ék-so-thos
toilet	toua-lé-ta
women's	yi-ne-kón
men's	án-dron

Shopping
store	ma-ga-zí
kiosk	pe-ríp-te-ro
open/shut	a-nik-tó/klis-tó
post office	ta-ki-thro-mí-o
stamp	gra-ma-tó-simo
letter	grá-ma
envelope	fá-ke-lo
telephone	ti-lé-fo-no
bank	trá-pe-za
marketplace	a-go-rá
Have you..?	É-hie-te..?
Is there..?	É-hi..?
How much is it?	Pó-so ká-ni?

It's (too) expensive
I-ne (po-lí) a-kri-vó
How much?	Pó-so?
How many?	Pó-sa?

What time does it open/close?
To óra anígi/klíni?

Emergencies
doctor	ya-trós
hospital	no-so-ko-mí-o
pharmacy	far-ma-kí-o
police	as-ti-no-mí-a
station	stath-mós
embassy	presvía

FURTHER READING

Flowers of Greece and the Aegean, by Huxley and Taylor. The standard work on the subject
The Bull of Minos, by Leonard Cotterell. The story of the archaeolgical finds.
The Cretan Journal, by Edward Lear. Record of the the artist's journey in 1864.
The Fall of Crete, by Alan Clark. Wartime Crete.
The Greek Islands, by Lawrence Durrell.
The Greek Myths, by Robert Graves.
The Villa Ariadne, by Dilys Powell. Foreigners who "discovered" Crete.
Zorba The Greek, by Nikos Kazantzakis. Best known work of Crete's best known author.

OTHER INSIGHT GUIDES

A dozen *Insight Guides* to Greece, are just some of more than 300 titles covering all parts of the world. Crete and Rhodes are also titles in Apa Publications' new *Compact Guide* series.

The three other *Insight Guide* titles to the country are: Greece, The Greek Islands and Athens. There is also an Insight Guide to Cyprus.

For the short-stay traveller, there are *Insight Pocket Guides* to Crete, Rhodes, the Aegean Islands and Athens.

ART/PHOTO CREDITS

INDEX